THE
VISION OF
BUDDHISM

Books by Roger J. Corless

The Art of Christian Alchemy (1981)
I Am Food: The Mass in Planetary Perspective (1981)

THE
VISION OF
BUDDHISM:

THE SPACE UNDER THE TREE

by Roger J. Corless

PARAGON HOUSE
New York

Published in the United States by
Paragon House
, 90 Fifth Avenue
New York, NY 10011

Interior design and Map by Virginia Norey

Library of Congress Cataloging-in-Publication Data
Corless, Roger.
The vision of Buddhism / by Roger Corless.—1st ed.
p. cm.
Includes index.
ISBN 1-55778-200-8
1. Buddhism. 2. Gautama Buddha. 3. Buddhists—India—Biography.
I. Title.
BQ4012.C66 1989
294.3—dc20   89-30447
                                                        CIP

Manufactured in the United States of America

The paper used in this publication meets the minimum requirements of
American National Standard for Information Sciences—Permanence of Paper
for Printed Library Materials, ANSIZ39.48-1984.

10 9 8 7 6 5 4 3

Table of
CONTENTS

Figures

Dedication

To my mother and father
who gave me
the fortunate human rebirth.

Acknowledgments

This book has been many years in the making and it is impossible to mention here all those who have obtained merit by assisting me to make myself clear.

The most important acknowledgment goes to my students at Duke University, for it was due to my attempt to teach an introductory course on Buddhism, and my frustration at the standard approach of the introductory textbooks, that I began what turned out to be the long drawn out project of writing this book. I developed a course called "Buddha and Buddhism" in which I tried out the idea of discarding history as the framework and using the model of the life of the Buddha. The undergraduates who signed up for the course found an experiment in which I invited them to participate. Throughout successive offerings of the course they patiently waited while I developed handouts, scribbled outlines, drafts of this and that chapter, and finally, an entire book. The responses of these students to what I gave them has been invaluable. As any teacher quickly realizes, we do not know whether we understand something until we try to teach it. My students made me see, repeatedly, that what I thought I remembered having meant to say was not what they believed they remembered hearing, and so they stimulated me into successive revisions until the text is, now, "test marketed" and clear enough to warrant a first edition. To all my students, then, some of whom have kept in touch but many of whom have gone their way, I give hearty thanks.

Many of my colleagues in Buddhology have offered suggestions from time to time, and have helped me to avoid errors, although it is a reflection on the state of the discipline that no one of my colleagues was able to spot errors in all fields of Buddhism. Mistakes, I think, still remain. Therefore, I request the gentle reader please to write to me or to the publishers with suggestions for emendations or amendations.

I received the most detailed professional help from Professor Jeffrey Hopkins of the University of Virginia, who made careful notes throughout the final draft of the manuscript. He has saved me from many an embarrassment in matters relating to Tibetan Buddhism, a form in which I have practical, but not professional, training.

As for secretarial help, I began the book before computers were in common use for word processing and, since my handwriting is quite illegible, I was forced to type most of the early drafts myself, but, when my Department purchased computers, I thankfully accepted, and hereby gratefully acknowledge, the help of the secretaries (many of whom have, like the students, now gone their way) in keying in the text. I would especially like to thank Robert Bright, an undergraduate who assisted me for a time on a work-study program. Because of his help I began to see that even I might be able to understand computers, and he made it possible for me to summon the courage to learn how to key in the final text myself.

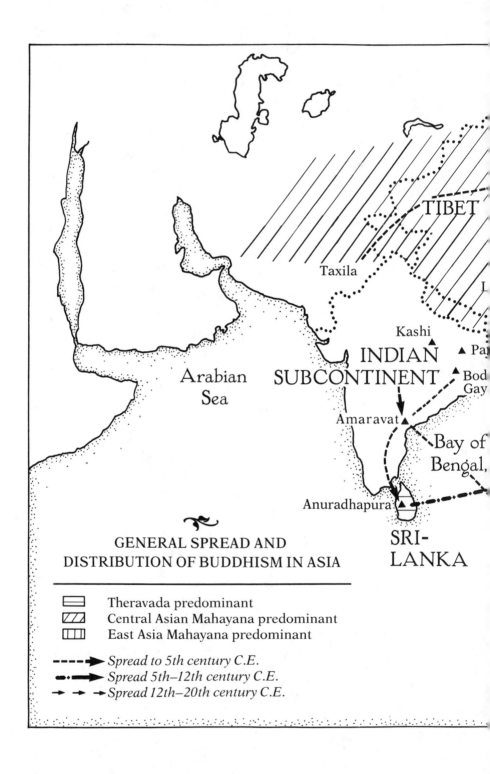

TIBET

Taxila

Kashi ▲   ▲ Pa

INDIAN   Bod
SUBCONTINENT   Gay

Arabian
Sea

Amaravat ▲

Bay of
Bengal,

Anuradhapura ▲

SRI-
LANKA

GENERAL SPREAD AND
DISTRIBUTION OF BUDDHISM IN ASIA

⊟	Theravada predominant
⊞	Central Asian Mahayana predominant
⊞	East Asia Mahayana predominant

----▶ *Spread to 5th century C.E.*
·—·▶ *Spread 5th–12th century C.E.*
· · → *Spread 12th–20th century C.E.*

Introduction

One and a half hours by rickshaw from the crowded Hindu pilgrimage town of Gaya in northeast India, a massive stone temple rises two hundred feet above the mud-and-straw cottages of the village of Bodhgaya; to the west of the temple there is a tree, and under the tree there is a space. To this space, it is said, came Prince Siddhartha Gautama, about the year 528 B.C.E., in search of true happiness. He had run away from his kingdom, wife, and family; he had studied under accomplished gurus; and he had nearly killed himself with a severe fast. Nothing had worked, nothing "led to the cutting off of desire." But now, fortified with just sufficient food, his body and mind were functioning smoothly, and he felt that if he sat beneath this tree, resolving not to move "even though flesh should drop from bone," he would break through the tangle of rebirth and become Buddha, the Awoken One. What he saw was at once so intangible and yet so obvious, like the space in which he sat, he at first refused to speak of it, believing it would be a waste of time. The gods, however, persuaded him that there were some beings "with little dust on their eyes" who could understand. Generations of his followers have since tried to wipe the dust from their eyes, see what he saw, and pass the vision on to others. The content of this vision has ranged from bulky lists of the Ultimate Constituents of the perceived universe, through sparkling, rococo panoramas of salvific paradises, to a fragile, mind-baffling silence, symbolized by a flower and a smile.

The tree under which the Buddha sat, now known as the Bodhi (Enlightenment) Tree, is said to have endured to the present day. Botanically, this is impossible. It is a specimen of the pipal *(Ficus religiosa),* a straggly species of fig tree with a distinctively heart shaped leaf, found growing like a weed all over India, and commonly regarded as housing a wood-sprite (yaksha), or as having a god on every leaf, or as containing all knowledge (veda). A pipal does well to live even a hundred years; it cannot live two thousand five hundred. Yet, by vegetative reproduction, from cuttings or portions of roots, it can spring up anew. Thus, there are offspring of the Bodhi Tree all over the world, carried home by pilgrims, and the tree at Bodhgaya is organically linked to its ancestor. It is neither the same tree under which the Buddha sat, nor different from it.

Buddhism revolves around this tree and this space and can be symbolized by it. The space, the vision, is finally incommunicable by descriptive means, it must be experienced: it cannot, say the Tibetans, be entered, and even the gods must fly around it. The attempts to encompass this experience, like the tree, have spread throughout Asia and the world, and none of the attempts is exactly the same as, nor completely different from, the original message.

Most introductory surveys of Buddhism written in the west use its history as an explanatory framework. But, when we do this, we fall into a terrible tangle, dragging down the reader too. An introduction to Buddhism by means of its history must begin with the exposition of the Buddha's original message, in so far as it can be recovered by historical means, go on to its elaboration and division into at least thirty-four competing schools, examine its codification in Sanskrit, Pali, Tibetan, and Chinese, as well as fragments in disused Central Asian languages such as Khotanese and Sogdian, continue with its confrontation with and modification of and by all the main cultures of Asia (and, now, of the west), and include the commentaries and popular stories from all the regional languages. It is not surprising that the beginning student of Buddhism, attempting to find the connection between all these complexities, gives up, suffering from intellectual indigestion. No wonder, the reader thinks, the gods had to persuade the Buddha to speak.

It took me some years of teaching Buddhism to discover what was wrong here. History is an academic discipline that has developed in the western hemisphere. The western hemisphere has been strongly influenced by the Abrahamic traditions (Judaism, Christianity, and Islam) and their conception of time as something created by God in and through which God manifests himself. On this view, time is meaningful. It has a beginning and an end, and the end is a goal, so that there is development, a progressive achievement of the goal. It makes sense to ask "What is the meaning of life?" A Christian hymn says "God is working his purpose out as year succeeds to year." As soon as we substitute the word Buddha for God in this sentence, however, there is a problem.

History as a secular discipline has many of the features of the Abrahamic tradition's view of time. God has been gradually eased out, and the notion of goal or purpose has become suspect, but the assumption that time is meaningful and that development is real does not seem to have been given up by even the most radical critics of the philosophy of history.

Buddhism, on the other hand, sees things as changing over time, but it does not see things as becoming more meaningful as they change. Change, for Buddhism, is a primary characteristic of cyclic existence (samsara), and history is just a lot of change. All that we can say about history, Buddhistically, is that as time goes on we get more of it.

Buddhism, also, does not regard time as existing independently of the consciousness which experiences time: time is different for different beings in different rebirths (see "The Triple World," appendix to chapter 6). What we call history is, at most, time as perceived by humans—and, we might add, only by post-Renaissance humans, that is, humans who do not live in mythological or (as Australian aborigines call it) dream time. Buddhism teaches indeed that nothing *at all* exists independently of the consciousness which perceives it (see chapter 7), that is, it teaches nonduality. Most western academic disciplines, including history, assume (with occasional unimportant modifications) a dualistic universe split between the independently existing observer and the independently existing observed phenomenon. Recently, al-

though it has become fashionable to wonder about the validity of
this split, it is nevertheless, when push comes to shove, received
academic dogma. But a dualistic tool, it should be clear, is unable
to discover non-dual reality; like stamping a blank page with the
statement "This is a blank page," the explanation destroys the
reality.

It is my contention that history, a western, post-Christian, academic discipline, is non-Buddhist, even anti-Buddhist. It is a
method of study that is alien to Buddhism and, hence, any attempt to explain Buddhism *primarily* by means of its history
obscures, and sometimes destroys, the reality, that is, the Buddhism that it is trying to study and explain. This is not to say that
history can never be usefully employed in the study of Buddhism. It is legitimate to write a history of Buddhism, but such
a book will be more history than Buddhism, and in order to
make sense of the history one should first have an understanding
of Buddhism.

This book is an introduction to Buddhism in terms of a meth-
odology that Buddhism itself suggests. The center of the book is
the space under the tree. This is a symbol of non-duality, reality
as it really is. It cannot be described, but it can be circumscribed,
pointed to, or manifested. The primary manifestation of the
space is the life of the Buddha. The secondary manifestation is
Buddhism, what Buddhism itself calls the Dharma, which radi-
ates out from the actions of the body, speech, and mind of the
Buddha, expanding through many cultures for two thousand five
hundred years and still growing. The life of the Buddha is, thus,
taken as a kind of genetic base information from which the
various forms of Buddhism may be seen to spring. The Buddhist
teachings and practices are herein dealt with according to topics
suggested by events in the life of the Buddha, without paying too
much attention to their chronological emergence or to a historical analysis of whether the Buddha actually taught them, and
without the denominational or lineage bias found in the traditional accounts that originate from within Buddhism itself.

By means of this method, I propose that I have, in effect,
reinvented the teaching of Buddhism, with a western audience
in mind. Buddhism is presented Buddhistically, that is, in terms
of its own reality, but it is also presented pan-Buddhistically, that
is, in a manner that is compatible with the post-critical reality of
the modern west.

The structure of the book is based on the Bodhi Tree, used as an allegory of Buddhism: its seed is the life of the Buddha, the space under it is the vision of reality as it truly is, and the tree is the historical reality we call Buddhism. The allegory produces the division of this book into three unequal sections corresponding to the seed, the space, and the tree.

The argument is circular rather than linear, and the central object of investigation, Emptiness or Transparency, is exposed in the center of this circle, but never expressed, since the circle cannot be entered, only known to be.

I recommend that the reader go through the first two sections in order. The third section, however, may be read in any order. Since it is circular, there is no necessary development, no historical plot, from one chapter to the next.

The reader may emerge from this book a little vague on Buddhist history, but should grasp Buddhism as an integrated, though complex, variation on the theme and vision of one life, and may even begin to glimpse the space under the tree which is, finally, the purpose of it all.

PART 1
THE SEED:

The Life of
Buddha

The Legends

The first accounts of the Buddha's life were oral. The oral transmission of sacred material is developed to such a high degree of precision in India that it is the normal or preferred method: what one has in one's head, one has surely and readily, whereas a piece of writing may be forgotten or mislaid. The Buddha probably spoke Magadhi, the language of the territory of Magadha, but he is said to have ordered his disciples to spread his doctrine in the vernacular of whatever region they entered. The first written accounts, which were in Pali, a language possibly similar to Magadhi, come from Sri Lanka (Ceylon), and are themselves already heir to a denominational bias, having been selected from a confusion of tongues and a variety of lineages. There can be no certainty that they reproduce, without modification, the earliest oral records. Undeniably, however, the Pali accounts are the oldest written texts that we have, and research into the Buddha's life frequently begins with them.

The Sanskrit tradition appears to have developed more or less independently. Almost a contemporary of the Buddha, though slightly after him, Panini systematized the Sanskrit language in a comprehensive, but cryptically dense, sutra. It became necessary thereafter to write in this elegant and rather artificial language in order to be taken seriously in academic and literary circles. Somewhat later than the writing of the Pali texts, Ashvaghosha composed the Buddhacharita, "Acts of Buddha," in the north of the Indian Subcontinent, employing a highly ornamental style of Sanskrit court poetry. It is highly literary, and clearly aimed at a cultured intelligentsia. Other accounts are written in a more vigorous style known as Buddhist Hybrid Sanskrit, which blends "official" Sanskrit with the common speech. They picture the Buddha as a great deal more exalted and transhuman than the Pali texts. It was this tradition that meandered through the Central Asian city-states—and their several languages—into China. Once translated into Chinese, which the Chinese regarded as the only civilized and truly comprehensible language, the source-language originals were destroyed. Fragments of Central Asian texts have since been recovered, but after the city-states decayed (apparently, in part, through a progressive decrease in the rainfall), and the region subsequently converted to Islam, the ancient Indo-Chinese link has been difficult to reconstruct.

The connection with Tibet is more secure. By the twelfth century C.E. a large body of Sanskrit Buddhist texts had been brought to Tibet and, under carefully controlled conditions of checking and counter-checking by bilingual scholars, translated into Tibetan. Although the Tibetan language is unrelated to Sanskrit, a series of linguistic conventions was invented so that the Tibetan texts may be re-translated into Sanskrit with a high probability of reproducing the lost original. Shortly after the Buddhist texts had thus migrated to Tibet, Buddhism (for reasons which are far from clear) died out in the Indian Subcontinent. Tibetans commonly claim that they are, therefore, the custodians of the total Buddhist tradition as it was known during its heyday in the northern Subcontinent. One might not wish to take this view quite as it stands, but there is something to be said for it.

What, then, is, "the legend of the Buddha"? The various traditions do not differ seriously in their broad outlines: the disputes are at the level of detail and interpretation. Since we are not concerned with the details (which would lead us back into a purely historical search), we can accept any version of the broad overview as our model, and the various interpretations may be fitted into it. The version commonly taught in Tibet is the most convenient, for it collates the various texts and organizes the life of the Buddha into twelve divisions called the Twelve Acts of the Buddha.[1] I shall use the broad outlines of this system as the structure of this book.

Western scolarship has established the date of the Buddha's birth as c. 563 B.C.E. and his final disappearance (conventionally called his death) as c. 483 B.C.E. The birthplace is traditionally located at Lumbini in what is now Nepal, and the death site at Kushinagar in what is now India. His life was spent in and around the Ganges basin, broadly between the regions of his birth and disappearance and the region near Gaya, India.

The Story of the Twelve Acts of the Buddha

What follows is a summary account of the life of the Buddha Shakyamuni, told according to the traditional stories, and divided into the Twelve Acts.

1. WAITING IN THE TUSHITA HEAVEN

The Buddhist cosmos is filled with a great number of heavens, hells, and intermediate states. Life in none of them is eternal, and a being will, because of the law of karma, be born in all of them at one time or another. Birth in the hells is clearly unfortunate, for immense suffering is endured there, but birth in a heaven (*devaloka*, literally "divine realm") is also unfortunate, since one's life is then so long and pleasant that one becomes slothful and drops back into the lower regions. Birth as a human is the most fortunate, for this state is at the junction of the divine and the animal, the point at which the web of karma is the weakest. Humans can make choices in ways that animals and deities cannot. Our brains have huge, empty spaces which allow us to learn and change to a greater extent than other beings. Therefore, a human has the best chance of realizing the nature of samsara and learning how to break out of it.

So, it was necessary for the life that was to become the Buddha to be born as a human. Just before that, due to his previously acquired merit, he resided in a divine realm called *Tushita*, "The Sated," where all joys are satisfied. However, he realized that this condition, though blissful, was long lasting but not permanent. Eventually it would change and he and all the other Tushita dwellers would experience the pain of loss. He knew that, to find release from suffering, he would have to descend to the human realm and work towards Buddhahood. His past stock of merit, painstakingly accumulated through myriads of good actions in the realms of animals, deities, and humans, was now large enough to ensure that, with one final great effort, he could break out of the circle. Appointing Maitreya as his successor, who would thus be the next Buddha after himself, he departed for Jambudvipa, the world-sphere of humankind.

2. GROWING IN THE WOMB OF MAYADEVI

At that moment, on Jambudvipa, Queen Mayadevi dreamt that a white, six-tusked elephant had entered her womb. By this she knew that she had conceived[2] a son whose life would be auspicious and powerful, for the elephant is a royal animal, white is auspicious, and six tusks signify wealth. As he grew in her womb, some texts say, he could be seen by her husband King Shuddhodana, and by her handmaidens, sitting in meditation, enclosed in a wonderful box that sparkled like jewels, yet was softer than swansdown. As the name Maya means "illusion" or "dependent existence," the poets write that the infant Buddha began to appear in the world through illuminating the material body of his mother like the moon shining through clouds.

3. BIRTH AS A HUMAN FOR THE LAST TIME

Mayadevi, knowing that her time was near, began to journey to her mother's home, where it was customary for a daughter to give birth. But on the way, she had to rest in a grove of tall and stately sal trees.[3] There, while standing in the classic S-bend of womanhood, and holding onto a branch with one hand, her son emerged painlessly from her side.[4] Her posture was that of the *yakshi,* a female wood-sprite connected with fertility, and indicates here the cosmic forces conspiring together to give birth to the One who will release them from bondage.

Her son, named Siddhartha, "Object Achieved," and later known as Shakyamuni, "The Shakyan Holy Man," took seven steps towards the east, the south, the west, and the north, pointed upwards and downwards, and proclaimed, "I alone in the world am the Honored One. This is my final birth." He thus claimed dominion over the entire realm of samsara, and the gods came down to bathe and honor him. On his body were a series of marks that a soothsayer interpreted to mean he was destined for universal earthly sovereignty. But, the soothsayer warned King Shuddhodana, Siddhartha would turn aside from this and seek spiritual sovereignty if he realized that worldly power was subject to decay.[5]

Within a few days, Mayadevi died and was reborn as a goddess, so that her sanctified womb would not bear again. According to some accounts, her womb was carried off to one of the heavens where it was enshrined and worshipped by the deities.

4. ATTAINMENT OF INTELLECTUAL AND PHYSICAL SKILLS

As a king's son, Siddhartha was assigned tutors to teach him literature and the arts of war. The story of his schooldays is a short one: he knew more than his teachers, without being taught. He wrote perfectly more scripts than his writing master had even heard of, could count higher than his mathematics master, and when there was an athletic contest for the hand of the lady who was to become his wife, he surpassed all in fencing and archery, wrestling, jumping, swimming, and running.

Indian culture proposes four goals for human life: *artha* (physical power and wealth), *kama* (enjoyment of sensuality), *dharma* (religious duty), and *moksha* (liberation). Siddhartha had thus far shown mastery in the first, and was to prove supreme in the remaining three.

5. MARRIAGE AND THE ENJOYMENT OF SENSUALITY

While Siddhartha was married to the beautiful Yashodhara, "Possessor of Radiance," his father took great care to insulate his son from discomfort, disease, decay, and death, in accordance with the warning he had received. He wanted his son to build on the foundation he had laid: it would not do for Siddhartha to become aware of decay and give up his right to the throne.

There are three seasons in India: hot, wet, and cool. Siddhartha was given a palace suitable for each. He was constantly attended by beautiful young men and women, could call for music whenever he wished it, and ate the most delicious food. Anyone who became ill was removed from his presence, all dirt and dead flowers were swept away. Everything was arranged to support a world-view of eternal, undying freshness.

Siddhartha, however, was vaguely uneasy. He fathered a son, whom he unflatteringly named Rahula, "The Chain." And, he was bored: he wanted to go out of his palaces and tour the countryside.

6. RENUNCIATION OF THE WORDLY LIFE

Shuddhodana could not deny this request, for fear of upsetting his son: yet he could not accede to it, lest Siddhartha come upon an instance of decay. He decided to let his son go out, but only after ordering the route cleared of all unlovely sights, sounds, and smells.

Siddhartha then sallied forth, and received the homage of the happy, youthful crowd. But somehow, a senile man broke through the cordon (some texts say he was a god in disguise). Siddhartha saw him with revulsion, and turned back to the palace to brood on the futility of a life that leads to such an enfeebled condition. Shuddhodana redoubled the forces of pleasure, and eventually his son seemed to forget the disturbing vision. But, twice more Siddhartha went out, seeing respectively a sick man and a corpse, and returned to brood as before. Finally, he went out a fourth time and saw a monk, serene, dispassionate, detached. In the life of this monk, he felt, was the answer to the problem posed by the first three sights. If he was going to find freedom from aging, sickness, and death, he would need to give up his involvement in family and property.

So, in the middle of the night, while his dancing girls lay strewn about the floor snoring and drooling, all their enchantments gone, he took one last look at his sleeping wife and child, and escaped. The gods, who were anxious to assist Siddhartha to become enlightened, so that they too might know how to emerge from the wheel of existence, muffled the sound of his horse and opened the city gates. Penetrating deep into the forest, he dismissed his faithful horse Kanthaka (who died of a broken heart and was reborn as a god), cut off his hair, removed his robes and ornaments, and, clad in homespun, searched for a spiritual teacher.

7. THE PRACTICE OF EXTREME SELF-DENIAL

The forests and mountains of the Indian Subcontinent, unpopulated by villages, have long been the home of the homeless—the *vanaprasthin*, "the one who has gone into the forest or wilderness" and *saññyasin* "the one who has completely gone away," i.e., completely renounced family and property—holy men (and occasionally women) searching for the key to existence behind the pressures and duties of family life. They are united only in their denial of the world of getting-and-spending: their teachings are endlessly varied, often alarmingly eccentric, and they seldom agree amongst themselves. Siddhartha is said to have sought out two of these teachers, Arada-Kalama and Udraka Ramaputra.

These masters seem to have taught some version of Samkhya–Yoga.[6] The basic rationale of Yoga is to establish a list (*samkhya*, "a counting") of the building blocks of the universe: when this is done, the cosmic mechanism is exposed, and escape from it is merely a matter of proper manipulation. Yoga posits a system of creation by evolution, and of liberation by devolution. Out of the Unimaginable there arises *Prakriti*, "First Formed," the prime matter, which is mysteriously "made to vibrate," or enlivened, by *Purusha,* "Spirit" and then modified by the *gunas,* "additions/modifications" to produce all the created universe. Liberation (moksha) is achieved by a successive reduction of psycho-physical activity until the ascetic merges again with the Unimaginable in eternal bliss. Arada-Kalama taught a method for returning to a condition called "the state of nothing whatsoever" *(akinchanyayatanam).* Siddhartha practiced hard, attained this state, returned to normal waking consciousness, and said, "That was merely the state of nothing whatsoever; it is not the destruction of desire."

Then, under Udraka Ramaputra he reached an even more subtle enstasis called "the state of neither–notions–nor–non–notions" *(naivasamjñanasamjñayatanam),* but again said, "This is not the destruction of desire." Siddhartha had gone to bhavagra the "limit of existence," the immeasurable vanishing-point from which the universe arises, and had declared (contrary to the views of Yoga practitioners) that this was still within the realm of conditioned, decaying things, it was not release from birth-and-death.

Siddhartha left his teachers, and wandered alone. He decided to try the practice of extreme bodily deprivation, sitting outside in all kinds of weather, not bathing or scratching himself, eating almost nothing until, according to one account, he could place his hand on his stomach and grasp his backbone. Heroic asceticism of this sort is commonly believed in the Subcontinent to lead to speedy liberation, and Siddhartha attracted five admiring disciples. However, of this practice he said, "It is not the destruction of desire."

He remembered that once, when he was a boy, his father had held a plowing festival. Not being very interested in the plowing, he had wandered away from the crowd and sat down under a tree and, his body and his mind at ease, had automatically fallen into a state of profound meditation; smoothly and skillfully his mind contemplated the rise and fall of things.

The disciplines of Yoga and *tapas* (self-denial) had only weakened him and brought him at most into a state of suspended animation in which his mind could not function. But he also felt: since the mind is what entraps me, only by the mind can I be released.

So, scandalizing his disciples by accepting an offering of food from a woman who apparently mistook him for a tree-sprite (he certainly must have looked quite bizarre), he went off alone again to find the proper place to sit in *relaxed attention*, confident that, this time, he would obtain release.

8. THE MARCH TO THE CENTER

A human and a tree are often mystically interlinked. A tree may be planted at the birth of a child; thenceforward both live in symbiosis. A tree may be regarded as the center of the world, and the support of the sky. Climbing a tree can be a symbolic ascent to the heavens.[7] The feeling "I have a tree somewhere" arises spontaneously in cultures that do not "officially" recognize the mythologem.

Siddhartha set out to find the Bodhi Tree, that particular specimen of *Ficus religiosa* under which, it is said, all Buddhas have realized enlightenment (bodhi). Finding it, he went around it to determine the Bodhi-maṇḍala, "the Enlightenment Circle," where he must sit. The ground sank and swayed on all sides except the east: here was the center of the earth for him. He made a sitting–pad of sacred grass, and composed himself on it with the firm resolve not to move until enlightenment had been attained. This was the source of power, the pivot which does not shift, the "still point of the turning world."[8] As long as he remained on it, he would be unconquerable.

9. OVERCOMING MARA

Anyone who wishes to obtain liberation must, according to Buddhism, defeat the Lord of Samsara, a powerful and cunning deity called Mara.

Thus, as darkness fell on the meditating Siddhartha, Mara came with a vast retinue to challenge him. First, Mara tried to unseat Siddhartha by fear and hate, setting horrible demons to rush upon him, and pelting him with rocks and arrows. But Siddhartha observed the phantasms with the serenity of one who knows it is only a nightmare, and by the power of his kindliness transformed the missiles into flowers as they came within range.

Secondly, Mara attempted to draw Siddhartha away by greed and lust, commanding his ravishing daughters to dance seductively, breathlessly urging him not to miss this rarely offered opportunity of consorting with them, the goddesses of the world of desire. This was a more subtle attack than that of hate. It is easy to recognize hate as negative, but lust may be mistaken for love and compassion. Siddhartha looked at the luscious ladies, realized that they were in fact skin bags of bone and excrement, only temporarily delightful, and saw them decay into repulsive old hags.

Mara was vanquished, but, bolstered by his huge army, he called upon the solitary Siddhartha to surrender, for he seemed to have no one to witness for him in the joust. "The Earth," said Siddhartha, "is my witness." He touched it with his right hand (a gesture often reproduced in Buddhist art) and it quivered in agreement. Mara left Siddhartha in peace.

10. ATTAINING ENLIGHTENMENT

In the middle of the night, Siddhartha began to observe his own former lives, the lives of others, and then the entire space-time continuum concentrated in an extensionless, eternal point.[9] He saw the universality of suffering *(duhkha),* the pain of cyclic existence, in which beings trap themselves in ignorance and desire, like an animal walking around in a circle in a cage. Cutting the circle at the right point would bring liberation: he relinquished desire (attachment), desirelessness (aversion), and indifference (mixed attachment/aversion), and, as dawn broke upon him, cried, "Now is birth-and-death finished! The ridge—pole of that house built over many lives is broken!"

11. TEACHING

The vision was overwhelming, and overwhelmingly simple. Space exists, but if someone does not believe that it does, how do you prove to them that it does? Where, and at what, will you point? Siddhartha, now become the Buddha, the Enlightened, decided that although he had freed himself it was useless to try to free others.

But the king of the gods, fearing that after all his trouble in protecting Siddhartha from adverse influences, he might not hear about what had been discovered, appeared before the Buddha and asked him to attempt to teach, out of compassion, for there were "those beings with little dust on their eyes." The Buddha saw that this was true, and began to teach. For forty-five years he traveled in the Ganges delta region, teaching any who would listen. The resulting record of what the Buddha said or is supposed to have said, and the commentaries on this, forms a considerable library, and is too extensive to be read by one person in a single lifetime. Yet, the main point is encapsulated in the short teaching traditionally said to have been his first sermon: The Sutra Turning the Wheel of Dharma (Dharma-chakra-pravartana–sutra), commonly called the Wheel Sutra.

This is said to have been spoken at Sarnath, a forest retreat on the outskirts of Kashi (now a park on the outskirts of Varanasi) the holiest of the Seven Holy Cities of Hindu India. There, in what may have been a test of his doctrine amongst the foremost pundits and holy men of the time, and in front of his five disciples, now restored to him, the Buddha formalized his vision into the Four Truths, the Eightfold Path, and the Twelvefold Cycle of Interdependent Arising. The Four Truths proclaim the existence of suffering (duhkha), its arising, its ceasing, and the path to its ceasing. The Eightfold Path elaborates the Fourth Truth, and the Twelvefold Cycle explains the cycle of ignorance and desire. If one fully comprehends this teaching, in both theory and practice, one has fully understood Buddhism.

12. FINAL NIRVANA

Supposedly on the site of a once-great city, the place where all Buddhas of the past had come to die, although all that could be seen was jungle, Buddha Shakyamuni lay down, ill from some rancid almsfood offered the day before.[10] The Samgha, the community of monks and nuns he had gathered around him, waited for his last instructions. He received one more monk into the Samgha, the last to be received by him personally, got an affirmative response to his question as to whether his doctrine seemed quite clear, and then said: "What was to be done has been done. Now, be your own refuges and your own lights. All things made of parts will drop apart. Work out your liberation diligently."

This passage has frequently been interpreted in the West as some sort of stoical call to stiff-upper-lip-ness: "Now you're on your own, chaps; do your very best for the honor of the school!" Such an interpretation is un-Buddhist, and can probably be attributed to the "muscular Protestant" bias of many of those who first put the Pali texts into English. What the passage is saying, in a rather compressed way, is that the Buddha, having sufficiently expounded true viewpoint (Dharma), established the monastic community (Samgha), and provided it with a rule of practice (Vinaya), is now handing over to the Samgha, as his deputy, the preservation of the Dharma, and the operation of the Vinaya. Henceforth, each day will begin with the formula "We go for refuge in the Buddha, the Dharma, and the Samgha." If a new monk or nun is to be received, a practicing monk or nun to be disciplined, or a point of teaching to be authentically interpreted, it is to be done by means of a Samgha-karma, an action in common of the entire community: thus, the monks and nuns are *collectively* their own lights and refuges.

Having thus spoken, the Buddha went into the deepest of trances, came partly out of it, went in again, and then attained final disappearance *(pari-nirvana).* [11] The Buddha did not strictly die, for death implies another birth within samsara, but "went out" as a candle "goes out." To ask, "Where did the Buddha go when he went into nirvana?" is as nonsensical as asking, "Where did the candle-flame go when it went out?"

His body was cremated, according to standard Indian practice, and the hard, bright lumps *(sharira)* which, it is said, all holy persons leave behind in their ashes, were distributed to the four quarters and to the heavens, to be enshrined in large reliquary-mounds (stupa) not unlike the Round Barrows of the Anglo-Saxons. The Buddha could not now be "pointed out as being here or there," but he still existed in the Dharma and the Samgha. Similarly, his relics cannot now be seen, hidden under the pile of earth, but they are present today in the perfectly ungraspable simplicity of the hemispherical stupa, and in the community of Buddhists which circumambulates it in worship.

Now, it must be asked: how can *we* come to see what the Buddha saw? And what did he see?

NOTES
to Part One

1. For the developed Tibetan tradition, see, for example, Bu-ston, *History of Buddhism*, trans. by E. Obermiller, 2 vols., Heidelberg: Harrassowitz, 1931–1932, Vol. 2, pp. 7–72. The convention of the Twelve Acts is derived from the Lalitavistara Sutra, an English translation of which has been published as *The Voice of the Buddha* (Emeryville, CA: Dharma Publishing, 1983, 2 vols.).

2. None of the legends give any suggestion that this conception was virginal. Many cultures believe that, in order to conceive, one must see (in waking state or otherwise) some specific thing such as a certain star or a particular animal or tree, in addition to cohabiting. The nature of the sighting indicates the nature of the conception.

3. The *sal* or *shala* tree is known in the West as the Bombay or Rosetta rosewood, or as the Indian or Malabar blackwood. It is a deciduous tree producing a hard wood very resistant to decay, and may grow as high as 25 or 30 feet. The botanical name is *Dalbergia latifolia* (Roxb.).

4. The birth of Jesus, as found in the Qur'an and some Apocryphal Gospels, the births of some Greek and Indian deities, and of Lao-tzŭ, is similar. It appears to be a widespread mythologem for the appearance of a *Wunderkind*.

5. In the Tushita heaven, he had known this. But intellectual knowledge and physical skills decay with the body that acquired them. The *aptitude* for them is retained, so that although the new body must re-learn them, it can do this more rapidly. (This is the Buddhist explanation of child prodigies.) Every Dalai Lama, though a reincarnation of himself, must go to school.

6. Samkhya-Yoga, as we know it, is generally said to have been founded by Kápila (perhaps prior to 6th century B.C.E.) and systematized by Patañjali (perhaps 2nd century B.C.E.), but its origin is really unknown. The classic formulation is in the Yoga Sutras of Patañjali, of which there are many English translations.

7. These and many other examples are documented in Mircea Eliade, *Patterns in Comparative Religion* (New York: Meridian Books, 1963), pp. 265–330.

8. T.S. Eliot, *The Four Quartets:* "Burnt Norton," canto II, line 16, *The Complete Poems and Plays 1909–1950* (New York: Harcourt, Brace, and World, 1952), p. 119. The whole of "Burnt Norton" is a seminal meditation on the unmoving middle.

9. A short story by Borges tries to capture the feeling of one who sees such a point, which he calls "Aleph" after the trans–finite number, any one of whose divisions is equal to its whole, discovered by Georg Cantor (1845–1918). See Jorge Luis Borges, "The Aleph," in *The Aleph and*

Other Stories, 1933–1969, ed. and trans. by Norman Thomas di Giovanni (New York: Bantam Books, 1971), pp. 3–17.

10. The preservation in the legends of this very unflattering cause of his death is a strong indication of its historical truth.

11. This "going up and down the scale" of the trances mentioned in all the legends, probably emphasizes again that even the subtlest trance is no more than the *limit of* existence *(bhavagra),* not *liberation from* existence *(moksha).* Something other than deep trance is required to get out of the circle.

PART 2

THE SPACE:

Transparent Reality

The experience of Buddhism is the experience of joy. Far from being the grim, pessimistic, and nihilistic *philosophy* it has often been mistaken for in the West, it is a supremely optimistic and positive *vision*. The Buddha discovered that his mind was, when fully allowed to be itself, intrinsically joyful, zestful, creative, loving, and wise. He then taught us—humans, deities, animals, ghosts, and demons—that our sufferings and frustrations, though very real, are no more than a sickness that has gripped our minds since beginningless time, and if we apply ourselves, we can be cured.

He identified the root sickness as ignorance. Of ignorance, all other diseases are symptoms. The principal symptom is attachment to external objects and people, and to something in me I call my Self. Ignorant of the true nature of reality, I freeze and compartmentalize it so that it seems (and *really* seems) to contain discrete things forever separate from each other and from Me. Then I try to gain happiness by collecting as many things as possible and fastening them to my Self so that it will be content and secure. As George Carlin has said, "A house is a place to keep your stuff while you go out and get more stuff."

But attachment does not work. I never seem to feel connected. I never seem to have enough stuff. If I am of a philosophical bent I may write ponderous tomes or grisly novels about how we are eternally locked into ourselves and must somehow put up with it. If I am not a philosopher, I just feel miserable and vaguely perplexed.

The Buddha discovered that this viewpoint is simply wrong. Having himself struggled with ignorance over thousands of rebirths, he finally saw the mistake. We make ourselves miserable by first closing ourselves off from reality and then collecting this and that in an attempt to make ourselves happy by *possessing* happiness. But happiness is not something I *have*, it is something I myself want to *be*. Trying to be happy by accumulating possessions is like trying to satisfy hunger by taping sandwiches all over my body. The Buddha found that happiness is intrinsic to a healthy mind, and to be happy we need to let go of our hold on people, places, things, and on our conceptions of whom we think or feel we really are, and *allow* ourselves to be happy. But we do not believe this, and we have not believed it since beginningless time. It seems wrong to us, very wrong indeed. This is the root sickness of ignorance. Getting rid of it is not easy.

Buddha taught one supreme Wisdom to combat this ignorance, and Buddhism has come up with various ways of attacking the hard shell of our stubbornness to expose the Wisdom within. The Wisdom is simply put in one word: shunyata (in Sanskrit) or suññata (in Pali). This word is often translated as Emptiness, but I propose the translation Transparency.[1] Reality, according to the Buddha, is not an illusion, it certainly exists, but its thing-ness, essence, or intrinsic autonomy cannot be found when it is analyzed. Reality is real, but its reality is *transparent to analysis.*

Reality is, for Buddhism, space-like rather than particle-like. A particle may be located in space, but space itself cannot be located. Space is non-locatable and non-referential: it does not have a beginning, a middle, or an end, an inside or an outside, it is not made up of anything or of nothing, and it cannot be packaged. It is that without which nothing could be, yet it is not itself a something or a nothing that causes anything to be or not to be. But, for all this indescribability, space indubitably and incontrovertibly *is.*

Space exists, but how it exists is indescribable. In fact, questions about how, when, and where it exists are unintelligible and incoherent. So, says Buddhism, although things (like apples) exist, while other things (like unicorns) do not exist, upon sophisticated and sustained physical, mental, and spiritual analysis, the how, when, and where of that existence or non-existence *cannot be found.* This is shunyata: Emptiness, Transparency, or, as the Chinese translate it, Spaciousness (*k'ung,* "vacuity").

Buddhism developed three major systems (with sub-systems that do not concern us at the moment) to demonstrate the truth of Transparency: Abhidharma, Madhyamika, and Yogachara.

Most Western surveys of Buddhism regard these systems as three progressive phases of philosophical development, but this view, of course, entails the historical presuppositions that I have claimed are non-Buddhist. The historical perspective would imply absurdly that Space develops, getting more space-like as time goes on.

From the point of view of the *Buddhism* of Buddhism, however, these systems are three ways of circling round the Space under the Tree, three ways of attempting to express the inexpressible vision. Each system has certain strengths, but, since they are descriptions of what is essentially indescribable, each system also has inevitable deficiencies. These deficiencies permit the system to be misunderstood such that it needs one or both of the other systems to correct it. When any one system has been learned properly, or all three have been learnt together, and this learning is combined with meditation and ethical conduct, we find ourselves firmly on the road towards the discovery of our own wisdom and compassion.

Abhidharma

Meditative introspection reveals that what I call my Self is made up of parts: a material (mostly visible and tangible) element (*rupa*, "form, color, materiality") and an invisible, mental element (*nama*, literally "name," i.e., all elements that are invisible but personal, like my name). Further introspection shows that these main parts are themselves made up of parts, e.g., my *rupa* has solid, liquid, and gassy aspects, and my *nama* contains bundles of intellectual and emotional elements both conscious and unconscious. None of these units, however, can be found to be existing autonomously. Everything is interconnected, and although the units do not always seem to cause each other they are always dependent upon the functioning of the other units. Each individual unit is found not to be a hard nugget of atomic reality, existing in and for itself no matter what, but a tiny and fleeting *functional concurrence of forces* that will be broadly the same whenever broadly similar forces create it.

In the Abhidharma or Further Dharma (i.e., Advanced Buddhism) system, these units are called dharma (literally "a holding"). Their momentary uniqueness is called *svabhava*, "own-being," and their individually recognizable profile is called *sva-lakshana,* "own-mark." The interdependence of their flashing into and out of existence is called *pratityasamutpada* (literally, "arising next to, or in relation to, each other") variously translated as conditioned co-arising, conditioned genesis, or dependent arising. I suggest calling it *interdependent arising.* Because of interdependent arising the dharmas are said to be *shunya,* empty or transparent to analysis since they are not found to exist independently but *interdependently.* Thus, Reality is transparent to analysis, or space-like.

This system was mistaken, by Buddhists themselves, as teaching that Reality was particle-like or granular, made up of infinite combinations of a finite set of simples, much as matter is understood in classical western physics as the interaction and combination of discrete atoms. The dharmas were regarded as simples, the word svabhava was taken to mean "intrinsic and inalienable being-ness" and svalakshana was interpreted as "unique and eternal property." The race was then on to see who could come up with the most plausible finite list of dharmas, each neatly pinned down and labeled with its svalakshana.[2] At the same time, this progressive philosophical rigidity was linked with a narrowing of spiritual effort concentrating on the liberation of oneself without regard to the liberation of others.

Madhyamika

Madhyamika ("Middle-ist," i.e., "the school of those who slip between all extremes of 'this' and 'that'") arose to combat the mistaken views of Abhidharma. First it made a public relations move and called itself the Mahayana ("Great Vehicle," implying big-heartedness and universalism) and its opponents Hinayana, "Inferior Vehicle." Then it used linguistic and logical analysis to show that svabhava and svalakshana, as understood by the Hinayanists, were self-contradictory and absurd, since everything is known and defined in terms of *itself and something else.* Svabhava and svalakshana are just names with no solid and irrefutable thing-ness underlying them. Therefore, the only svabhava and svalakshana that any dharma can have is that of shunyata, Emptiness or Transparency. Reality, therefore, is not granular but space-like. This is true also for the self, and if it is the case that my inner "I" is known and defined only in terms of *myself and someone else,* then it is nonsense for me to concentrate on my own liberation to the exclusion of that of others. Compassion must then be the primary inspiration of Buddhist practice.

The Madhyamikas, however, who did not suffer fools gladly, were almost too successful.[3] By bringing shunyata out of the ranks and promoting him to commander-in-chief of the Mahayana attack force, they created the impression that they were preaching Nihilism. "Nothing exists really" became, in the eyes of those who misunderstood them, "nothing really exists." Whatever such an assertion might mean—and perhaps only a philosopher could make sense of another philosopher proclaiming that he does not exist—it was denounced (especially by Hindu opponents) as ethically and spiritually paralyzing.

A similar mistake was made by Western observers of Buddhism, with similar effects. Philosophers and missionaries and, indeed, some of the great pioneer Buddhologists, called Buddhism nihilist and world–denying, and pointed to the calm repose of many Buddha images as proof that the Buddha himself was a cold fish. Shunyata was translated as "The Void" and became much beloved of the more incomprehensible Western occultists. Jack Kerouac's novel *The Dharma Bums* illustrates the moral confusion of "nothing matters" consequent upon the view that "nothing really exists." A more troubling result is the catatonic depression that may be suffered by those who, having read a couple of books on Zen, decide they should meditate and see The Void. Alarmingly, some people can actually do this and they succeed in experiencing a pervasive nothingness. But, Nihilism is one of the viewpoints consistently *denied* by Buddhism. Transparency, like space, is opportunity and connectedness, not cosmic blankness and isolation.

Yogachara

In order to correct the disastrous confusion of shunyata with *abhava,* "non-existence," the Yogachara school, as its name "Practice of Yoga" suggests, turned back to meditation and reintroduced the *dharma* list. Its dharmas, however, could not be misunderstood as atoms in a naively objective sense, for they were said to be produced by the mind. Its slogan was "just mind," *(chitta-matra),* but it assumed that we would know that this meant mind in the context of meditative practice (yoga), not "just mind" in general.

Most forms of Buddhism have a system of meditation, or mind training, which uses the aid of an *alambana,* "support." Suppose I want to meditate on an image of Shakyamuni Buddha in order to focus my mind and emotions on his good qualities. I begin with a physical copy—a statue or a picture—and study it attentively and receptively. Then I avert or close my eyes and try to see the same image mentally. When I can do this comfortably, I purify the image by removing all the defects which will inevitably be part of a statue or painting, and make a generalized, perfected image free of any physical faults. Then I play with this image, expanding it so that it fills the universe and contracting it so that I can hardly see it, yet without losing any of its details.

This exercise in mind training is compared to catching and training a wild elephant. In the west, we might prefer the analogy of taming a horse. A wild horse is no use to me, it goes wherever and does whatever it wants. When it is caught, it seems at first to become wilder as it tries to escape, but eventually, with the proper techniques, I bring its will into conformity with mine so that we work together as partners. Similarly, an untrained mind is useless to me, unpredictable and dangerous. As I try to bring it under control, it resists and appears to become even more distracted, but if I keep up my meditation I will find it gradually becoming calmer and more pliable until the full extent of its awesome power is under my control. In this exercise, the physical Buddha image is the rope, the corral, and the technique, as it were, that I use to tame my mind.

Now, the Yogacharin slyly asks, what have I tamed? The object that I call a Buddha image? Clearly not, it has just sat there quietly all along. I have tamed my *perception* of the Buddha image. I had thought that I had transferred the object to my consciousness, but I now realize that the "object" has from the very beginning of the exercise been an object-in-consciousness. This is no valid reason for me to deny the object's existence, but I must accept that the object, as far as I am concerned, depends upon my consciousness, just as much as my consciousness of the object depends upon the object. In Yogacharin terms, the object and the perception of it arise simultaneously, produced by a single seed *(bija)*. I could demur and say that the universe would not disappear if I were not to exist. How could I conceive of this? Because I can imagine a completely dead, materialistic, and unconscious universe. But where does such a universe exist? In my consciousness! So, we arrive at the surprising but altogether compelling conclusion that a completely materialistic universe, so beloved of nineteenth-century science and still in good favor, is a *fiction created by consciousness.* This is what is meant by chitta-matra, "just thinking," or *vij-ñapti-matra,* "just recognition." In other words, the objective universe exists but its *independent* existence, separate from its subjective perception, *cannot be found.* Reality, once again, is shown to be spacelike.

This system was misunderstood in its turn. In China and Japan the mists of Taoism bewitched the Yogacharins more and more to claim the illusory nature of the shifting world and to recognize mental events as alone real; in the West Yogachara was straightforwardly identified with philosophical Idealism, and it was presumed that Yogachara overturned the nihilism of Madhyamika by teaching the supremacy of Universal Mind. "Just mind" was misinterpreted as "Mind Only."

Madhyamika (Ritornello)

Buddhism produced no further correctives, but it did not need to. By applying Madhyamikan linguistic analysis to chitta-matra, both the object and the perception of the object are emptied of intrinsic and inalienable being-ness (of svabhava in the Hinayana sense), and Transparent Reality is once again rescued for our inspection. This is exactly the maneuver made by the Gelugpa lineage of Tibetan Buddhism, which teaches Madhyamika after Yogachara.

The Space

This chapter has been a quick spin around the impenetrable Space to give you the characteristic flavor of Buddhism before we delve into some of the complexities in which the simplicity of the Space has necessarily been wrapped so that we might have a hope of seeing it. "My teaching" said the Buddha, "is like the sea. It is wide and deep but it has only one taste. The taste of the sea is salt. The taste of my teaching is freedom."

NOTES
to Part Two

1. I considered this suggestion to be mine alone but, as I was revising this book for publication, I discovered that, by a convergence of karmic fruiting, Lama Govinda also proposes Transparency as a translation of Emptiness. He writes: "If *shunyata* hints at the nonsubstantiality of the world and the interrelationship of all beings and things, then there can be no better word to describe its meaning than *transparency.* This word avoids the pitfalls of a pure negation and replaces the concepts of substance, resistance, impenetrability, limitation, and materiality with something that can be experienced and is closely related to the concepts of space and light." Lama Anagarika Govinda, *Creative Meditation and Multi-Dimensional Consciousness* (Wheaton, IL: Theosophical Publishing House, 1976), p. 51.

2. That this interpretation of Abhidharma was a distortion is shown by the fact that it is only taught by the Mahayana as an elementary system (the Hinayana or Inferior Vehicle). Theravada, which continues to teach Abhidharma (it calls it, using the Pali language, Abhidhamma) as a living system, consistently maintains that the dharmas (dhammas) are empty *(suñña)* and is realistically vague about their number. See Nyanaponika Thera, *Abhidharma Studies* (Kandy, Sri Lanka: Buddhist Publication Society, Third edition, 1976), especially pp. 36–47. Also, see the discussion of Abhidharma and Abhidhamma, below, in chapter 5.

3. This point, and the consequent view of Madhyamika and Yogachara as complementary rather than contradictory, is made by Janice Dean Willis in her introduction to *On Knowing Reality* (New York: Columbia University Press, 1979), especially pp. 13–19.

PART 3

THE TREE
AND ITS FRUITS:

Buddhism

Chapter 1

THE BIRTH OF BUDDHAS

(Acts 1, 2, and 3 of the Buddha)

Introduction

Where do Buddhas come from? How many Buddhas are there at any one time?

Whenever we ask a question like this, of the form "What is the Buddhist view of X?" we need to picture a medicine or tool chest model of Buddhism and realize that the question is only meaningful when rephrased as "What is the view of X for Buddhist B at time T and place P?" In this book, I concentrate as far as possible on what links the various forms of Buddhism together, but I cannot ignore the differences entirely and still pretend that I am speaking of Buddhism as it actually exists.

In regard to the question of the origin of Buddhas in particular, different, and apparently contradictory, answers are given by different Buddhist lineages. The two chief lineages are

Theravada (dominant in Southeast Asia) and *Mahayana* (dominant in north, central, and east Asia). If you are not familiar with these terms, you may wish to turn to the appendix, "The Story of the Dharma," before reading on.

The Theravadin and Mahayanist views on the origin of Buddhas may be summarized under three heads:

1. THE BIRTH OF BUDDHAS IN ETERNITY

According to Mahayana, Buddhas are not really born and do not really die. Everything, in fact, is Buddha, but since unliberated beings do not see this, the Buddhas make a show of appearing in the phenomenal world: living, teaching, and dying.

2. THE BIRTH OF BUDDHAS IN THE INDIVIDUAL

Theravada teaches that Buddhas are highly evolved beings. They were not always Buddhas, as the Mahayana teaches, but began as ignorant life forms, such as animals or humans, and, since they attained Buddhahood, they hold out the hope that we also, in fact all sentient beings, may eventually become Buddhas. While the Mahayana also maintains this, it teaches that Buddhahood should not be a personal goal, but should be put off until all other beings have attained Buddhahood before one has oneself, while, paradoxically, all beings are Buddhas already.

3. THE BIRTH OF SHAKYAMUNI BUDDHA AT A PARTICULAR TIME

Both Mahayana and Theravada teach that the life of Shakyamuni Buddha, when viewed from the human standpoint, is bounded by historical space-time, and that he is, within the continuum that we call history, the latest Buddha to have appeared. However, Theravada maintains that only one such Buddha appears at a given time, and that his death is a real disappearance, whereas Mahayana holds that many Buddhas appear simultaneously, and all of them, whether presumed to be extinct or not, are still in contact with us.

This controversy has not been resolved. Theravadins and Mahayanists simply disagree. What seems to be going on is a difference of opinion over what the word "Buddha" really means. For Theravada, it means a person of high attainment, and must necessarily refer to a particular person at a particular time, even though they say that one who is a Buddha is totally free of limitations and so cannot be called a "human" except in conventional, everyday language. For Mahayana, the word "Buddha," while being identified with particular persons, has, in addition, a larger meaning, referring to "pure mind" or "reality as it really is," and since it is nonsense to talk of reality "being born" or "dying" one cannot, at that level of discourse, speak of Buddhas as "appearing" or "disappearing."

Risking a generalization on this sensitive issue, I propose that we might say that the Theravada teaching is that a Buddha *has* "pure mind" (not "a" pure mind, for it is not a personal possession); while the Mahayana teaching is that "pure mind" *is* (not "are") the Buddhas. The pure mind that a Buddha has is the purification of the mind that all living beings (human and non-human) have. Theravada sees this mind as pure only in the Buddhas. Mahayana maintains that, although it may manifest as defiled, mind is intrinsically pure wherever it occurs, and so it can say "all things are Buddha."

In this book we are not taking sides, but trying to understand Buddhism as a whole. Therefore, we will look at how these apparently contradictory opinions can be seen to arise from the same data and be, on their own terms, individually coherent. The three main views on the birth of Buddhas can be related to the first three Acts of Buddha as follows.

In Act One, the life that is to become Shakyamuni Buddha waits as a deity in the Tushita Heaven, where, it is said, one day is equivalent to four hundred human years and each being lives for four thousand Tushita years, i.e., five hundred and seventy-six million human years. This is, from our standpoint, such a long time that it can serve us as a symbol of the birth of Buddhas in eternity. In Act Two, Shakyamuni grows in the womb of his mother and so can be seen as a symbol of the birth of Buddhas in the individual. Act Three is, straightforwardly, the birth of Shakyamuni Buddha at a particular time.

Figure 1, "The Origin of Buddhas," charts the three views in terms of the first three Acts.

Act One is symbolic of the *synchronic* origin of Buddhas, that is, the origin of Buddhas without reference to serial space-time. This is a specifically Mahayana view, and it has two major forms. In one sense, the Mahayana teaches, everything already *is* Buddha. Since, on this view, nothing is really happening, I call it the *static synchronic model.* We shall look at its explanation accord-

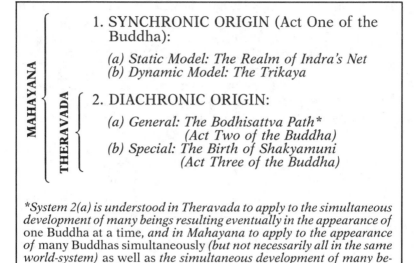

Figure 1: THE ORIGIN OF BUDDHAS

ing to the simile of "The Realm of Indra's Net." But in another
sense, Buddhas appear, they incarnate in the phenomenal realm,
and are seen as particular people at particular times and places.
I call this the *dynamic synchronic model,* since something is
"coming to be." Although dynamic, it is still synchronic, since the
"coming to be" and "ceasing to be" are appearance only. The
Mahayana teaching on the way Buddhas "move towards us without moving" is called the Trikaya, "Triple Embodiment."

Acts Two and Three are related to the teaching that there is,
contrary to the synchronic model, an evolution in space-time
from ignorance to enlightenment. This I call *diachronic,* or
movement through time, and I distinguish two forms of it. Since
all Buddhists say that all living beings have the potential to
become Buddhas, the path of the Bodhisattva, of the being who
has resolved to be a Buddha, is open to all. This is the *general
diachronic model,* and it is accepted by both Mahayana and
Theravada. However, where Theravada accepts that Shakyamuni was a Bodhisattva up to the time of his enlightenment, and
that there may well be many individuals now who, although not

recognized as such, are bodhisattvas because they are moving towards enlightenment in a similar way, Mahayana holds up the bodhisattva path as an ideal for all Buddhists and strongly advocates that they should take the Bodhisattva Vow or Resolve (*pranidhana*, "earnest application of the mind").

Finally, Act Three, the birth of Shakyamuni in time, which is accepted by both Theravada and Mahayana, relates directly to Shakyamuni's life in the human realm. I call it the *special diachronic model* since it is a special case of the general teaching that all sentient beings can eventually become Buddhas.

Synchronic Origin of Buddhas (Act 1 of the Buddha)

STATIC MODEL

Pure mind is easy to experience. Suppose we are in a very noisy place, like a construction site, for a long time. At first, the noise is bothersome, but eventually we get used to it and hardly notice it. Then, suddenly, the noise stops. It is quitting time. If we are aware of our minds we will experience, at that moment, a brief flash of total openness. There is no time or lack of time, no observer, nothing observed, and no observing. There is neither nothing nor everything, for either "nothing" or "everything" would be a limitation, an obstruction, and what we have experienced is limitlessness, unobstructedness. The experience will seem to have happened of itself, although in fact, Buddhism says, it is caused by our virtuous actions performed, perhaps, very long ago. Shakyamuni experienced such a moment of openness when, as a boy, he wandered away from the plowing festival and sat down under a tree. He realized, later, that this openness was the fruit of many ages of practice in previous lifetimes.

But, if this moment of openness is no more than the fruiting of karma,[1] and we have not learned how to cultivate it (as Shakyamuni did when, as an adult, he sat under the Bodhi Tree), the moment disappears almost at once. We become aware of the silence and think "Oh, good, it's time to go for a beer." Thoughts crowd in and obscure the openness, like clouds massing and obscuring the sky.

This state of total openness is Emptiness or Transparency. It is free of all limitations and cannot be labeled. At the time that it occurs no explanation of it is possible or necessary, but after the event we label it so that we can speak of it. Labels such as *Tathata*, "Thusness," *Tattva*, "Thatness," *Yathabhutam*, "As-it-is," and *Asamskrita*, "Incomposite," have been proposed by various Buddhists at various times. The Chinese monk Fa-tsang (643–712 C.E.) preferred the word *Fa-chieh* (Sanskrit: *Dharmadhatu*), "Realm of Dharma," and tried to show us what reality would be like if we saw it always as the Dharmadhatu, that is, if we saw everything as Buddhas and Buddhas in everything. In 704 C.E., he preached a dense little sermon before a vigorous usurper of the Dragon Throne of China, a lady who insisted on being addressed as Emperor (rather than Empress) Wu Tse-t'ien. He called it *The Essay on the Golden Lion*.[2]

Fa-tsang had been preaching on the Avatamsaka, ("Flower Garland") Sutra, an enormous scripture in which Shakyamuni Buddha, manifesting in a celestial form just after his enlightenment, presides over nine gatherings at seven different places (only the first and last being terrestrial) and causes a number of Bodhisattvas to speak at length on all aspects of Mahayana doctrine.[3] This Sutra, translated into Chinese as the Hua-yen Ching, became the basis of the Hua-yen School, founded by Tu-shun (557–640 C.E.). Its characteristic doctrine, as systematized by Fa-tsang, is the unobstructed interpenetration of the realm of liberation and the realm of suffering. The realm of liberation is called *Li*, a character meaning the veins in a piece of jade, and one of the many Chinese words roughly equivalent to English "essence," and is a synonym of Emptiness or the Dharmadhatu. The realm of suffering is called *Shih*, meaning "service, activity, manifestation," and is the world as we ordinarily see it. Li and Shih are said mutually to interpenetrate in every possible way. It was at this point, apparently, that "Emperor" Wu became puzzled. So, Fa-tsang pointed to one of the golden statues of a lion contained in the palace hall. The gold, he said, is like Li, and the lion is like Shih: both the basic substance (gold) and the conditioned manifestation (lion) are needed to produce the total reality (golden lion). There is no knife which can separate the lion from the gold, yet they differ, and there is no concept that can divide a conditioned manifestation from the universal Buddha-Nature, yet they are not the same. Fa-tsang builds and ornaments and rebuilds and reornaments this identity-in-difference until, in the seventh part of the seventh section of his sermon, he presents the following rococo picture:

*In each of the lion's eyes, ears, limbs, etc., even in every
one of its hairs, there is a golden lion. Every lion in
every hair penetrates simultaneously and
instantaneously into a single hair, such that all of them
contain all of them, interpenetrating equally. This is the
principle of Unobstructed Interchange spoken of in the
verse:*

   A Buddha's realm in every mote;
   A Buddha sits in every pore.

*In every hair there are limitless lions. Every hair feeds
back these limitless lions into a single hair, such that all
of them contain all of them, interpenetrating constantly.
This is the principle of Unobstructed Mutual Presence
spoken of in the verse:*

   A boundless sea in every hair
   Of Buddha-realms with lotus thrones.

*So it is, again and again without end. It is like the
jeweled net of T'ien-ti, who is known in Sanskrit as
Shakrodevanam Indra, the jeweled net of the Loving
Lord of Heaven, the net of pure jewels of Him Who
Guards the Hall of True Dharma. Using the endless
interchange of brilliancies as a simile, we call this, "The
Principle of the Realm of Indra's Net." The Large
Commentary says: "If two mirrors reflect one another,
their images bounce off each other."*[4]

Shakrodevanam Indra, "Indra, the Strong One of the Gods," is
the leader of the gods of storm and war in the Hindu pantheon.
In Buddhist texts, he frequently appears as the King of *all* the
gods, and so is called T'ien-ti, "Emperor of Heaven," in Chinese.[5]
His jeweled net is the night sky, each star a faceted diamond
enmeshed in a celestial web, sparkling with the reflection of
itself. In a similar way, Buddhas are in everything, and everything is a Buddha. Fa-tsang's students, less intelligent (or more
honest?) than "Emperor" Wu, could not understand. So, Fa-tsang
set up a lighted statue of Buddha in the middle of ten mirrors,
positioned at the four cardinal points, the four intermediate
points, the nadir and the zenith—i.e., "everywhere" according to
Buddhist cosmological convention. Figure 2 shows eight of these
mirrors: one must imagine another at the rear of the diagram
and one more in front of it. The Buddha image could then be

seen reflected in all the mirrors, and these reflections again reflected, up to the physical limit of the show–and–tell device. In
reality, there is no limit, and the smallest piece of the realm of
suffering thus contains an infinity of Buddhas. This is what it
means to say "All things are Buddha," or, "All things have Buddha Nature."

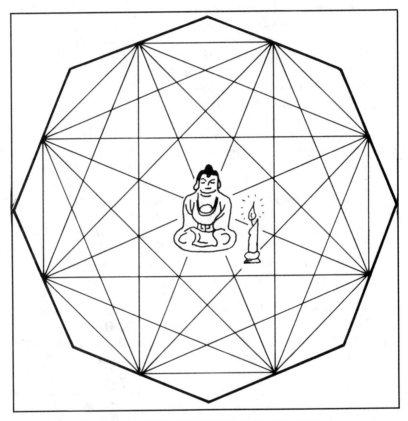

Figure 2: THE REALM OF INDRA'S NET

How the universal Buddha-Nature and a particular human
Buddha are related is explained by the next model.

DYNAMIC MODEL

Another term for universal Buddha Nature, or pure mind as
Mahayana understands it, is *Dharmakaya*. The term is used

when we wish to speak of universal Buddha Nature as it dynamically relates to our world of imprisonment in the passions. It means "Dharma Body" and is related to two other terms: *Sambhogakaya*, "Enjoyment Body," and *Nirmanakaya*, "Transformation Body." All Buddhas possess (according to the Mahayana) all three "bodies" simultaneously. (See figure 3.) The Dharmakaya is, like space, unclassifiable, and nothing can be said about it. The Sambhogakaya and Nirmanakaya have classifiable properties, and can be described. Taken together, they are called the *Rupakaya*, "Form Body," to distinguish them from the Dharmakaya, which is, of course, formless.

FORM→ SYMBOL↓	Dharmakaya (Formless)	Rupakaya (with Form)	
		Sambhogakaya Divine Form	Nirmanakaya Human Form
MENTAL STATE	*Deep Sleep*	*Dreaming*	*Waking*
BODILY ORGAN	*Heart*	*Mouth*	*Eyes*
ACTIVITY	*Mind*	*Voice*	*Body*
TEACHING SOURCE	*Dharma Wheel*	*Tanka*	*Lama*

Figure 3: THE TRIKAYA

The Sambhogakaya is awe-inspiring, gigantic, and glorious. It is a celestial or divine form; in the Buddhist sense of these words: the deities are said to have similar bodies, but not as magnificent as those of the Buddha. The Sambhogakaya is capable of moving through the universe at will, for it does not depend on the laws of physics as humans experience them.

The Nirmanakaya is the human form. It looks, feels, smells, sleeps, eats, walks, defecates, laughs, and cries just like a human.

It *is* a human. Sometimes a Nirmanakaya is called an "incarnation" or a "Living Buddha." These are not very helpful terms but they indicate an apparent similarity between the Christian doctrine of the Incarnation and the Buddhist teaching of Nirmanakaya. Whether there is any real similarity is a point that is not yet clear.

Figure 3 plots the three bodies against four sets of symbols of them.

Ordinary beings go through *mental states* which are analogous to these three "bodies." In deep, dreamless sleep our condition is similar to that of the formless and universal Dharmakaya. When we begin to dream, our consciousness manifests as a subtle body unfettered by physical laws, similar to the Sambhogakaya. And when we awake, we emerge into the world of physical reality, like a Nirmanakaya. We are not three different people in these three states, nor are we quite the same person in each state. In a much fuller and more real way, a Buddha or Great Bodhisattva also manifests in the triple "body" without either really changing or quite remaining the same.

Three of our *physical organs* are symbolic of the operation of the three bodies, and these are related to the *three activities.* The heart, which is regarded as the seat of deep mind, is a symbol of Dharmakaya or mind in its pure, primal, or pristine state. The mouth, which produces speech, is a symbol of the Sambhogakaya since it gives form to our thoughts and yet it is not as limited as the physical body. We can tell stories containing events which are not limited to the world of our everyday experience. The eyes locate us in a particular space-time and give us a sense of embodiment here and now. The eyes are most closely related to our present bodily condition, and therefore symbolize the Nirmanakaya.

Within the context of *receiving the teaching* of the Buddha (as it is communicated in the Tibetan tradition) the Dharma Wheel (often misleadingly called a "prayer wheel") is a symbol of the Dharma in its purest form, since it contains mantras. Mantra (see chapter 10) is Dharma manifested as, embodied or incarnated in, sound. A mantra may be a word, that is, a sound that has a meaning; but meaning is not its essential feature. Mantra is closer to music than to speech since its effect is in itself, in its sound, not in that to which its sound refers. A mantra communicates Dharma directly to the mind without the mediation of concepts. A Dharma Wheel spreads Dharma when it is rotated just as when a record is rotated it spreads music, except that the music of Dharma is silent, for it is purely mental. A *tanka,* or sacred picture, is a symbol of the Sambhogakaya since it depicts an entity, such as a Buddha, in an anthropoid, yet not a human, form. The body in the painting has a boneless, weightless, dimensionless quality and is more highly colored than anything we see on the human level. Finally, the lama, or teacher, is our human focus for the Dharma. Some lamas are regarded as Nirmanakayas in their own right (for example, the Dalai Lama is said to be a Nirmanakaya of Avalokiteshvara, the Bodhisattva of Compassion), but any lama can be an appropriate human focus for the teaching and can therefore be regarded as if they were Nirmanakayas in their own right.

Diachronic Origin of Buddhas General: The Bodhisattva Path (Act 2 of the Buddha)

The Sanskrit word bodhisattva is found in its Pali form of *bodhisatta* in the Theravada texts. As mentioned above, both Mahayana and Theravada refer to Shakyamuni before his enlightenment as a bodhisattva, and, in general, use the word to mean anyone who is definitely on the path to final enlightenment. The difference between Mahayana and Theravada on this point lies in the *explicit* presence of the bodhisattva ideal in the Mahayana as against its *implicit* presence in Theravada. Theravada reveres the bodhisattva *ideal,* but does not, except in very rare instances, identify any one *person* as a bodhisattva. Mahayana not only reveres the bodhisattva ideal but goes so far as to recommend it to all Buddhists, even to the point of suggesting that someone who has not formally taken the Bodhisattva Resolve is not a serious practitioner of Buddhism. Mahayana, in short, identifies the Bodhisattva Path with true Buddhism.

The main idea is quite straightforward. A bodhisattva is one who puts others' happiness before his or her own. In our usual ignorant state we look after ourselves as "number one" and concern ourselves with other sentient beings as a secondary matter. The bodhisattva practices the reverse of this. The Tibetans call it *dak-shen-jay-wa,* "exchanging self for other." Suppose two people are eating cake, and there is one piece of cake left. The one who says to the other, "Please have the last piece of cake," and really means it from the heart, saying it without any regrets and simply because the other's feelings are experienced first, is a true bodhisattva. An ordinary person will want the last piece of cake and not care whether the other wants it or not. Someone who has been practicing the bodhisattva path for a time may want the last piece of cake, then recognize this feeling, and offer the piece out of consideration for the other. Such a person has begun to practice the bodhisattva path.

Although a bodhisattva may begin practicing with pieces of cake, he or she has a much more noble, and more final, purpose. The heart of the Bodhisattva Resolve, which the Mahayana practitioner makes in a formal liturgical ceremony, is the determination that one will lead all other sentient beings without exception into final and complete enlightenment, into the end of all suffering for ever, before one allows oneself to attain complete enlightenment and the final end of suffering. This means, in effect, putting off one's own nirvana, even though one has become pure enough to attain it, for anything approaching the imaginable future. The bodhisattva dedicates his or her practice, in this and all subsequent lives, for the good of all sentient beings, "until samsara is emptied."

The Mahayana texts go into great detail about the stages or levels (*bhumi*, "ground") of the Bodhisattva Path. There are, however, many other texts and traditions about how many levels there are, what their qualities are, and how long it takes to go through them to perfect enlightenment. The Avatamsaka Sutra speaks of ten levels, and this has become the most popular teaching. Each level, it says, is associated with a particular degree of mental purity, a particular virtue, a particular meditative state, a particular power, and a particular state of rebirth (amongst humans or in one of the divine realms). The whole sequence is preceded by a "Preparatory Stage" and followed by a "Buddha Level" both of which are outside of the sequence of the ten levels. The precise explanation of all this, however, does not seem to matter in practice. When the bodhisattva ideal is taught, the emphasis is on altruistic action and not on checking up on one's progress. Even the highest teachers do not seem to be unambiguously identified as having attained a particular bodhisattva level.

A simile that is used to explain the progress as a whole involves the refining of gold. As gold is first extracted from ore, then further and further refined, then worked into an ornament, then into a more and more precious ornament—for a king, an emperor, a divine king, a divine emperor, and so forth—so the bodhisattva's mind is purified from the dross of its ignorance and made more and more charming and powerful.[6]

Certain bodhisattvas are identified by Mahayana as "Great Bodhisattvas." They function essentially as Buddhas and are accorded regular worship. Some of the best known are as follows.

1. Avalokiteshvara: *The bodhisattva of perfect compassion, who takes a variety of forms, and (in Sino-Japanese Buddhism, though not in Tibetan Buddhism) may be female, and may have eleven heads and a thousand arms. Always he/she "listens to the prayers of the world" (hence the Chinese and Japanese names* Kuan (shih) yin/Kan (ze) on) *and "always has his eyes open" (hence the Tibetan name* Chenrezig) *so as to be able to assist in any difficulty. As the servant of Amitabha Buddha (the Buddha of the Western Paradise—see the sections on Vajrayana and Pure Land Buddhism in chapter 10), he has a representation of Amitabha in his crown, but, even when he has this feature, he sometimes appears as an independent figure. The Dalai Lama is a Nirmanakaya (Tibetan:* tulku) *of Avalokiteshvara.*

2. Mañjushri: *The bodhisattva of perfect wisdom, who holds a book, from which he teaches, and a sword, with which he destroys ignorance, and rides a lion, whose voice silences all other animals. He is popular as a patron of the Zen meditation hall (wherein the wisdom of insight is sought) and of Dharma study (that is, of the wisdom aspect of Buddhist practice) in general.*

3. Samantabhadra: *The bodhisattva of perfect conduct, whose Bodhisattva Resolve focused especially on acts of devotion to all the Buddhas and the other Great Bodhisattvas, and pledges of untiring liberative action. He rides an elephant, which symbolizes the mind, as it is considered to be the wildest of all animals when out of control but the most docile of all when trained.*

*4. Achala: The bodhisattva of perfect stability. He symbol-
izes the eighth bodhisattva level. Surrounded by flames and
standing firmly on a rock, he glares fiercely at the evil in
and around his worshippers and prepares to snare the demons with his noose. In Japan, where he is known as* Fudo
Myo–o, *"Immovable Wisdom King," he was popular with
the samurai, who prayed to him that they might be able to
stand their ground and fight bravely. Many ordinary Japanese today seek his protection in the cut and thrust of rush
hour traffic by hanging his amulet in their cars.*

Question: Synchronic or Diachronic?

There is an apparent contradiction between the synchronic
vision of Fa-tsang and the diachronic model of the Bodhisattva
Path. Two ways of resolving this conflict are found in, respectively, the Tibetan and the Zen traditions.

THE TIBETAN RESPONSE

On reaching the final level of the Bodhisattva Path, Pure Mind
manifests, and reality is seen as it really is. That is, the Dharmadhatu is seen as the Avatamsaka Sutra and Fa-tsang describe it.
Since the Dharmadhatu is reality seen as non-dual, dualistic
notions such as "diachronic" and "synchronic" are abandoned in
it. One's progress was real at the time that one went through it,
but having attained the goal, both "goal" and "progress" disappear as the samsaric conditions that supported these concepts
vanish.

Attaining (according to the general diachronic model) the
Dharmadhatu vision (the static synchronic model) is the same as
obtaining the Dharmakaya (the dynamic synchronic model).
Simultaneously with the Dharmakaya, the appropriate forms of
the Rupakaya are obtained. The Tibetans identify the Dharmakaya with wisdom and the Rupakaya with compassion. Wisdom, that is Transparency, is always just what it is—it is, therefore, synchronic. Compassion, however, is active, always
moving to the assistance of suffering beings. It is necessarily
diachronic. At enlightenment, then, the diachronic and synchronic aspects of becoming and being a Buddha are seen to be
non-dual.

THE ZEN RESPONSE

The Soto lineage of the Zen tradition takes a different approach, but arrives at an essentially similar answer. Zen Master Dogen (1200–1253 C.E.) made it his life-work to answer the conundrum: "If all beings are already Buddhas, what is the point of struggling so hard to become a Buddha?"

Born into the distinguished Japanese family of Fujiwara, Dogen ran away from home to escape a proposed secular career, and became a monk near Mount Hiei, the center at that time of the powerful Tendai lineage (see appendix for the important place of Tendai [Chinese: T'ien-t'ai] in Far Eastern Mahayana). By solitary meditation, study, and learned enquiry, he attempted to solve the puzzle of so many people earnestly striving to become what they already were. After nine unsuccessful years of this, he left for China, where he felt sure there would be a monk who could answer his question, but, wandering from temple to temple, he still seemed no nearer, and two years later he decided to return to Japan. However, he revisited the monastery where he had stayed on first arriving in China, and practiced under its new abbot, Ju-ching. Ju-ching was strict, and practice was intense: monks frequently fell asleep during the arduous nighttime meditation sessions. During one of these, Ju-ching awoke a monk with the remark "Shin shin datsuraku,"[7] "Body and mind drop off!" that is, in order to realize Buddha Nature, one must discard the illusion that one is either one's body or one's mind. The remark is a commonplace of Zen, indeed of all Buddhism, but it struck Dogen, at that moment, with clarifying force. "Datsuraku shin shin!" "Drop off body and mind!" he replied, reversing the command. If one's body and mind are *really* to be dropped off, one must also drop off the *idea* of dropping them off. The question "Why try to become Buddha if you are already Buddha?" is insoluble as long as it is seen as a question looking for an answer. A question looking for an answer is a function of dualistic, or unliberated, mind. For unliberated mind, innate Buddha Nature (Japanese: *hongaku*) and becoming a Buddha (Japanese: *shikaku*) are two different things. But Buddha Nature is not concerned with duality. The "answer" lies in the dispersion of the dualistic delusion, and therefore the disappearance of the question. Practice and attainment, said Dogen, are non-dual: "Therefore, I sit in meditation not to *become* Buddha but because I *am* Buddha."

Diachronic Origin of Buddhas
Special: The Birth of Shakyamuni (Act 3 of the Buddha)

THE JATAKA

And now, dear reader, since you have been good and have listened quietly without fidgeting, I will tell you a story.

Once upon a time, that which was eventually to become the Buddha Shakyamuni was born as a rabbit. He was a very good rabbit indeed, kind and generous, and most particular to observe all the laws of his religion (he was a Hindu at the time). Telling the days by the moon, he realized that a fast day was near, so he called together his friends Otter, Jackal, and Monkey.

"We must fast tomorrow," he told them. "If you find any food, you must not eat it, but give it in alms to anyone who asks."

"Very good, friend Rabbit," they said, and they all went away to their homes.

Next day, a priest (brahmin) came by, and Otter, Jackal, and Monkey all offered him what they had in their larders, but he would not take anything. When the priest came to Rabbit, Rabbit had no food at all, so he offered himself.

"If you will build a fire, Priest, I will jump into it and you can eat roasted rabbit."

And that is just what he did. But the fire did not burn him. The priest took off his disguise and revealed that he was Indra, King of Gods, come down to test the reports he had heard about Rabbit's virtue. And since Rabbit had passed the test, Indra took the juice of the cosmic mountain and drew a picture of Rabbit on the moon. So, when anyone tells days by looking at the moon, he sees Rabbit, and remembers how well he fasted and how kind and generous he was. So it was, and so it is, and so it will be until the end of the world.[8]

This improving little tale, with its simple, nursery-rhyme quality and nanny-ish sense of propriety, is typical of the stories called *Jataka*, "Pertaining to That-Which-Was-Born." Usually called "Birth Stories," they are really "life stories," portraying the previous lives of Buddha Shakyamuni. The stories come from the vast stock of Indian tales that, via the Muslim world, have become part of Western culture as Aesop's Fables, the Arabian Nights, Grimm's Fairy Tales, and so forth. Each country and age has remade them to fit its own purposes: the Hindus, for instance, have a quite different explanation of why there is a rabbit-mark on the moon, and some say it's a deer, while Westerners call it a man.[9] Buddhists use the stories as catchy sermon material when speaking to the general laity, and especially children,[10] about basic Buddhist teachings and practices, such as the value of giving alms, being kind, the law of cause-and-effect (karma), or the mechanism of rebirth.

Jatakas typically, though not always, have the following general structure:

1. The occasion for recounting the Jataka, called "the story of the present." An incident in the life of Shakyamuni causes him to tell an appropriate story about a previous life. In the Rabbit Jataka, the liberality of a benefactor prompts the tale of the liberality of the Rabbit.

2. The Jataka itself, or "the story of the past." This is told straightforwardly. It may include verses (gatha) as well as the prose narrative.

3. The identification of the dramatis personae, called the "connection" (samodhana). Shakyamuni identifies each of the characters in the story with one of the people in the audience. So, in the Rabbit Jataka, Shakyamuni was Rabbit, Ananda (his chief attendant) was Otter, Mahamaudgalyayana and Shariputra (two of the most distinguished disciples) were respectively Jackal and Monkey. This identification demonstrates the law of karma and its effects on re-birth.

4. The Moral. This is the main point of the story. In the Rabbit Jataka, it is the virtue of liberality (dana) even at the risk of one's own life. The moral is explicitly stated and may be encapsulated in a brief mnemonic jingle.

These stories are generally accepted as likely, if not literally true, episodes in the long, laborious process by which That-Which-Was-Reborn evolved into the human called Shakyamuni, who then further evolved, in that one last lifetime, into the Buddha.[11] For Theravada, this is the only way that Buddhas come to be: they evolve out of lower forms of life. Mahayana also subscribes to this idea, but the story of the personal evolution of a Buddha is seen as the unfolding of the eternal seed of pure Buddha Mind rather than as the discovery of something new.

According to the Tibetan tradition, Shakyamuni begins his upward path when, as a hell-being drawing a flaming chariot yoked to another hell-being, he has compassion on his yoke-fellow and offers to pull the chariot by himself. Some Buddhists also say that because of the merit gained in each lifetime as an animal or human, Shakyamuni had many lifetimes in the realms of the deities. A Chinese tradition says he was born as the King of the Gods thirty-three times. The only divine rebirth that is commonly mentioned, however, is in the Tushita heaven just prior to his birth as Shakyamuni.

THE LAKSHANA

The infant Siddhartha, appearing in time, showed certain significant marks on his body, called *lakshana*, "mark," and *anuvyañjana*, "minor mark," which, found by the soothsayer Asita at his birth, indicated Siddhartha's destiny as a *Mahapurusha*, "Hero." It is common for Indian children to be examined at birth, in a manner related to palmistry and phrenology, in order to determine their future. Asita, finding thirty-two lakshana and eighty anuvyañjana[12] on Siddhartha, predicted that he would be either a world emperor *(Chakravartin)* or a Buddha: possession of the marks indicates power, but does not indicate how it will be used. The list of marks is very curious,[13] and has given the commentators a great deal of trouble: some are bodily traits desirable in any hero (broad chest, lionesque stature, etc.), others have symbolic value (prints of wheels, the symbol of power, on palms and soles), while a few are quite odd (webbed hands and feet like a duck). Many of the marks are seen on statues of Buddha, and indeed some of the marks may have been invented after the fact to accommodate the mechanical expediency of the statuary (e.g., webbed fingers don't fall off easily), rather than the other way round. The most distinctive features of the iconography, and their significance, are as follows (see figure 4):

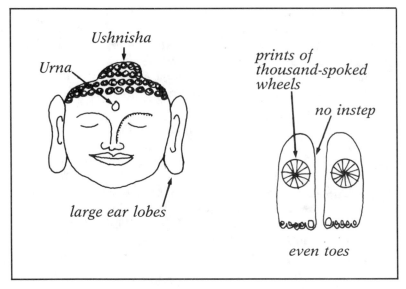

Figure 4: HEAD AND FEET OF A BUDDHA

1. The ushnisa-shirsha: *Literally meaning "cap-head" or "turban-head," it is depicted in the earliest statues as a topknot made from long flowing hair; later it becomes a large bump on the head, covered with short curly hair. In Thailand, it is elongated into a flame, symbolizing the light of inner consciousness, whereas in Zen pictures, with their more naturalistic conventions, it is often merely a very high forehead. Tantric Buddhas may wear a crown, symbolizing the identity of kingship and Buddhahood, i.e., of samsara and nirvana.*

2. The urna: *Described as a curl of white hair between the eyebrows, it is frequently shown as a dot, similar to the tilak seen on married Hindu ladies and some devout Hindu men, and later as an eye placed vertically in the middle of the forehead, the "eye of Dharma" which sees that which is invisible to the physical eyes. In Mahayana texts, the urna emits a piercing beam of light which can illuminate the entire universe.*

3. Large earlobes: *Although this mark is not in any of the lists, it is invariably in the iconography. It is normally explained as a sign of kingship, since Indian kings used to wear large earrings, similar to those depicted in Mayan art, which distended the lobes. Persons with large earlobes are generally regarded in Buddhist countries as very wise.*

4. Rounded body: *The entire body of a Buddha is full and rounded, with no concave surfaces (e.g., between the shoulder blades), massive yet sinuous, strong yet somehow boneless. This rather androgynous physique, with the stress on sedate, elephantine power rather than hard, well-defined musculature, is a persistent feature of Indian heroes, from the ancient legends down to modern Hindi movies. It is regarded, in Indian esthetics, as a mark of beauty, and it gives the impression of a being who has transcended duality.*

5. The feet: *Feet are an object of worship in India. On greeting or taking leave of one's parents, teacher, or guru, it is proper to kiss their feet, or touch their feet with one's right hand and place the dust of their most dishonorable member (feet) on one's most honorable member (head). In the absence of the feet themselves, an object marked with the prints of the feet may be similarly reverenced. Footprints of the Buddha, real, supposed, or imitation, are a common iconographic feature. Since they have no insteps (no concave surfaces) and are marked with wheel prints, they are quite unmistakable. In early Buddhism, the feet served to represent the presence of Buddha whose form, considered to have disappeared into the non-phenomenal, could not be pictorially delineated. The iconography of the complete Buddha did not arise until later, with the rise of the Mahayana teaching of the non-duality of samsara and nirvana, allowing for the representation of qualities on an essentially qualityless being.*

The question naturally arises as to whether these bodily marks are, or were, actually visible or not. Unfortunately, there is no simple answer. Both the Theravada and Mahayana texts generally speak as if they are visible, and the iconography of both traditions always shows them. However, the evidence is ambiguous.

In at least two places, the Theravadin texts mention that the signs were clearly visible, but, apparently, only to certain people. In the Lakkhana Sutta, a disciple tracks the Buddha by his distinctive footprints, and in the Ambattha Sutta a brahmin sees all but two of them, the "concealed member" (the Buddha's penis is said to be in a sort of sheath) and the tongue (which is unusually long). For the brahmin's benefit, the Buddha sticks out his tongue and, by his superior powers, makes his penis visible (though, the commentary assures us, only "the shape, the shadow" of it).[14] There are indications that people see the signs only if they know what they mean. Perhaps we can make sense of this by an analogy with language: one cannot hear a language one does not know, that is, one would not hear words, only noises.

The Mahayana tradition is clearer, but only slightly. The signs are always represented in the iconography because, the Tibetans say, the *tankas* depict the celestial form *(sambhoga-kaya)*, which, in order to impress the deities, appears superhuman. This leaves open the question of whether or not the human form *(nirmana kaya)* has the signs. From personal experience, I would say it does not: I have seen the Dalai Lama and other *tulkus,* and none of them had head-bumps, although one high lama (since deceased) from whom I took teachings, had such large ears that he reminded me of Yoda, the Jedi knight in Star Wars. But, Mahayana seems to tell me that I *would* see the bodily signs if I were in the proper state of consciousness. It does in any case require me to visualize a lama, while he is teaching, as a particular Buddha or Bodhisattva, but it is unclear as to whether, or under what circumstances, I might actually see the lama as that Buddha or Bodhisattva. At the beginning of the Larger Sukhavitvyuha, a fairly late Mahayana text, the disciple Ananda sees the Buddha as shining brightly, and the Buddha asks him if he sees this himself or if the gods have told him. Ananda answers that he sees it himself. Thus, he, as a human, seems to be seeing the celestial form, just as the deities regularly do.

Perhaps this all comes down to the Sufi saying about the saint and the pickpocket: if a pickpocket looks at a saint, he only sees his pocket. That is, unless my consciousness is sufficiently open and purified, I could be sitting next to a Buddha on a cross-town bus, and not know it.

NOTES
to Chapter One

1. Karma, in Buddhism, is the moral law of cause and effect. It is not fate. What happens to me now is the result of what I, in this life or previously, have bequeathed to myself.

2. For an abridged translation, see Garma C. C. Chang, *The Buddhist Teaching of Totality* (University Park, PA: Pennsylvania State University Press, 1971), pp. 224–230.

3. The English translation by Thomas Cleary runs to 1,459 pages, exclusive of introductory and explanatory material: *The Flower Ornament Scripture* (Boulder: Shambhala, 3 vols., 1984–1987). Thomas Cleary has given a summary of the sutra in his *Entry into the Inconceivable: An Introduction to Hua-yen Buddhism* (Honolulu: University of Hawaii Press, 1983), pp. 171–205.

4. My translation from the Taisho Tripitaka (T.XLV, 665c19–666a2).

5. Indra, as king of warriors, may have been regarded as the supreme god by the Kshatriya (warrior) caste, to which the Buddha belonged.

6. sGam po pa, *The Jewel Ornament of Liberation*, translated by H. V. Guenther (London: Rider, 1959; reprinted by Shambhala, 1971 and subsequently), pp. 241–251.

7. This is the Japanese pronunciation of Ju-ching's Chinese, in which the remark is usually quoted by Soto Zen teachers.

8. Retold from the Pali. For a translation of the original, see Henry Clarke Warren, *Buddhism in Translations* (Cambridge, MA: Harvard University Press; Atheneum reprint, 1953 and subsequently, of the 1896 edition), pp. 274–279.

9. Since we are so accustomed to seeing "the man in the moon" it may take a little practice to see the rabbit. He is sitting upright, with his front paws raised and his left side towards us. Look for the long "V" shape of his ears, and the rest of him should suddenly become clear.

10. Dharma Publishing of Emeryville, California, has produced a dozen of the more popular Jatakas in child's picture-book form, e.g., *The King and the Mangoes*, 1975 (suitable for ages 3–6) and *The King and the Goat*, 1986 (suitable for ages 4–7).

11. The precise number of Jatakas is difficult to determine. Both Theravada and Mahayana possess books of collected Jataka identified as such, but tales of the Jataka type are also found scattered throughout the literature. Some stories seem to be duplicates or variants of each other, or they may just be similar. The main didactic point, however, is that the past lives of the Buddha (as of any being) are innumerable, but only those that carry a clear moral or doctrinal message are used in teaching.

12. This is the earliest known list. Later accounts mention, though mercifully not in detail, 32,000, 84,000, or even larger numbers of marks.

13. For the list and a discussion of its possible translations, see Har Dayal, *The Bodhisattva Doctrine in Buddhist Sanskrit Literature* (London: Routledge, 1932; reprinted, Delhi: Banarsidass, 1970), pp. 299–305.

14. For this information I am indebted to Professor George Bond of the Department of the History and Literature of Religions, Northwestern University (letter dated September 24, 1988).

Chapter 2

THE VALUE OF
WORLDLY SKILLS

(Act 4 of the Buddha)

A fighting Buddhist may seem to be a contradiction in terms. Are not Buddhists committed to non-violence? Yes, and no. The first precept (see next chapter) is non-harming, but this does not mean pacifism. It is said that the best gift is the gift of the Dharma, that is, of final liberation from all suffering, but physical needs must be met first, or people will not have the leisure to understand Dharma. If the body is too weak from excessive fasting, the mind cannot function. (We will examine the Buddhist argument against extreme asceticism in chapter 5.) Similarly, if there is starvation or war in a land, the people have no energy for hearing or practicing Dharma. Buddhism, therefore, involves itself in politics, revolutions, and wars, but (ideally) only insofar as this creates a space in which the teaching of final liberation from samsara can flourish, and it is concerned with the maintenance of justice in society.

The Buddhist Ruler

King Ashoka Maurya, whose decrees were said to have been always for the betterment of the Teaching and never for the expansion of his own power, has become the symbol of the perfect Buddhist ruler. Many Buddhist rulers have aspired to be like Ashoka, and it is a high compliment to compare a sovereign with "righteous Ashoka." A fair amount is known about Ashoka, for he left behind him a number of inscriptions on rocks and memorial pillars: neither monsoon nor termite could destroy these records.[1] He ascended the throne at Pataliputra (now the Kumrahar ruins in the city of Patna, the capital of the northeast Indian State of Bihar) about 269 B.C.E. He found himself in control of most of the subcontinent, from present-day Kashmir in the north to Mysore in the south, but he added Kalinga (modern Andhra Pradesh and Orissa) to the empire. As a result of the campaign, he recorded that over a hundred thousand people died, and a hundred and fifty thousand captives were taken. Instead of exulting in this slaughter, as is the way with most kings, he became sorrowful *(shoka),* and resolved henceforth to follow Dharma (meaning, as he understood it, righteousness, piety, or religious duty). Ruling benevolently according to Dharma, he became "Not-Sorrowful" *(ashoka):*

King Priyadarshi[2] now thinks that even a person who wrongs him must be forgiven for wrongs that can be forgiven.[3]

His people were to have confidence in his generosity, but were not to suppose that all laws were about to be abolished:

He reminds them, however, that he exercises the power to punish, despite his repentance, in order to induce them to desist from their crimes and escape execution. For King Priyadarshi desires security, self-control, impartiality, and cheerfulness for all living creatures.[4]

Ashoka's function, as he saw it, was to maintain an army to insure against invasion, and a police force to ensure domestic peace. With peace and prosperity, the people could be exhorted to morality, and the monks and nuns could proclaim true teaching.[5] Ashoka separated matters concerning the present life (i.e., physical well-being), which he dealt with directly, from matters concerning future lives (i.e., final liberation), which he delegated to the monks and nuns. This relationship between the ruler and the monastics is a special case of the symbiosis between monastics and laypeople in general (see chapter 3). The ruler is the righteous protector of righteous monastics: unworthy monastics may be returned to lay life by the ruler, and worthy monastics may ostracize an evil ruler, effectively making him a "non-Buddhist" and endangering his future lives.

Political Buddhism

Buddhism often goes further in supporting the state than it did under Ashoka. In Southeast Asia, particularly, it has been used for the legitimation of power.[6] Wars have even been fought on the pretext of defending the Dharma. Some western apologists for Buddhism have maintained that there has never been a Buddhist war. This is, at best, a half-truth. There has not been any war in the Buddhist world as dramatic as the Christian Crusades, but there have been wars supported by Buddhist principles.

The problem is simple. Suppose that you are the ruler of a country that is not only Buddhist, but also, as far as you can see, the only truly Buddhist country, or, at any rate, the most truly Buddhist country in the region. Then, if your country is attacked and defeated by a non-Buddhist country, the Dharma will be destroyed. If the Dharma is destroyed, the liberation of sentient beings will be imperiled, or, at the very least, long delayed. Therefore, you opt for the lesser evil of killing non-Buddhist humans in the hope of preserving Buddhist humans and, consequently, the Dharma and the chance of liberation for all sentient beings—Buddhists and non-Buddhists, humans and nonhumans.

If the problem is simple, the solution is not, for in real life it is never quite clear how things will turn out. The conquest of Tibet by the Chinese, for example, seemed at first to signal the death of Tibetan Buddhism. Monks and nuns were imprisoned, tortured, and killed; monasteries were looted and destroyed. However, since many monks and nuns, including the fourteenth Dalai Lama, were able to escape to India and elsewhere, Tibetan

Buddhism is experiencing a renaissance as it puts down new roots outside of Tibet.

Since the Dharma is "the way things are," it is essentially eternal, but when it is proclaimed, and so comes into the phenomenal world, it partakes of the nature of samsara and begins to decay.[7] So, on the one hand, the disappearance of Buddhism is inevitable, but, on the other hand, when it does disappear the way to nirvana will be lost. Therefore, the Buddhist whose country is attacked must weigh the evidence carefully, and wisely discern whether the time has come to fight, surrender, or escape. This is not an easy decision, and it must be admitted that kings, being what they are, may decide to fight no matter what the circumstances, and monks can often be found who will support them.

It is not only rulers who use Buddhism for the ambiguous legitimation of their actions. Colonized or otherwise oppressed people may also use it when they rise in revolt. This was the case in Burma,[8] Sri Lanka,[9] and, perhaps best known because of the extensive media coverage, Vietnam. Many westerners, watching the war on their television screens, were startled to see what they wrongly considered to be "pacifist" and "world-denying" Buddhists actively campaigning against a government they considered corrupt. But this was not, in fact, something new. Buddhism in Vietnam has a long history as the vehicle of nationalist reaction against foreign domination.[10] Here also the justification was that unless a peaceful Buddhist state, free of strife and famine, was established, the best gift of the Dharma, the really helpful gift of final liberation from all suffering, could not be offered.

When the archipelago that we now know as Japan began to come together as a single country in the 6th century C.E., it quite explicitly enlisted the help of Buddhism, basing itself on the Suvarnaprabhasottama Sutra or Konkomyokyo.[11] Chapter 6 of this sutra is called "The Four Great Kings" and features the four powerful deities who are the guardians of the four cardinal directions: Vaishravana or Kubera to the north, Dhritarashtra to the east, Virudhaka to the south, and Virupaksha to the west. These deities are known in some form or another in all Buddhist lineages. In Burma, for example, they are called, respectively, Kuweira, Daterata, Wirulaka and Wirupeka.[12] In Japan they have various names, some of which are merely translations of their functions (e.g., Hoppoten, meaning God of the Northern

Quarter) while others are translations of their Sanskrit names (e.g. Jikokuten, meaning Protector of the Land, for Dhritarashtra) and, collectively, they are known as the Shitenno, "Four Divine Kings."

In chapter 6 of the Konkomyokyo, the Shitenno pay honor to the Buddha and promise that they will, first of all, protect any monks who recite this sutra, and, furthermore, they will protect the king who protects such monks. A human king who acts in this way is assured that whenever a foreign power moves against him the Four Divine Kings will fight with their heavenly armies against the invader so that the intruder will not even be able to enter the land which the Divine Kings are protecting. Conversely, any country which, having heard of this sutra, neglects to honor it by having it liturgically recited, will be deserted by the Divine Kings and left open to invasion.

Reading this, the Prince Regent Shotoku Taishi, who wrote the first Japanese Constitution and is honored by Japanese Buddhists as a great Bodhisattva, built the Shitennoji "Temple of the Four Divine Kings," in 593 C.E. In 741 C.E., Emperor Shomu went even further. He established two temples in every province, one for monks and one for nuns, to be supported by the state (therefore called *kokubunji*, "State Temples") as long as the monks and nuns recited, as a major part of their practice, the Konkomyokyo. Thus, Buddhism became part of the Japanese defense system. By the time of the Meiji (1868–1911) this principle had become enshrined in the slogan *goho-gokoku*, "When Buddhism is protected, the State is protected."[13]

Social Buddhism

There are two forms of Buddhism that, in very different ways, emphasize social action above all else:[14] the Nichiren Shoshu of Japan, and the reform movement of Dr. Ambedkar in India.

NICHIREN SHOSHU

Nichiren Shoshu, "The Orthodox Nichiren Lineage," is nothing if not clear, organized, and motivated. It claims to have the true Buddhism, proves it by its physical success, and aims at the destruction of all other forms of religion.[15] Its roots are in a medium length Mahayana Sutra, Saddharmapundarika Sutra or Sutra on the True Dharma which is like a White Lotus, called the

Lotus Sutra for short.[16] This text presents Shakyamuni in his gigantic-sized, Sambhogakaya form preaching the Mahayana doctrines that had been withheld from the Hinayana. It may have been written about the beginning of the Christian era. Partly perhaps because it was chosen by the Chinese monk Chih-i (531–597 C.E.) as the perfect expression of Mahayana,[17] it has become one of the most popular texts of Far Eastern Buddhism. It was studied by Nichiren (1222–1282 C.E.), a Japanese Tendai monk practising on Mount Hiei. He seems to have decided that the scholastic exegesis of the Lotus Sutra had become over-sub-tle, and that its main points had been missed. The Sutra was not concerned, he felt, with voluminous doctrinal formulae, but with the victory of the oppressed under the leadership of the Bodhisattva Vishishtacharitra ("He of Superlative Action"; known as Jogyo Bosatsu in Japan), who is mentioned in chapter 15[18] of the Lotus Sutra as the leader of a vast army of Bodhisatt-vas who emerge from below the earth to worship the Buddha. Coming out of the earth signified, for Nichiren, the release of the lowly from injustice, and he identified Vishishtacharitra with himself. Later followers came to regard Nichiren as the pre-eternal Buddha, superior to all other Buddhas. Only by cleaving to the supreme doctrine of the Lotus Sutra could anyone be free, either relatively (i.e., within samsara) or absolutely (i.e., by leav-ing samsara). He expressed his contempt for competing forms of Buddhism in four staccato phrases:

1. "Nembutsu muken": *Those who recite the Buddha's Name in the hope of paradise will be reborn in hell.*

2. "Zen temma": *The practitioners of Zen are deluding de-mons.*

3. "Shingon bokoku": *The Tantric Buddhists, who say they are protecting the country, are traitors.*

4. "Ritsu kokuzoku": *The Buddhists who punctiliously ob-serve the monastic regulations are rebels.*

The government attempted to execute Nichiren as a trou-blemaker, but he was saved by a miracle, and exiled to the island of Sado between 1271 and 1274. He founded two temples before he died, and began the *Hokke Shu,* "Lotus Lineage" which emphasized the great merit of reciting the mantra *NAM'MYO–HO–REN–GE–KYO,* "Hail to the Lotus Sutra." Since the Lotus Sutra says that reciting a single phrase from it earns as much merit as reciting all of it, and since, according to classical Chinese thought, the essence of a book is encapsulated in its name or title, those who recite *NAM'MYO–HO–REN–GE–KYO* will find that they get all that they need.

After Nichiren's death, the lineage did not have a large following until Toda Josei (1900–1958 C.E.) became president of the *Soka Gakkai,* "Value-Creation Society," in 1951. Soka Gakkai is a lay organization that grew out of the educational theories of Makiguchi Tsunesaburo (1871–1944) who, in his four-volume work *Soka Kyoikugaku Taikei,* "A System of Value-Creation Education," written between 1930 and 1934, offered the unexceptionable idea that education should increase the student's sense of values. Toda befriended Makiguchi, both joined the Nichiren Shoshu (an outgrowth of the Hokke Shu), and, after Makiguchi's death, Toda whipped up what had been a study circle into a tightly run missionary society. He vowed to obtain the conversion of seven hundred and fifty thousand families before his death, and far exceeded his goal.

Today, Soka Gakkai is a potent force in Japanese society, able to stage breathtakingly unified mass meetings and, through the *Komeito,* "Clean Government Party," it is powerfully influential in the Diet (the Japanese parliament).[19] Its militancy alarms non-members, who may argue that is is not really Buddhism. Soka Gakkai claims, for instance, that Japan lost the Second World War because the Four Divine Kings deserted Japan when the Lotus Sutra was neglected. Soka Gakkai also has a world mission, with an American headquarters near Los Angeles and branches throughout the United States. Members of Soka Gakkai in America, where it is called Nichiren Shoshu of America (N.S.A.), attribute such varied practical benefits as release from drug addiction, a happy sex life, improved sports performance, good business deals, and successful hitch-hiking to the persistent recitation of the mantra *NAM'MYO–HO–REN–GE–KYO.* Unlike most Buddhists, they make great efforts to gain converts, and may claim that other Buddhists are not "real" Buddhists. And, whereas Nichiren himself originally claimed the Lotus Sutra as the salvation of Japan, American devotees patriotically use it to pay homage to the Stars and Stripes, sometimes with fife-and-drum bands.

AMBEDKAR BUDDHISM

The Indian reform of Dr. Ambedkar is a less startling development. It is not exclusivist, and lays no claim to world domination. Its activities are concentrated on raising the morale and the standard of living of the so-called "Scheduled Castes" or Untouchables in Indian society.[20]

Dr. Bhimrao Ramji Ambedkar (1891–1956), known to his followers as Babasaheb, "Honored Father," was himself of the Scheduled Castes but, through education,[21] he became a lawyer and a member of the colonial Constituent Assembly (parliament). As Law Minister of the first Government of post-British India, he chaired the drafting committee of the Constitution and was instrumental in the passing of the bill on April 29, 1947, which stated "Untouchability in every form is abolished and the imposition of any disability on that account shall be an offense." Abolition in theory, however, is very different from abolition in fact. Although one does not notice much of a problem in the larger Indian cities, where money is what counts, the violent murder of village Untouchables who, for example, might attempt to use the caste Hindu well when their own has dried up, is still not uncommon. Dr. Ambedkar attacked the problem of untouchability in two ways: education, and conversion to Buddhism. He founded the People's Education Society of Bombay in 1945. A passage from its Silver Jubilee souvenir booklet neatly defines the relationship of education and Buddhism to each other, and their practical utility:

> *The People's Education Society derives its inspiration from the teachings and ideals of the Lord Buddha; it believes in the principles of social equality and justice. Its primary aim has been to promote higher education among the poorer people in general and the scheduled castes, scheduled tribes and other backward classes in particular. Its motto is "Knowledge and Love" for, "Knowledge is Power." Its founder, Dr. B. R. Ambedkar, believed that education was the only effective lever for the uplift of the down-trodden.[22]*

Education in India tends to be the preserve of the caste Hindus. Dr. Ambedkar had used education to break the caste barrier himself, and he prescribed it as a general remedy. Buddhism, mainly that of the Pali Suttas, was chosen (after some flirting with Sikhism) as an ideological vehicle because it is natively Indian yet anti-caste. Dr. Ambedkar's understanding of the Suttas is presented in his *The Buddha and His Dhamma,* published posthumously in 1958 by the P.E.S. Especially characteristic is part V, "What is Saddhamma," in which true Buddhism *(saddhamma)* is said to consist of ethical conduct, universal education, and social equality, without deities or "priestcraft." Shri M. B. Chitnis, a close co-worker of Dr. Ambedkar and Principal Emeritus of Milind Mahavidyayala, Aurangabad, Maharashtra, in an interview he graciously granted me at his home on June 26, 1974, stressed the pivotal importance of the following passage from *The Buddha and His Dhamma:*

> *Dhamma is righteousness, which means right relations between man and man in all spheres of life. From this it is evident that one man if he is alone does not need Dhamma. But when there are two men living in relation to each other they must find a place for Dhamma, whether they like it or not. Neither can escape it. In other words, Society cannot do without Dhamma.*[23]

Ambedkar Buddhists may hold *pujas* (worship services), weddings, festivals, etc., that are not exotically different from those of their caste Hindu neighbors, and so can conduct themselves with equal dignity. Finally, however, the aim is not to raise one's caste, but to abolish the entire caste system. For this reason, Ambedkar Buddhists are eyed with distrust by caste Hindus, one of whom, otherwise charming and scholarly, did not hesitate to describe them to me as "traitors."

The Martial Arts

The Buddha was of the warrior *(kshatriya)* caste. In his youth, he surpassed all others at wrestling, archery, and athletics, and at the crucial moment of his enlightenment, he sat firm on the Bodhi-mandala, "Enlightenment-Space," and defeated Mara, the worst of all opponents. When Bodhidharma, a semi-legendary Indian monk, brought Zen to China around 470–520 C.E., he is said to have taught a method of fighting that, anchored in the Buddha-mind, would be invincible. He took up his quarters in the Little Forest Monastery *(Shao-lin Ssŭ),* and instructed its monks in the art of repelling brigands. They were to fight only as much as was necessary to allow law-abiding people to work at their jobs in peace: destruction of evil, not conquest, was the aim. In succeeding centuries, many different styles of fighting have been developed, and they have passed into Korea, Japan, and elsewhere, undergoing further modifications as they traveled. Some of the best known are:

1. Kung-fu *(Chinese: "Powerful Ability"): Based on circular body-movements and allied with native Chinese methods of breath-control, this method may employ weapons fashioned from farming implements, or dispense with weapons.*

2. Karate *(Japanese: "Empty Hands"): A development of Kung-fu with more linear body-movements, always without weapons.*

3. Judo *(Japanese: "The Way of Yielding"): Another development of Kung-fu, in which the combatant yields to his opponent in such a way that the force of the opponent's attack becomes the force of his own defeat.*

4. Kendo *(Japanese: "The Way of the Sword"): The professional form of fencing with a large two-handed sword, used by the Japanese samurai.*

5. Kyudo *(Japanese: "The Way of the Bow"): Archery, using the Japanese bow, which is held above the head and drawn by bringing the outstretched arms down to the level of the shoulders.*

The single most important Buddhist teaching underlying the martial arts is that of "No Reflective Thinking" (*wu-hsin* in Chinese, *mu-shin* in Japanese).[24] When we are asked "Which is the way to Washington, D.C.?," we stop and think before we answer: the mind "moves," like a computer scanning its memory bank or like a juke-box selecting a record. However, when we touch a hot stove, we remove our hand "automatically," only later thinking "How hot that *was!*": the mind is "unmoving," there is no sense of an ego, of a thinker, intervening between the touching of the stove and the movement away from it. Indeed, frequently, even the pain and the dualistic thought of a self thinking itself to have been burnt comes later. The enlightened mind of Buddha acts with no thought of an actor, and it is this mind that must control the successful fighter's movements.

Some of this can be developed simply by overlearning, patiently doing and redoing basic exercises, until they come together naturally as a series of learned reflexes in actual combat.[25] But, though one may remove one's hand from a hot stove by an unlearned reflex, and move a sword by a learned reflex, one cannot get to Buddhahood by any sort of reflex. Over and above this is the practice of meditation, which disperses all clinging at "me" and "mine" so that, eventually, the combat is done, but "no one" does the combat. Eugen Herrigel, practicing Kyudo, asked his Master:

> *"How can the shot be loosed if 'I' do not do it?"*
> *" 'It' " shoots," he replied.*[26]

One day, "It" shot. Herrigel said:

> *How it happened that (the shots) loosed themselves*
> *without my doing anything, how it came about that my*
> *tightly closed right hand suddenly flew back wide open,*
> *I could not explain then and I cannot explain today.*[27]

It should be clearly noted that the action of *mu-shin* bears only a surface similarity to the sub-rationality of the reflex. It is in fact *outside of* rationality. It is non-referential. *Mu-shin* acts out of Emptiness. A reflex action is, precisely, *conditioned,* and therefore intra-samsaric.

This basic Buddhist doctrine is allied with a devotion to Achala Bodhisattva (Japanese, *Fudo Myo-o*)[28]; with various compatible ideas from Taoism such as "unmoving movement" (e.g., *Tao Te Ching,* chapter 47) and "naturalness" (Chinese: *tzŭ-jan*); and with, in Korea and Japan, the simple love of a good fight. Martial arts are disciplined means to enlightenment for those of an athletic or martial disposition.

Buddhism and Art

Among the kingly arts at which the young Bodhisattva Shakyamuni excelled were those of writing, music, and cultured entertainment. Wherever there has been Buddhism, there has been Buddhist art. Buddhism has never been iconoclastic. Although the actual form of the Buddha may at times be left out of a picture, there remains a picture nonetheless. The Dharma is "lovely in its beginning, lovely in its continuation, lovely in its ending" (Vinaya–piṭaka 1:21). The Pali texts call nibbana (nirvana) *ehipassiko*, "inviting of inspection," literally "come-and-see-ish." Buddhist monasteries are often noteworthy for their architecture and for the art which they contain. Most Japanese temples, for example, have a treasure house that visitors see as a part of the regular tour.

Japan has intregrated art into daily life, almost to the point of identifying aesthetics with religion. In the west we might say "It's not really religious, it's just art." This would not be very comprehensible in a Japanese context. We might ask, for instance, what is religious about a frog jumping into a pond? The poet Basho (1644–1694 C.E.) tells us in this famous haiku:[29]

$$\frac{\begin{array}{l}\textit{Old Pond}\\ +\ \textit{Frog}\end{array}}{=\ \textit{Splash}}$$

If everything is Buddha, then an old pond, a frog, and the splash it makes are all Buddha. But, of course, not from the point of view of ordinary, defiled consciousness. All these things are Buddha only when they are themselves seen with the observer's Buddha Mind, and then, all notions of observer, observed, and observing, disappear. What Basho had, and what he is trying to make us have, was a moment of enlightenment (satori), a moment something like that in the construction site when the noise suddenly stopped. Clear Mind, Pure Mind, or Buddha Mind, suddenly manifests, apparently spontaneously.

This, analogous to the martial arts, is the motivation for the so-called Zen Arts of painting, calligraphy, composing haiku, flower-arranging *(ikebana)*, gardening, and, especially, serving tea *(chado* or *cha-no-yu)*.

Chado means the Tao of Tea, and is sometimes translated "Tea-ism." A number of books on Chado are available in English,[30] but to understand it one has to experience it, for it is a "way" (a Tao), not a theory of aesthetics.

Japanese monks who traveled to China brought tea back with them. At first it was a curiosity, an elegant diversion at the imperial court. But the Zen Master Eisai (1141–1215 c.e.) recommended tea for everyone, as, he claimed, a more healthful beverage than sake. Why, he asked, are we Japanese skinny, sickly, and short-lived, while the Chinese are healthy and long-lived? Because, he answered himself, we do not drink tea. Tea stimulates the heart, which, according to the medical theory which Eisai had learned, is the primary organ controlling health. By drinking tea, we become "good-hearted."[31] There is a legend that tea was invented by Bodhidharma (whom we have seen is also credited with the invention of the Sino-Japanese martial arts). The story is that, as Bodhidharma was meditating one day, he began to feel drowsy. Try as he might, he could not keep his eyes open. So, in desperation, he tore his eyelids off and threw them onto the ground. They took root and became the tea plant. Thus, tea keeps our eyes open because it is the sacrament of Bodhidharma's wakefulness. It is not uncommon for a wake-up cup of tea to be served in Zen temples before the early morning meditation session.

Chado developed outside a monastic, or even a Buddhist, context. It brought with it, from China, elements of Taoism and Confucianism, and blended them with Shinto, the indigenous religion of Japan. As practiced today it is difficult to call it "religious" without qualification. I have taken tea as part of the tour of a Zen temple in Kyoto, but also had it served to me by a Maui housewives' association in a Japanese supermarket in Honolulu, and found elegant little cafés in Japan that serve "quicky" formal tea off of individualized electric hotplates. Its most important cultural function in Japan today, perhaps, is as a refined accomplishment of young ladies, making them more marriageable.

At its most formal, however, a tea ceremony is like a concert, or a ballet, in which all the participants are simultaneously performer and audience. It takes place in the deceptively simple setting of a hut in a small garden, meticulously and expensively arranged so as to look poor, rustic, and natural. The dress, behavior, and speech of the participants is strictly prescribed by custom and the particular lineage in which the Tea Master or Mistress was trained. The utensils are carefully chosen so that, like naturally occurring objects, they complement each other but do not match. A slightly asymmetrical tea bowl, which looks more "natural," is admired over a perfectly round one. When one shops for a tea bowl, it is said that you do not choose it: the right one chooses you. The sights, sounds, and smells accompanying the ceremony are carefully attended to. The whole idea is to be *in* the process of preparing and drinking tea. It is this, perhaps, that makes it appear "religious" to a westerner. The Eternal Present spoken of by people we tend to call mystics is the ideal condition in which to be when participating in a tea ceremony. This moment is called *nen* in Japanese Buddhism, a Chinese character meaning "remember" and composed of the element for "now" and the element for the mind or heart: *nen* is the heart-mind in the now.

The formality of the tea ceremony derives from Confucianism, the acquired spontaneity of the formality from Taoism, the appreciation of natural surroundings from Shinto, and the attitude of *nen* from Buddhism. As the martial arts are a skillful means to enlightenment for those of a military disposition, so Chado and the other "Zen Arts" are a skillful means for persons who are more attracted to art than war.

NOTES
to Chapter Two:

1. For texts and translations, see G. Srinivasa Murti and A. N. Krishna Aiyangar, *Edicts of Aśoka* (Madras: Adyar Library, 2nd edition, 1951). An accessible introductory selection in English translation is N. A. Nikam and Richard McKeon, *The Edicts of Asoka* (Chicago: University of Chicago Press, 1959).

2. "Handsome," a common epithet of Ashoka.

3. Rock Edict 13. Translation of Nikam and McKeon, op. cit., p. 28.

4. Ibid., pp. 28–29.

5. As would be expected in India, all teachers of all religions were allowed to preach freely, though Ashoka seemed to have a strong bias in favor of Buddhism.

6. See Bardwell L. Smith (ed.), *Religion and Legitimation of Power in Sri Lanka* and *Religion and Legitimation of Power in Thailand, Laos and Burma* (Chambersburg, PA: Anima Books, 1978); Trevor O. Ling, *Buddhism, Imperialism and War: Burma and Thailand in Modern History* (London: Allen and Unwin, 1979).

7. The notion of the decay of the Dharma, and how it is handled by various Buddhist lineages, will be dealt with in chapter 10.

8. E. Sarkisyanz, *Buddhist Backgrounds of the Burmese Revolution* (The Hague: Nijhoff, 1965).

9. H. A. I. Goonetileke, "The Sri Lanka Insurrection of 1971: A Select Bibliographical Commentary" in Bardwell L. Smith (ed.), *Religion and the Legitimation of Power in South Asia* (Leiden: Brill, 1978).

10. Thich Nhat Hanh, *Vietnam: Lotus in the Sea of Fire* (London: SCM Press, 1967).

11. English translation by R. E. Emmerick, *The Sutra of Golden Light* (London: Luzac, 1970).

12. Melford E. Spiro, *Burmese Supernaturalism* (Englewood Cliffs, NJ: Prentice Hall, 1967), p. 44.

13. For alerting me to this slogan I am indebted to Professor Winston Davies, Department of Religion, Southwestern University.

14. A phenomenon known as Engaged Buddhism, in which social action is emphasized more than it is in traditional Buddhism, but is not made the primary activity, is beginning to take shape, especially in North America (where it is, in particular, allied with the peace movement) and Southeast Asia (where it tends to exhibit "Third World" concerns of aiding the socially disadvantaged). For North America, see *The Path of Compassion: Contemporary Writings on Engaged Buddhism*, edited by

Fred Eppsteiner and Dennis Maloney, 2nd edition (Berkeley, CA: Parallax Press, 1988). For a Southeast Asian example, see Joanna Macy, *Dharma and Development: Religion as Resource in the Sarvodaya Self-Help Movement* (West Hartford, CT: Kumarian Press, 1983). A Buddhist approach to ecology is also beginning to emerge. See *Tree of Life: Buddhism and Protection of Nature* (text in English, Tibetan, and Thai), published in 1987 and available from Ms. Nancy Nash, Buddhist Perception of Nature, 5-H Bowen Road, 1st Floor, Hong Kong.

15. Studies of Nichiren Shoshu and its offshoot Soka Gakkai are numerous, but most treat it only as a fanatical social movement. A book which explores it more religiously is Kiyoaki Murata, *Japan's New Buddhism* (New York: Walker/Weatherhill, 1969).

16. In the Far East the Lotus Sutra is usually read in the Chinese translation of Kumarajiva (c. 350–410 C.E.). This has been translated into English by Leon Hurvitz as *Scripture of the Lotus Blossom of the Fine Dharma* (New York: Columbia University Press, 1976); by the Buddhist Translation Society, San Francisco, with an extensive commentary, running to many volumes, by Master Hsüan Hua, as *The Wonderful Dharma Lotus Flower Sutra* (1977 and subsequently); and by Bunno Kato, *et al.*, in *The Threefold Lotus Sutra* (Tokyo: Kosei Publishing Company, 1975) (distributed in the U.S.A. by Weatherhill). Hendrik Kern's *Saddharma-Puṇḍarika or The Lotus of the True Law,* published as volume 21 of *The Sacred Books of the East* (Oxford, 1884) and reissued by Dover Books, New York, (1963 and subsequently) is a translation from the Sanskrit, which differs significantly from Kumarajiva's version.

17. See below, chapter 9.

18. Chapter 14 in the extant Sanskrit version.

19. There is no official connection between Soka Gakkai and Komeito, but Soka Gakkai members seem to block-vote for Komeito candidates.

20. "Scheduled Castes" was the term used by the British administration for what are generally known as "untouchables," or outcastes. Since 1938, under Mahatma Gandhi's influence, the designation *Harijan*, "God's People," has become official, but Ambedkar Buddhists are opposed to this "giving a dog a sweet name" and commonly refer to themselves as *Shedulika*, Indianizing the British pronunciation of "schedule."

21. His record is by any standards distinguished, and, for an Untouchable of the time, remarkable: B.A., Elphinstone College (Bombay), 1913; M.A. (1915) and Ph.D. (1916), Columbia University; M.Sc. (Econ.), University of London, 1921; D.Sc. (Econ.), University of Bonn, 1923; called to the Bar, London, 1923; Honorary LL.D, Columbia University, 1952.

22. *Silver Jubilee Celebrations of the People's Education Society (1945–1970) and the Siddharth College of Arts and Science, Bombay (1946–1971) on 14th. and 15th. January, 1974.* No publisher, date, or pagina-

tion given. Latest reports indicate that, education having had some success in conferring a sense of dignity on the Shedulika, more obviously Buddhist subjects such as meditation are now being taught.

23. Quoted from p. 316, without the editorial enumeration.

24. Frequently translated as "No-Mind," though it has nothing to do with zombies. It means no *defiled* mind.

25. The celebrated cellist Pablo Cassals said, at the age of ninety, "Every morning I begin with the scales and the arpeggios, and end with a Bach sonata."

26. Eugen Herrigel, *Zen in the Art of Archery* (New York: Vintage Books, 1971), p. 76.

27. Ibid., p. 77f.

28. Since the practitioner is immovable like the Buddha when he battled Mara, the practice-hall is called *Dojo*, a Japanese translation of *Bodhimandala*. Achala's function as a patron of motorists has been noted in chapter 1.

29. *Furu ike ya*, "as for an old pond," *kawazu tobi-komu*, "frog jumps in," *mizu-no-oto*, "water's sound." Stephen Beyer's translation into Concrete Poetry, in his *The Buddhist Experience* (Encino, CA: Dickenson, 1974), p. 248, comes very close to the egoless apprehension of the Japanese original.

30. The best introduction is still *The Book of Tea* by Kakuzo Okakura, published in 1906 and reprinted by Dover (New York), 1964 and subsequently. One of the more complete accounts in English is *Cha-no-Yu: The Japanese Tea Ceremony* by A. L. Sadler, published in 1933 and reprinted by Tuttle (Rutland, VT), 1962.

31. Eisai's tract is called *Kissa Yojo Ki*, "An Account concerning Nourishing Life by Drinking Tea." There is a selection from it in English translation in *The Buddhist Tradition in India, China and Japan*, ed. Wm. Th. de Bary (New York: Modern Library, 1969 and subsequently), pp. 365–367.

Chapter 3

BUDDHISM IN FAMILY LIFE

(Act 5 of the Buddha)

Before Shakyamuni left home to become a monk, he had married and fathered a child. Monasticism is very important, and very visible, in Buddhism, but it is neither possible nor desirable for every Buddhist to enter a monastery. And, although the monastic life is held up as an ideal, it is never said that one must be a monk or nun in order to get to nirvana. It should be easier to be virtuous and meditative in the controlled environment of the monastery, but there is also the danger that the monastic will become slack and proud without the daily challenges of ordinary life. In all countries where Buddhism is prominent, a symbiotic relationship has developed between monastics and laypersons.

Symbiosis of Monastics and Laypersons

The monk or nun has no property, no family, and no income, and is therefore dependent on the layperson to provide lodging, new recruits, and food. Since certain kinds of work are forbidden to the monastic, such as agriculture or handling money,[1] there must be laypeople to help. The layperson, on the other hand, does not have as much leisure as the monastic to study or meditate, and is in need of education and wise counseling: for all these things, the layperson looks to the monastic. Broadly, the monks and nuns concern themselves primarily with liberation from samsara, while the layperson is principally concerned with living this life. The layperson can, therefore, assist the monastic by providing temporal necessities, while the monastic, in return, teaches Dharma. The details of this interrelationship are quite complex: some of its more important aspects are diagrammed in figure 5,[2] which, though largely based on the Theravadin situation, is broadly relevant to the Mahayana also.

In Theravadin countries, the most obvious expression of this symbiosis is seen each morning, when the monk (as is explained in the next chapter, there are no nuns in Theravada) calmly and recollectedly goes from door to door of the laity's houses. The layperson (often the wife) who wishes to gain merit comes out of her house with food. The monk "opens" (i.e., takes the lid off) his bowl and "receives" (the bowl is a "receiving bowl," not a begging bowl) whatever food is offered without regard to what the food is or who is offering it. The layperson, having been thus granted the opportunity of gaining merit, then says "thank you" by foot worship or some other appropriate act. The monk, who is merely the instrument of the layperson's merit and is himself supposed to be unconcerned whether he eats or starves, does not acknowledge the gift, but silently passes on. Mahayana countries have largely abandoned this practice, lay support coming mostly from endowments, but it is preserved by the Zen lineage, where it is regarded as an exercise in humility. The Zen receiving round is not performed daily, but on definite, pre-set and publically announced occasions on which bags of uncooked rice are accepted from the laity and put into the monastery's storehouse.

In all countries in which Buddhism has penetrated, a funeral is an important time for lay/monastic interchange. Buddhism regards death as the great moment of opportunity: depending

ACTIVITY	LAY	MONASTIC
DONATIONS:	Food; clothing; temples; land; sons and daughters.	Maintenance of temples and the monastic life.
MORAL CENSURE:	Popular criticism of bad monastics; occasional government investigations of lay monasteries	Criticism of individual laypersons; occasional "excommunication" of a ruler by "inverting the bowl."
DHARMA:	Listening to teachings; making retreats and pilgrimages; worshipping.	Teaching; conducting worship and funerals; blessing and excorcising.
EDUCATION:	Donating libraries.	Free schools.
SOCIAL SERVICE:	Donating and endowing buildings for hospitals, orphanages, etc.	Running hospitals, orphanages, etc.; chanting services for controlling the weather.
COUNSELING:	[Good monks and nuns are regarded as wise and impartial.]	Personal counselling; legal advice; assessment of government policies.
COMMERCE:	Working in a monastery.	Lending and donating money and goods.
CULTURE:	Attendance at festivals, etc.	Literature; providing space for (Theravada) and performing (Mahayana) art, music, festivals.

Figure 5: THE SYMBIOSIS OF LAYPERSONS AND MONASTICS.

on one's actions in life, and one's attitude at death, one will go to an unpleasant rebirth, a pleasant rebirth, or final liberation. In Tibet, the Book of the Intermediate State[3] carefully details the proper procedure for a successful passage through the gate of death, and emphasizes the crucial role of a lama as a guide *in extremis*. It is often believed that a Buddhist funeral is best, even if in life a person has been an enthusiastic practitioner of, say, Confucianism or Shinto. "The Buddhists know the most about what happens after death," one frequently hears.

The relationship between a Buddhist ruler and the monastic order is a special case of the lay/monastic symbiosis. The king is in a position to endow the most magnificent shrines and may favor some Buddhist groups over others. In Japan, there have been fierce competitions between the lineages for the emperor's approval. In Theravadin countries, kings have convoked, and arbitrated at, Buddhist councils. Some Theravadin kings have ordered the return to lay life of an entire body of monks they considered irregular, and, in some cases, the destruction of their monastery. Conversely, monks who regard a certain king as notoriously immoral may assemble outside his palace as if to receive offerings. When the offerings appear, they refuse them by inverting their bowls, and walk away. This breaking of the symbiosis is a form of excommunication, for unless the king can give to the monks, he cannot gain merit, and he is destined for an unpleasant rebirth, possibly in the hells. He also loses popular support.

A monk is not necessarily a better Buddhist than a layperson: both need each other for mutual growth. A layperson who is wealthy but unattached to the wealth is nearer nirvana than a monk who is fiercely attached to the few objects which the monastery lends him for his use. The real community (samgha) is not just the order of monks and nuns (bhikshu-bhikshuni-samgha), but the assembly of the "saints" or persons of high attainment (arya-pudgala-samgha). This idea is expanded in the Mahayana, especially in the Teachings of Vimalakirti, one of the funniest Buddhist scriptures.[4]

Vimalakirti is a layman, yet his spirituality exceeds that of the monks. Becoming ill, he is visited by a few friends: eight thousand Bodhisattvas, five hundred Hinayanists, hundreds of thousands of gods of all kinds, and the Bodhisattva Mañjushri. "Come in," says Vimalakirti. His room is ten feet square. Even by Indian standards, this is absurd, and his guests object that they cannot. "But," responds Vimalakirti, "if you can't all fit in, it means you are stuck in duality, ignorant that things are not, in their true nature, either large or small." They enter, and there is plenty of space left. Vimalakirti's superior comprehension of Dharma is vindicated. This scripture was very popular with the Chinese, who had grave Confucian doubts about the unfiliality of giving up home and family to become a monk.

Accumulation of Merit

Punya ("good work," "merit") is the life-blood of practical Buddhism. In some ways, it can be regarded as a spiritual currency that can be gained, lost, donated, or invested.[5] But, since it is a non-material energy, it also functions in non-material ways. Like love and happiness, the more we give it away, the more of it we have. "Punya-sharing," which is basic to ordinary, everyday Buddhism, can be thought of as sharing our happiness as we progress towards nirvana. Punya will not by itself propel us into nirvana, but without sufficient punya we will not meet with Dharmically favorable circumstances from which we can attain nirvana. The chief means by which punya is gained are proper conduct and worship.

1. CONDUCT (SHILA)

The complete practice of Buddhism is triple: conduct, meditation, and study (see chapter 9). These three elements are interdependent, and no Buddhist who is serious about practice would entirely ignore any of them, but a layperson (who is earning a living and may have a family) may find that the emphasis falls upon conduct, with meditation and study being fitted in as time allows.

When conduct is discussed, it is customary to begin with the rules of restraint, expressed negatively as the five basic or grave precepts, and then to go on to the more positive formulations of the six or ten perfections *(paramita),* and the four pure abidings *(brahmavihara).*

Rules of Restraint: The Five Precepts

The basic precepts of Buddhism are known as *Pañcha-shila* (abbreviated as *Pansil*), "the fivefold (moral) conduct." They are couched in negative form and taken as resolutions to oneself and other beings, rather than as vows to a God. Breaking the resolutions is an act of disservice to others and unfaithfulness to oneself: it leads, through the law of karma, to unpleasant results at some time in the future. Holding to the resolutions builds up punya. Pansil is regularly recited as a liturgical formula. The text, in my English translation, is as follows:

1. I take upon myself the discipline of abstaining from harming sentient beings.

2. I take upon myself the discipline of abstaining from taking that which is not offered.

3. I take upon myself the discipline of abstaining from sexual misconduct.

4. I take upon myself the discipline of abstaining from false speech.

5. I take upon myself the discipline of abstaining from stupefying drink.

1. ABSTAINING FROM HARMING SENTIENT BEINGS

In so far as we harm, so shall we be harmed. The fruiting of karma mirrors back to us (with magnification) a world that we have created. Thus, a Buddhist strives for the well-being of all sentient beings—animals, ghosts, demons, deities, and other humans, i.e., all beings who have consciousness and will be reborn as each other. A "sentient being"[6] is any entity that observedly tries to avoid pain and obtain pleasure. Manifestation of this activity is regarded as proof that an entity has mind or consciousness. It is not taken to entail that the being has *self* consciousness. Many beings, such as insects, can be seen to run away from pain and towards pleasure, but it does not appear that they know they are doing this. We might say that they do it because of "instinct" (whatevever that is). A Buddhist explanation would be that, in the insect rebirth, the fruiting of karma is very powerful, and an insect-being does not have much choice as to how it will act. The Buddhist could then use this observation to reflect on the auspicious fruiting of karma that leads to rebirth in the human realm, where choice is relatively much easier.

The principle of abstaining from harming other beings is called *ahimsa,* quite literally meaning "non-harming." Nothing is killed just because it is in the way. A fly is rescued from drowning in a tea-cup, a mosquito is not swatted, and even a scorpion may be simply thrown out. It is said that if we bathe all creatures in thoughts of friendship *(maitri),* even venomous snakes will be pacified. (Protective mantras are available for those of us whose friendship is underdeveloped.) Because of the cycle of rebirth, one's mother may be reborn as a mangy, stray dog. If, then, one is followed by a stray dog, one might ask oneself, "Why me? And why this particular dog? Who might it have been in a previous life?" In fact, since time is beginning-less, it is said that all beings have been reborn numberless times as the mothers of all other living beings. All beings are then our mothers. Although a being might be trying to harm us today, at some time in the past it has nurtured us as our mother. Therefore, we should repay its kindness by seeking its welfare now.

Some Buddhists, especially monks and nuns of the Chinese tradition, basing themselves upon chapter eight of the Lan-kavatara Sutra,[7] interpret this precept to mean that Buddhists should be strict vegetarians, getting all their protein from soy-beans. Theravada monks say that their rule requires them to accept whatever food is offered, and they will therefore accept meat just as long as it is a left-over and has not been specially prepared for them. They point out that the Buddha accepted all offerings of food, even, reportedly, eating a leper's thumb acci-dentally dropped into his bowl, and that he died after eating bad pork.[8]

Other Buddhists accept meat eating matter of factly as a part of the omnivorous human diet, and seek to minimize rather than eliminate the killing involved. Tibetans prefer to kill one animal rather than many animals to feed a given number of people, so they will eat beef (yak meat) but not fish.[9] Japanese eat fish rather than beef, but apparently just for economic reasons: the stricter monks and nuns abstain from both.

The focus of the precept is not the harm done to the sentient being. Tibetans point out that even agriculture harms, and often kills, the insects and other beings that live in the ground—the monastic code, strictly interpreted, forbids the monk to dig the ground—and, since both insects and cows are sentient beings, there is no essential difference in "being" between an insect and a cow.[10] The focus of the precept centers on the hate in the mind of the eater, and then, as a consequence of the lessening of hate, on the non-harming of a being. Hate and killing form a con-tinuum. In so far as my mind is loving, I will naturally seek the good of other beings.

2. ABSTAINING FROM TAKING THAT WHICH IS NOT OFFERED
This is a slightly more precise way of saying "abstention from stealing." We can invent all sorts of ways of obtaining a desired object without actually stealing it. Extreme admiration of a friend's possession, contantly sighing, "How I wish I had something like that!," protestations of undying gratitude if one were to be given it, etc., all may cause the property to transfer from one's friend to oneself, especially in cultures where etiquette requires a host to offer the guest anything highly praised. Legally, this is not stealing, but mentally, it is, laying the seeds of unwholesome karma. Non-attachment to the property of others obtains punya.

3. ABSTAINING FROM SEXUAL MISCONDUCT
Buddhism tends to endorse the established sexual ethics of whatever country it is in, and uses those conventions as a basis for the teaching of non-attachment to sex. For the layperson, monogamy, sometimes with limited concubinage, is the norm. Monks and nuns are required to be celibate (although there are, in Tibet and Japan, certain "monks" who, often to the scandal of Buddhists of other traditions, are married): fornication, bestiality, and masturbation (strictly, the intentional emission of semen, though it is usually regarded as applying to nuns also) are explicitly forbidden. Nocturnal emissions (in the case of the monk) are discussed in the monastic code, and the Buddha is represented as deciding that they are not willed actions, and so not an offense.

Homosexuality is implicitly forbidden to the monk, since it involves the intentional emission of semen. The fear of illness through losing semen, endemic to the Indian Subcontinent, has spread to other parts of South Asia. But this does not seem to trouble the Japanese, where many samurai were known to be homosexual.[11] Courtesans were the leaders of fashion, and the red-light district of Tokyo was only dimmed in the nineteenth century, after the American admirals found it disgusting.

The Chinese horror of any kind of public acknowledgment that human beings might have sexual organs seems to be dependent upon Confucianism. In private, all kinds of sexual activities are likely to be practiced. They may be regarded as private entertainment (as it tends to be seen in modern America), or as a slightly disreputable form of Taoism. Buddhism was able to please both Confucianism and Taoism by stipulating public propriety while allowing private amusement, such as allowing lay visitors to their monasteries the comforts of the local inn, where it was understood that all bodily needs would be satisfied. The ladies of the inn were expected to attend the sermons of famous visiting monks, so that they could discourse intelligently with their pious customers much like the hetaerae of ancient Athens.

The Tibetan Master Gampopa gives a detailed list of sexual misdemeanors, which seem to break down into three major groups: their similarity to stealing, their relationship to scandal, and their addictive nature.[12] Sexual misconduct is similar to stealing when, for example, we commit adultery and so "steal" another man's wife. Certain acts are regarded as scandalous, but these vary from culture to culture. At other times, we may find our sexual activity out of control and recognize that we are addicted to it. In practice, Tibetans seem to be particularly offended by any sexual activity that takes place in a room containing sacred images.

Sex is an all-consuming passion. When we are involved in it, our minds may become muddy and confused. We may kill in order to obtain a particular sexual partner, or even kill the partner if he or she refuses our advances. The line between consent and rape (i.e., harming) is easily crossed. This precept warns us to watch out for the mental turbulence which often attends sex and, when in doubt, to refrain from it.

4. ABSTAINING FROM FALSE SPEECH

This precept is primarily against lying. Since the Buddhist sees the origin of suffering in ignorance, and the cause of release in knowledge, it can only hinder our progress to speak against the truth. However, the precept is also understood in a broader sense as referring to slander, backbiting, and other ways in which we can harm beings by our speech.

5. ABSTAINING FROM STUPEFYING DRINK

"Buddha" means "Woken Up."

Alcohol, however, after an initially stimulating effect, quickly deadens the senses, plunging us further into ignorance and even outright sleep. Indeed, that is the attraction of alcohol: it is a medicine for reducing stress. It does not, however, deal with whatever it is that is causing the stress; it only decreases our awareness of it, and every time we decrease our awareness we move backwards along the path to enlightenment. It can, moreover, cause loss of self-control, such that one breaks one or all of the other four precepts (especially the third precept, since sexual indulgence is also an ally of confusion and ignorance).

Alcohol is a socially acceptable drink in some Buddhist countries: Tibetans drink a form of beer called *chang,* and Japanese drink rice wine (sake), but observant monks and nuns abstain. Tea is regarded as an acceptable drink (see chapter on Japanese Buddhism). I have been at social gatherings of Tibetans where buttered tea (to non-Tibetans, definitely an acquired taste!) was served while the monks were present but, when they left, beer was produced.

The precept of abstinence says nothing about marijuana (known in India as *bhang*), hashish, opium, or psychedelic drugs, but it is commonly interpreted as a prohibition against them. The reasoning is that they are external to the mind. It is the mind itself that must be changed. Any high obtained from a drug is dependent on the drug. When the drug is not used—as it cannot be after death—the mind will revert to the state it was in (or a worse one, since the root of the problem has not been dealt with) before the drug was taken. All drugs have one bad side effect: they wear off.

A NOTE ON SAMSARA AND ADDICTION

I wish to suggest that it is helpful to understand the Buddhist analysis of the world as samsara, how we create it, why we are trapped in it, and how we get out of it, on the model of addiction.

Addiction is said to be present when a person, place, thing, or substance, which is not a basic requirement of life, is so important to someone that they give their lives over to it and it becomes the focus of their energies. Furthermore, rather than obtaining the pleasure that they seek, addicts find that increasing contact gives decreasing pleasure, so that more and more of the drug is needed, and the quality of life in general deteriorates, perhaps to the point of insanity and death.

For Buddhism, it is samsara itself that is the basic drug, and

addiction to samsara is the basic addiction. We keep rolling
around in birth and death, sometimes getting high but, always,
eventually deteriorating and dying. Tibetan Buddhism compares
this to drinking salty water: the more we drink, the thirstier we
get.

The great breakthrough in understanding and treating addiction came in the 1930's in Akron, Ohio, with the founding of
Alcoholics Anonymous (AA).[13] The new insight, which has
proved so successful that it has been copied by many other pro-
grams, was that alcoholism (and, we may say now, addiction in
general) is a spiritual disease, needing a spiritual remedy. This
remedy was called "God" by the founders of AA but, from the
Buddhist point of view, "higher power" can mean anything
"extra-samsaric." A well-known Buddhist teacher who is a recovered alcoholic says that he substitutes the Triple Jewel (the Buddha, the Dharma, and the Samgha) for what AA members call
"God."

We might say, Buddhistically, that addiction occurs whenever
an intra-samsaric phenomenon (even a necessity like food) is
mistaken for a means of escaping from samsara. This mistake is
easily made in a culture that assures us that, for example, a new
detergent will bring permanent happiness. Twentieth-century
America may, indeed, go down in history as the most addicted
society to date, voraciously consuming far more than its share
of the planet's resources, and still feeling miserable. For this
reason, some Buddhist teachers have predicted that Americans
are in danger of being reborn as hungry ghosts (*preta;* see
"Realms of Rebirth" in chapter 6), endlessly trying to fill their
enormous stomach through mouths the size of pin heads.

Giving our lives over to this intra-samsaric phenomenon, we
bind ourselves to its decay, disappearance, and repetitive mean-
inglessness.

To get off the cycle, we need to say "no" to it. But, as the
founders of AA knew only too well, saying "no" to an addictive
substance is about as effective as saying "no" to the weather:
sometimes there may be a difference, but it has nothing to do
with the addict's will power. However, the founders of AA discovered that if something *outside* the circle of addiction was
appealed to, the addiction could be arrested.

Saying "no" to samsara by means of the five precepts is not
enough. Whenever Pansil is recited, it is preceded by a formula

of homage to the Buddha, and the taking of refuge in the "higher power" of the Triple Jewel.

If this model of samsara as addiction is correct, it might explain some of the differences in attitude towards the third and fifth precepts in various parts of the Buddhist world. The total prohibition of alcohol, and the great uneasiness with sex, in Indian Buddhism and its derivatives (Theravada and Tibetan Mahayana) may be due to a general and ancient fear amongst the peoples of the Subcontinent that it is impossible to drink alcohol, or to have sex, without the danger of addiction.[14] In China and Japan, on the other hand, the approach to sex and alcohol is more pragmatic, even to the extent that addiction may not even be recognized as such. The reality lies somewhere in between. As alcoholism counselors put it, "Ten percent of those who drink alcohol consume eighty percent of the alcohol"—and a similar ratio may be true for sex.

Thus, when the five precepts are read in the cultural milieu of twentieth-century United States, and we are trying to find the "middle way" that is truly Buddhist, it may be helpful to ask, "To what extent am I liable to become addicted to this activity if I indulge in it?" We need to be thoroughly honest when we ask ourselves this, for a part of addiction is the denial that we are addicted—in Buddhist terms, the basic ignorance (avidya) which controls samsara.

VIRTUE: THE PERFECTIONS AND THE PURE ABIDINGS

The perfections (paramita, "gone across," i.e., gone out of samsara, therefore, "actions that take us and other beings out of samsara") are listed either as six or ten. The list of six appears to be basic, with the remainder as supplemental. In Theravada, the six are giving, conduct, restraint, wisdom, energy, and patience. The Mahayana list is the same, except that meditation is included instead of restraint, and the order is different.[15] For convenience, I will discuss the Theravadin list,[16] and relate the Mahayana list to it.

1. Giving

Giving things away is perhaps the most obvious way towards, and proof of, non-attachment. But this giving is not indiscriminate: to gain the most punya, the recipient must be worthy.

Giving to an observant monk is better than giving to a lax monk. Giving a flower to a Buddha is better than giving a complete meal to an ordinary person. Mahayana assigns much more punya to one who reverences a Mahayana Sutra on a single occasion than to one who spends his entire life in non-Mahayanist good works. The point is that assisting the Dharma is more beneficial to more beings over a greater period of time than other good acts. It follows that the most common recipient of liberality is the monastic order, and items associated with it: food and clothing for the monks, temples, books, etc.

Where the monastic order is not so important, as in Mahayana, giving is directed towards enlightenment. The Jatakas (see chapter 1) are full of stories in which the Buddha-to-be gives his life or limbs out of compassion for others, since the concern is with ultimate enlightenment rather than temporary comfort. Mahayana, generalizing the Bodhisattva life as the ideal for all Buddhists, points to self-sacrifice as the royal road to release. The Lotus Sutra advocates burning off a finger, or even total self-immolation, as a sure way to gain large amounts of punya and liberation from bodily attachment. Finger burning and self-immolation were taken literally by Chinese, and some Japanese, Buddhists. Recently, the practice was revived in Vietnam (which has a strong historical connection with Chinese Buddhism) as a means of gaining punya and applying it towards the removal of injustice and the ending of war. This self-sacrifice may, however, be interpreted symbolically: giving one's head means helping someone think out a problem, giving one's tongue is counseling someone, giving one's arms is helping someone move things about, etc.[17]

The liberation of captive animals or people is a popular practice which also partakes of the virtue of non-harming: animals which might otherwise have gone to the butcher are set free. In Theravada countries, boys sit outside temples, ready to release, for a financial consideration, a small animal or bird they have trapped—a practice with benefits for all concerned: the donor gains punya, the boy gets money, and the animal gets its liberty. The Chinese and Japanese observe a yearly festival of Assembling to Liberate the Living (Chinese: *fang-shêng hui;* Japanese: *hojo-e*) when, after a certain amount of ceremony and chanting, a quantity of animals (usually birds and fish) is set free. Under the auspices of the City of Ten Thousand Buddhas in Talmage,

California, this is now being practiced in the United States. Buddhist rulers may gain punya by declaring an amnesty to prisoners on such occasions.

The main effect of giving is that it releases the giver's grasp on the sense of self. One who gives is less grasping and, as a consequence, more joyful. In Charles Dickens' story "A Christmas Carol," the miserable Scrooge becomes rosy cheeked and Christmassy when he discovers the value of giving.

2. Conduct

This is *shila,* and has already been discussed under the heading of the five precepts.[18] When it occurs in the context of the perfections, the list is the same, but the emphasis is on taking responsibility for one's actions. Instead of grasping, selfish conduct which exploits other beings and objects, one acts out of compassion and true concern for their welfare.

3. Restraint

This perfection is a drawing in, a counsel of simplicity. I ask, "What is really necessary?" If my main objective is the happiness of others and my and their final liberation from cyclic existence, a lot of needs will be seen as superfluous. If I am buying a house, for example, I consider not how grand it looks and what a prestigious neighborhood it is in, but whether it has more rooms than I would ever, given the size of my family, be likely to use, and if so, I look for a smaller one.

The monastic requisites are four: food, clothing, shelter, and medicine. Even as a layperson, if I have adequate supplies of these four, I am well provided, and in a position to concentrate on helping others.

Instead of restraint, Mahayana lists meditation. (See chapter 6.)

4. Wisdom

In Mahayana, the perfection of wisdom (prajña-paramita) becomes central. It means understanding and teaching Transparency. It is taught in all Mahayana systems, but especially in Madhyamika. (See "The Silence of the Philosophers" in chapter 9.)

For Theravada, the perfection of wisdom *(pañña-paramita)* is more a way of using the intellect than a teaching about reality.

It is using our mind wisely, for the sake of our own and others' liberation, rather than obsessively or discursively, frittering its energy away on trivial matters. The wasteful use of *pañña* is, perhaps, the most notable failing of professors who pile up books and articles on merely intra-samsaric subjects.

5. Energy

Energy puts into action what has been determined by wisdom to be beneficial. Energy without wisdom becomes busyness or workaholism. The Zen Roshi, Abbess Jiyu Kennett, says that before she developed wisdom she was "a centipede with a wash-cloth in each foot." But, wisdom without energy produces the armchair activist who is always reading about how to do things without ever actually doing them.

6. Patience

We remain ignorant of reality as it really is partly because we do not stay with any one thing long enough to find out much about it. This is particularly the case with pain. Especially in our society, which tries to have a pill for everything, we run to the medicine cabinet as soon as we feel any sort of twinge. We do not have the patience, or the endurance, to stay with the pain and look at it. In meditation, one observes pain as it comes up, goes into it, and watches it. There will certainly be bodily pain, and there probably will be mental pain. The meditation has not produced this pain, it has only created the environment in which, as it comes up, we can notice it and investigate it.

As we concentrate on the pain, we will note, first of all, that there *is* pain, and that this realization is something we have been trying to escape. Then, we will note that pain, like everything else, changes. We discover that the pain (unless it is very serious or life-threatening) is endurable, and that the suffering of pain comes largely from our panic and attempt to escape it. When we become friendly with pain, welcome it, and learn from it, we find it is a great teacher.

This friendliness with our pain is patience.

Perfections 7 to 8

The remaining four perfections are given by Theravada as truthfulness, resolution, friendliness, and equanimity. Truthfulness is a humble honesty: who is really to blame, is it "them" or is it me? Probably it is I who have created my own suffering. Resolution is similar in function to energy. Friendliness and equanimity are also listed as two of the four pure abidings. (see below).

THE PERFECTIONS

Theravada		Mahayana	
1. Giving	dana	1. Giving	dana
2. Conduct	shila	2. Conduct	shila
3. Restraint	nekkham-ma	3. Patience	kshanti
4. Wisdom	pañña	4. Energy	virya
5. Energy	viriya	5. Meditation	dhyana
6. Patience	khanti	6. Wisdom	prajña
7. Truthfulness	sachcha	7. Skillful Means	upaya
8. Resolution	adhiṭṭhana	8. Resolution	pranidhana
9. Friendliness	metta	9. Strength	bala
10. Equanimity	upekha	10. Knowledge	jñana

THE PURE ABIDINGS

metta	*Friendliness*	*maitri*
karuna	*Compassion*	*karuna*
mudita	*Sympathetic Joy*	*mudita*
upekha	*Equanimity*	*upeksha*

Figure 6: THE PERFECTIONS AND THE PURE ABIDINGS

The Mahayana list is skilfull means, resolution, strength, and knowledge. Skillful means is a primary virtue of a Buddhist teacher (See chapter 9). Resolution and strength are similar to energy, but resolution, in Mahayana, refers especially to constancy in the Bodhisattva Resolve. Knowledge (jñana) is sometimes (especially in Theravada, where it is written ñana) said to be a synonym of wisdom (prajña or pañña) and sometimes (especially in Tibetan Mahayana) taught as superior to wisdom. In

the latter case, prajña is said to be the removal of basic ignorance, and jñana the supreme knowledge of reality as it is, so that
it might then be better to reverse the translations, calling prajña,
"knowledge" and jñana, "wisdom"—but other Mahayana teachers seem to disagree with this. The translation I have given is, I
think, reflective of the most common teaching.

The Pure Abidings

The same list is taught by both Theravada and Mahayana:
friendliness, compassion, joy, and equanimity. There is, however, a difference between Theravada and Mahayana regarding
the order in which it is recommended that they be cultivated.

Theravada says that we first need friendliness *(metta).* We go
out to other beings as if they were our friends, and try to do what
is best for them. Then, we can empathize with their suffering,
feeling their pain as if it were our own: this is compassion
(karuna). Later, we can rejoice with them in "sympathetic joy"
(mudita)—feeling genuinely happy at others' good fortune is a
higher accomplishment than feeling sad at their misfortune—
and finally we can develop equanimity (*upekha,* literally "equal
eye-ness") so that, whatever happens to us, and whether others
praise or blame us, we are not diverted from the path to liberation.

Mahayana understands the terms slightly differently, and
therefore teaches them in a different order. Karuna is taught
first, as it is explained as the wish to remove suffering from
beings. Then one goes on to friendliness *(maitri),* which is taught
as the wish that all beings may be happy. Compassion is, for
Mahayana, the removal of sickness, and friendliness is the giving
of health. The last two abidings, joy at others' happiness and
equanimity as what happens to oneself, are said to imply each
other, and are taught, effectively, as a single virtue.

Suggestions, not Commandments

It is important to note that all of the above precepts and virtues
are *suggestions* rather than *commandments.* Only when we
become Buddhas will we observe them perfectly. Until then, we
observe them as well as we can, and we discover they give us, at
least, a foretaste of the peace of nirvana. If we do not observe
them, no one is going to wag a finger at us and tell us we are
naughty children, we will just delay our own progress to true joy.

In Buddhism, we may make a mistake and wish to correct it, but we do not have to feel guilty.

2. WORSHIP (PUJA)

Things come from previous thoughts, are led by thoughts, are composed of thoughts: if one speaks or acts with pure thought, then happiness follows like a never-leaving shadow. [19]

Worshipping the worshipful is intrinsically valuable, automatically gaining punya, but it also helps to direct the mind, the pilot of the psychosomatic bundle, towards release. Its function in the latter case is not very different from meditation, and, indeed, worship before and after meditation sessions is a universal Buddhist practice. It is the best way to begin collecting the thoughts together, aiming them one-pointedly at the ultimate goal. Laypeople, who may not have time for regular periods of meditation, can at least spend a few moments each day in worship, either in a temple or before their personal shrine. In order to aid concentration, use is made of images, ritual implements, and liturgies in varying amounts: generally speaking, Theravada, Zen, and Pure Land Buddhists rely the least on external paraphernalia, while Tibetan Buddhists use them the most. None, however, entirely dispense with it except in the most unusual circumstances.

The question then arises, "Is the image being worshipped for what it is, or for what it symbolizes?" The answer varies with the image, the lineage of Buddhism, and the individual worshipper.

Images can be of a Buddha, a Bodhisattva, a Patriarch or former teacher, or a god or goddess. Worship of the image of a god or goddess is fairly straightforward. Although Buddhism has always denied the existence of a supreme and eternal God (Ishvara), it has never denied that there are beings in the heavens who live a long time and are powerful, and whom humans call "gods" (deva). Since the gods are powerful, they can be called upon to help us, but since they are mortal (although very long lived), their help is limited; they may give riches, protection, and children, but they cannot give nirvana, for they also are seeking it. The Buddha is said to have converted many of the gods and so put them under an obligation to assist humans who are Buddhists. In the previous chapter, we saw how the Four Divine Kings, having become Buddhist, vowed to protect Buddhist countries.

The list of gods and goddesses worshipped throughout the Buddhist world is quite large, normally including all important local deities and a number imported from India. The most thoroughgoing integration of non-Buddhist deities into Buddhism has occurred in Tibet, where Padmasambhava, a colorful Indian missionary often regarded as a form of Buddha Shakyamuni, "subdued the demons," i.e., challenged the regional tutelary deities to a fight, defeated them with superior magic, and converted them to zealous Protectors of Dharma *(Dharma-pala)* by a sermon. The Japanese developed a beautifully balanced list of correspondences, wherein every native deity was an alternative form of a particular Buddhist entity, or vice versa, but it remained little more than a legal fiction.[20] Devotion to Hindu deities, especially by performance of the Indian epic Ramayana, is common amongst Buddhists of Southeast Asia.

The worship of Bodhisattvas and Patriarchs is not dissimilar to the worship of gods. Bodhisattvas, of course, are only worshipped by the Mahayana: they are commonly regarded as superior to the gods but inferior to the Buddhas. They may have specific functions, e.g., Mañjushri is invoked for wisdom, Kshitigarbha (Japanese: *Jizo*) for the protection of dead children, Avalokiteshvara for a successful (and, these days, an unsuccessful!) pregnancy. Patriarchs, or former saintly or influential monks, receive an ambiguous worship in both Mahayana and Theravada that seems best regarded as an extension of ancestor worship: the person is accorded dutiful respect, sometimes (especially in Tibet) being regarded as a Bodhisattva, but sometimes (especially in China and Japan) without any clear idea as to whether he is actually able to receive it or respond to it. Kukai (774–835 C.E.), the founder of Shingon (Japanese Tantric Buddhism) is a curious and special case: he is popularly believed to be sitting in his tomb on Mount Koya in an immensely deep trance, a sort of hibernation, from which he will emerge to lead Japan at the proper time.

The worship of a Buddha image in Mahayana and Theravada may appear identical to the casual observer, but the mind-set of the worshippers is usually different. The general procedure for the consecration of the image is broadly similar: it is protected by mantras (called *parittas* by the Theravadins); humans and gods are invited to the ceremony; its eyes are ritually opened. But then, Mahayana regards it as an image that may be addressed in its own right (since it has become a vessel for the Buddha invoked), whereas Theravada (believing that the Buddha of this cosmic cycle is now out of the phenomenal world) claims that it is no more than a legitimate focus of pious attention. The ordinary worshipper may not be aware of this scholarly distinction.

The ritual of worship is similar to that of Hinduism, and retains a pronounced Indian flavor throughout the Buddhist world. It strives for the total involvement of the worshipper with the worshipped. All the senses are employed, and the image is treated as a person to be honored, addressed, washed, clothed, and fed, although the lavish lustrations with all kinds of unlikely substances, so common in Hinduism, tend to be restrained, symbolic, or absent in Buddhist worship. Lights are offered for the sense of sight, flowers and incense for the sense of smell, bells for the hearing, food for the taste, water for the touch, and chanting texts for the mind.[21] Some offerings affect more than one sense, e.g., flowers can be seen as well as smelt, and many offerings emphasize impermanence, e.g., the candle burning down. Worshippers use their entire bodies by adopting appropriate postures such as standing or prostrating, and prescribed gestures, such as joined hands. Shoes are always removed on entering the sanctuary. If the image is surrounded by an ambulatory, it is worshipped by clockwise circumambulation. Adoration, confession of faults, rejoicing in merits and thanksgiving is almost universally made. Petitionary prayer is restricted in Theravada to the worship of gods. It is more common in Mahayana. Worship is normally concluded by some formula transferring the punya gained by the ceremony to some special intention (such as the fate of a dead relative) or a general intention that all beings might be assisted to gain enlightenment.

Tantric worship is much more elaborate, both in theory and practice, than this general plan. Since it sits most firmly astride the thin partition between worship and meditation, we shall deal with it along with other meditation systems, in Chapter 6.

Distribution of Merit

Punya that has been gained by the foregoing practices may then be directed towards favorable outcomes in the future, either for oneself or for another. At the popular level, this procedure often takes on a pronounced mercenary tinge of "purchasing" rewards, a practice often discouraged by more sophisticated Buddhists, but never denied. The commonest rewards that can be purchased, with varying amounts of different sorts of punya, are:[22]

1. Rescue from present suffering.

2. Certainty of a favorable rebirth (particularly desired for deceased relatives or friends).

3. Good fortune, now and in the future.

4. Rebirth as a god (i.e., in one of the heavens).

5. Liberation from samsara.

It is common practice to enter upon the performance of any good work (such as worship) with the intention, "May this good work be for the well-being of so-and-so," and concluding the work with a similar formula, very much like the Roman Catholic practice of paying for a Mass "for" a certain person.

It is important to notice that this list of rewards ascends from good to better to best. Removal from samsara is clearly supreme, but aiming for happiness or life as a god is not condemned, and is in fact the commonest hope of most ordinary Buddhists. The happiness is not gained selfishly (only selfless action gains merit) and when it is gained, it is understood that one's resulting power and wealth will be used in the service of others. It is in this spirit that the Zen monk's table grace says:

The first morsel (of food) is to destroy all evils.
The second morsel is to practice all good deeds.
The third morsel is to save all sentient beings.
May we all attain the path of Buddhahood.[23]

NOTES
to Chapter Three

1. This rule is kept by Theravadins, but relaxed or modified by Mahayanists.

2. This chart is distantly based on a seminar presentation of Peter Le Sha at the University of Wisconsin at Madison, February 1968. See also Jane Bunnag, *Buddhist Monk, Buddhist Layman* (Cambridge: Cambridge University Press), 1973.

3. The *Bar do thos grol* is unfortunately known in English as *The Tibetan Book of the Dead,* although its Tibetan title literally means "Liberation" *(grol)* through hearing *(thos)* in the Intermediate State *(bar do).* An Intermediate State is any state of "between-ness" and its resulting confusion—between jobs, between love affairs, or between lives. The confusion of the Intermediate State is not total, its general energy is predictable, and it is the job of the *Bar do thos grol* to be a guidebook to the confusion. Theravadins do not teach an Intermediate State between lives, but say that the last moment of consciousness in an embodiment is followed at once by the first moment of consciousness in a new embodiment. For the Tibetan view of death and rebirth in general, see *Death, Intermediate State and Rebirth in Tibetan Buddhism* by Lati Rinbochay and Jeffrey Hopkins (London: Rider; Valois, NY: Snow Lion, 1979). For a translation of the *Bar do thos grol,* see *The Tibetan Book of the Dead: The Great Liberation through Hearing in the Bardo,* translated with commentary by Francesca Fremantle and Chogyam Trungpa (Berkeley and London: Shambhala, 1975), which is to be preferred to the version of Evans-Wentz and Lama Dawa-Samdup (Oxford, 1927). Also useful is the collection of texts assembled by Glenn H. Mullin, *Death and Dying: The Tibetan Tradition* (Boston: Arkana, 1986).

4. *The Holy Teaching of Vimalakirti: A Mahayana Scripture,* translated by Robert A. F. Thurman (University Park and London: The Pennsylvania State University Press, 1976).

5. A large number of the Buddha's disciples were of the merchant *(vaishya)* caste, to whom a fiscal model of spiritual advance would be especially appealing.

6. The Pali is *pana,* literally "breather," breath being an indication, according to a common Indian philosophical viewpoint, of life or mind. Tibetans translated the word as *sempa,* "mind-possessor," from which the English "sentient being" is derived. The Chinese decided on an explanatory translation, *tuo-chung shêng-ssŭ* (usually abbreviated to *chung-shêng*), "many births and deaths."

7. *The Lankavatara Sutra,* translated by Daisetz Teitaro Suzuki (London: Routledge, 1932 and subsequently), pp. 211–222.

8. The fact that the pork was bad and killed the Buddha is an instance of the fruiting of unwholesome karma, to which even he was not im-

mune. Far from teaching that we should not eat pork, the story is taken to mean that the monk should accept all food, whether it is tasty, fresh, and vegetarian, or not.

9. A collection of liturgical texts for western practitioners of Tibetan Buddhism, *Rites and Prayers: An FPMT Manual*, edited by Martin Willson (London: Wisdom, 1985), p. 47f., gives a mantra and says, "When you have meat, if you put this mantra onto it, recited seven times, the fault of eating meat is stopped and the sentient being whose flesh it was will be reborn in a happy destiny, it is taught."

10. The distinction that westerners tend to make between, for instance, abortion in humans and similar practices in animal husbandry, and their concern for whales but not for bats, may have its origins in the Aristotelian view, as adopted and adapted by Christianity, of the Great Chain of Being. According to this, God is Being Itself, and other beings "be" by participation (less and less as one goes down the chain or ontological pyramid from angels through humans to animals) in God. In its most extreme form, this philosophy teaches that animals do not have souls (i.e., minds) and that their observed behavior in regard to pleasure and pain is purely mechanical. Buddhism, holding to the circular view of rebirth, cannot make any sense of this assertion.

11. Ihara Saikaku (1642–1693) wrote *The Great Mirror of Male Love*, which became a classic of Japanese literature. For a partial English translation (via the French), see E. Powys Mathers, *Comrade Loves of the Samurai and Songs of the Geishas* (London, 1928: reprinted as 2 vols. in 1, Vermont: Tuttle, 1970). A complete translation directly from the Japanese has been prepared by Paul Gordon Schalow, *The Great Mirror of Male Love* (Stanford University Press, 1989) dissertation. Schalow read a diverting paper on a legend that the Japanese Tantric Master Kobo Daishi (for whom see "Buddhism as the Best Religion" in chapter 5) granted a vision of himself to a worthy disciple in which he revealed complicated techniques for seducing young male acolytes ("The Priestly Tradition of Homosexual Love in Japanese Buddhism: The Legend of Kūkai," American Academy of Religion, Boston, December 7, 1987). At the same panel, Leonard Zwilling presented a paper, subsequently published in Amalā Prajñā: *Aspects of Buddhist Studies*, edited by N.H. Samtani, (Delhi: Indian Books Centre, 1989), "Homosexuality in Indian Buddhist Texts."

12. *Jewel Ornament of Liberation*, trans. by H.V. Guenther (Shambhala, 1971 and subsequently), p. 76.

13. Various pamphlets and books on the history of AA are published by AA World Services in New York, but the most satisfactory account is *Not-God: A History of Alcoholics Anonymous* by Ernest Kurtz (Center City, MN: Hazelden, 1979, revised as *A.A.: The Story*, Harper, 1988). Kurtz plots the spirituality of AA within the context of American Pietism. His attempt suggests that a larger study, from the standpoint of History of Religions, would be worthwhile.

14. The temples at Khajuraho are often cited as an exception. But this is exactly the point: they are an exception. The riotous, athletic sexuality of the temples appears out of and disappears back into the history of Indian art like a wave on the seashore. Most Indians regard them as quite obscene, and must resort to special pleading to justify their preservation.

15. For comparison, the lists are presented side by side in figure 6 with the technical terms in Pali and Sanskrit.

16. This discussion is indebted to a teaching on the ten perfections, according to the Theravadin tradition, given by Ven. Ajahn Sumedho Bhikkhu, at a retreat in Switzerland in May 1982. For a detailed scholarly discussion of the perfections in the Mahayana texts, see Har Dayal, *The Bodhisattva Doctrine in Buddhist Sanskrit Literature* (Delhi: Banarsidass, 1970; originally London: Routledge, 1932), chapter 5.

17. On this whole question, see Jan Yün-hua, "Buddhist Self-Immolation in Medieval China," *History of Religions* 4:2 (Win 65), 243–268. I am indebted to my colleague at Duke University, Professor Harry B. Partin, for drawing this article to my attention.

18. The presence of an element in two or more different lists is frequent in Buddhism. It indicates that the elements are operational definitions with no inherent existence of their own. See Abhidharma, chapter 5.

19. Dhammapada 1:2. My translation.

20. Alicia Matsunaga, *The Buddhist Philosophy of Assimilation* (Tokyo: Sophia University, dist. by Tuttle, 1969).

21. The mind is regarded as a sense-organ.

22. List modified from *Buddhist Soteriology: The Teacher-Saviours,* an unpublished paper by the late Richard H. Robinson.

23. D. T. Suzuki, *The Training of the Zen Buddhist Monk* (New York: University Books, 1965), p. 146. Note the progression from self-benefit to other-benefit.

Chapter 4

THE MONASTIC LIFE

(Act 6 of the Buddha)

The monks and nuns are the eyes of Buddhism. They are professionally involved in studying, contemplating, and explaining Dharma. "Where there is the Samgha [i.e., the monks and nuns], there is the Dharma," said King Ashoka. However much it is true in theory that laypersons may outdo the monastic in knowledge of Dharma, in practice only professional meditators have the opportunity to devote most of their time to Dharma.

The word "monk," though commonly used, does not adequately translate bhikkhu (Pali) or bhikshu (Sanskrit). Literally, bhikkhu means beggar or mendicant: the bhikkhu has given up all family and personal property. He is celibate, and lives (normally) in a community of other bhikkhus, called a vihara or "lodging," i.e., theoretically a temporary resting place. In this, he resembles a Christian monk. But the bhikkhu does not usually live far from normal human society, as is ide-

ally the case for the Christian monk: the vihara is nearly always close to a village or city, and frequently is right in the
middle of it, for it functions as a kind of "parish church" for
the laity. So, the bhikkhu is also similar to a Christian priest.
The rarely used word "hieromonk" (priest-monk) or the more
common "friar" comes closer to expressing bhikkhu in English,
but "monk" seems to have become the accepted translation,
and it will do as long as one remembers its wider meaning. It
should also be noted that there are many officials, especially in
Tibet and Japan, who may seem at first to be "monks," but who
are married, and are therefore better regarded as "priests."
Every Buddhist country has developed its own elaborate hierarchy, differing from that of the others in extent, classifica-
tions, and terminology. Rather than draw the reader into this
exotically proliferating bureaucracy, I shall use the term
"monk" for an official who is celibate, and "priest" for one who
is not. Women who follow a similar life-style are called bhikkhuni (Pali) or bhikshuni (Sanskrit), that is, "nuns."[1]

The Origin and Development of Buddhist Monasticism

Leaving home to search, either alone or with others, for ultimate values is regarded as eccentric in modern America. In the
Indian Subcontinent, *pravrajya*, "going forth"—a word with a
sense of adventure to it—is a (although sometimes reluctantly)
socially approved option. Today, as in the past, the streets of
India, especially in the Hindu pilgrimage cities, are filled with
"wanderers" *(parivrajaka),* those who have left their temporal
homes to seek the Eternal, living on alms and sleeping in temples
or Dharmashalas (religious hostels). Frequently, these men[2]
have come from comfortable backgrounds, and they may be
quite learned. Siddhartha, in the legend, had all his desires ful-
filled, was attractive, intelligent, and admired. But, as Aldous
Huxley once said, "There comes a time when one asks, even of
Beethoven or Shakespeare, 'Is that all?'" A disadvantaged youth
is likely to seek physical comforts. One who has all possible
comforts and yet feels unsatisfied is liable to "go forth" to seek
true happiness elsewhere. The best monastic tradition, east or
west, rejoices in the delights that come *because of* the renuncia-
tion of material pleasures.
It seems there have always been homeless wanderers in the

Indian Subcontinent: monasticism may even be an Indian invention. The only religions that have monks and nuns are Hinduism,
Jainism, Buddhism, Taoism, Christianity, and Islam. Of these,
the first three are native to the Subcontinent. Taoist monasticism
demonstrably arose as a reaction against Chinese Buddhism.
Islamic monasticism is almost certainly modeled on Christian
monasticism, and there are (albeit muted and subterranean)
indications that Christianity got the idea from India. Therefore,
although the origin of Indian monasticism is a puzzle, it is quite
natural to find the Buddha, and then Buddhists, accepting it. The
history of Buddhist monasticism begins with its modifications of
Indian monasticism.

The basic modification, from which the others follow, is the
down-grading of the solitary and leaderless wanderer life-styles.
Wherever we find the Buddha, we see him surrounded by his
gana (flock) or samgha, "community." Individual monks (not,
usually, nuns) may go off to meditate alone, or be sent on solitary
teaching circuits, "wandering alone like the rhinoceros," but
they seem always to have been regarded as members of the
samgha of a particular area, to which they returned when the
rains began.

Traveling in the Indian Subcontinent during the refreshing,
but torrential, monsoons is sometimes impossible even today:
paved roads are washed away, airports are flooded, railroad
tracks are submerged. In the sixth century B.C.E., the wet months
(approximately June, July, and August) were not for travel. Con-
fined to one place, the monks built huts against the weather,
engaged in discussion, and meditated. This practice was called
Vassa (in Pali) or *Varsha* (in Sanskrit). At the end of Vassa, clad
in fresh robes, physically and spiritually revived, they once more
set out on their wanderings. Gradually, the amount of wandering was cut down, and it became normal to live constantly in the
vihara, though a formal convoking and dismissing of Vassa is
still observed today.

The democratic and *ad hoc* organization of the primitive
Vassa hardened into a more definite hierarchy, somewhat
resembling the *laura* of early Christian monasticism: a federa-
tion of cells in which the monks were ultimately alone yet con-
gregated frequently. Later still, the laura gave way to the fully
unified monastic community (what Christianity calls the *coe-
nobium*), each monk forming an essential element of a total

organism, with an established bureaucracy. This is now the rule throughout the Buddhist world, though there were hermits in Tibet before the recent Chinese invasion, and the Zen novice is called *unsui,* "clouds-and-water," because he performs a (largely symbolic) wandering, like the clouds and rivers.

The organization of the monastery often reflects that of the society in which it develops. For example, in China, monks and nuns arrange themselves in the manner of a Confucian family, with the abbot as the father, the retired abbot as the grandfather, and the deceased abbots as the ancestors or patriarchs. Male kinship terms are even used by the nuns: an abbess, for instance, is called *Shih-Fu,* literally "Teacher-Father."[3]

Buddhism gave shape and solidity to the shifting, individualistic, often highly idiosyncratic, Indian ideal of monasticism. Beginning as a private experiment, it became a public institution. A network of monasteries, often very large, with extensive landholdings, imposing buildings, and considerable libraries, inhabited by accomplished practitioners of Dharma, covered the Indian Subcontinent, and then all of Asia. The monasteries had all the virtues and vices of centralization: they were powerhouses, irradiating the countryside with sound teaching and morals, but if they were destroyed by wars or persecutions, or if they decayed into idyllic retreats for unspiritual drones, Buddhism was lost. The disappearance of Buddhism in India, which is still a problem for historians, must have been at least partly due to the destruction[4] and/or decay of the monasteries, and Chinese Buddhism never regained its ascendancy after the persecution by Emperor Wu-tsung in 845 C.E., which was aimed principally at the monasteries.

Monastic Initiation

Becoming a monk or nun is a *rite de passage,* a ceremony of transition from one life-style to another, a symbolic death and rebirth.[5] The initiates shed their old identity and put on a new one, renouncing their biological lineage and entering the *Buddha-kula,* "family of Buddha."

A candidate for monastic initiation must be free from worldly obligations such as debts, military service, spouse, or dependent parents. One who wishes to be a monk should be healthy, male, and a human being.[6] In Thailand, the ceremony may begin dra-

matically with a triumphal procession around the village or
town, the candidate becoming "king for the day," reenacting the
early life of Siddhartha, and bidding farewell to his parents. The
initiation proper,[7] inside the monastery, takes place in the presence of other monks and a head officiant of proper seniority. It
is a community act (samgha-karma), not a private affair, though
when the Buddha was alive, his word alone was sufficient for
initiation.

Continuing with the symbolic reenactment of Act Six of the
Buddha, the candidate's head is shaved (long hair being considered an adornment) and the secular clothes are replaced with the
monastic habit, provided solely for reasons of modesty and protection against the weather. The earliest robes were pieced together from cast-off material that, though clean, might be yel-
lowed with age (*kashaya*, "earth colored"). Gradually, robes
have evolved that are specifically made for the purpose. Broadly,
there are three varieties of robes: the Theravadin, which is yellow, and closest to the primitive form; the Tibeto-Mongolian,
which is maroon; and the Sino-Japanese, which is black, dark
brown, or light grey. The Tibeto-Mongolian and Sino-Japanese
customs have preserved the original yellow, patchwork garment
as an outer robe worn especially on ceremonial occasions.[8]

Finally, in the initiation ceremony, the candidate is given a
new name, the Dharma Name. In Theravada, this is expressive
of a Buddhist virtue, such as Wimala, "purity" or Dhammaviriya
"strong in Dhamma." The Chinese abandon their parental sur-
names (their *hsing*) and take a Buddhist family name such as
Shih,[9] an abbreviation of Shakyamuni in Chinese transliteration, adding a personal name *(ming-tzŭ)* of (usually) two characters indicating a Buddhist virtue. Because they thus lose the
name of their biological family, the Chinese translate *pravrajya*
by *ch'u-chia*, "leaving the family or clan." In the full Chinese
ordination, indifference to pain is marked by placing a burning
incense stick at twelve places on the shaved head.

After the ceremony, the candidate has become a *samanera*
(Pali; feminine *samaneri*) or *shramanera* (Sanskrit; feminine
shramanerika) "one who exerts him/herself." By analogy with
Christian monasticism, such a person is sometimes called, in
English, a "novice." In this state, one tests one's vocation, and
may relinquish it without stigma. Temporary life as a samanera
is common in Theravada countries. It is regarded as a valuable

component of a boy's education, and may be a prerequisite for the king's coronation. This is another of the lifelines joining the monks and the laypeople. If the samanera decides to remain in the monastery, he may seek *upasampada,* "full attainment," by which he "becomes a bhikkhu or bhikshu" *(bhikshu–bhava).* The ceremony is a more solemn version of the *pravrajya* by which he became a samanera. Upasampada does not normally occur before age twenty. Withdrawal from the bhikshu state is, in some countries, regarded as a more serious matter than giving up the samanera state.

The new monk is visibly different from his former self. Shorn, clad in unflattering clothes,* living apart from family residences, bearing a Buddhist name, he moves recollectedly through the early morning bustle of the wakening village. If he should stop by the door of his parents' house for food, his father or mother, to whom he once respectfully deferred, will instead pay honor to him. Faring alone, with his focus chiefly upon his future lives and eventual liberation, and homeless, the son becomes the model for the parents, as all alike search for true happiness and peace.

Monastic Rules

A sincere Buddhist voluntarily takes on the Pañcha-shila (see previous chapter). Monks and nuns bind themselves to additional rules, called Vinaya, "that which leads away," the guidebook for the journey to nirvana. It is the most treasured possession of Buddhism, for without it the monks may go astray, taking the laity with them, and the true Path will become overgrown and forgotten.

In the classical age, Chinese monks would courageously travel through the deserts and mountains of the barbarian West, attempting to reach India. Many did not make it, victims of exhaustion, storms, or brigands, but others did, and became the stuff of legend.[10] Frequently, the motivation for these heroic journeys was the recovery of the true Vinaya. Inspiring sermons on how everything is Buddha, which is really Transparency, are

---

* For extended discussion of monastic clothing see appendix to chapter 4.

all very well, but they do no more than erect the target: how one shoots at it is the business of Vinaya.

The importance of Vinaya resulted in its becoming the earliest form of the teaching to be written down, and the one least modified by time. The practice of Buddhist monastics, whatever their lineage or doctrinal views, is everywhere very similar.

The simplest form of Vinaya is a set of five precepts added to the Pañcha-shila, making ten in all. The additions are:

1. Not to eat after mid-day.

2. Not to watch secular entertainments (dancing, singing, theater).

3. Not to use perfumes or ornaments.

4. Not to use a high couch or bed (i.e., not to use a luxurious bed or to use sleep indulgently).

5. Not to handle gold or silver (i.e., not to become involved in commerce).

These five are sometimes reduced to three by combining the second and the third and omitting the fifth, producing a total of eight precepts. Their main intent is to exclude luxuries and distractions. They are observed by the samanera and by any earnest layman *(upasaka)* or laywoman *(upasika)* who has formally taken the precepts and who may reside temporarily or permanently within the monastic enclosure. Commonly, the layperson will prefer to take the eight precepts (for example, on a daily basis during a retreat) while the ten precepts will more often be taken by Theravadin women who desire to live as nuns, as a substitute for (the impossible, because unavailable) full ordination (see footnote 1). Such women are called *dasasilavanti* ("those living under ten precepts") and may be addressed as "Ayya" ("aunt" or "sister"). They shave their heads and wear the same robes as monks.[11]

The bhikkhu must observe a great many more rules: 227 in the Pali text and 253 in the Sanskrit text. Nuns are bound by further restrictions (from 8 to 111, according to the tradition of their particular lineage), making them subordinate in all matters to the monks.[12] These rules are called Patimokkha (Pali) or Pratimoksha (Sanskrit), a word which may mean "bond." In its present form, the Patimokkha is a liturgical text.[13] It is recited every half month of the lunar calendar by the monks in common, as a means of purification. The day of its recitation is called Uposatha (a word borrowed from Hinduism for the day before a sacrifice when the gods came to "dwell near," but irrelevant to its Buddhist usage) and laypeople are urged to make a retreat on Uposatha day. For a time, Sri Lanka adopted Uposatha day as its "day of rest," but since the remainder of the world seemed to prefer the Sunday of the Christian solar calendar, the experiment was dropped as impracticable.

The recitation of Patimokkha begins with all the monks assembled, those unavoidably absent sending acceptable excuses. A list of four grave offenses is read out: fornication, theft, murder, and false (or prideful) claims of insight and attainment. "Are the brethren quite pure in these matters?," the officiant asks. Silence means "yes." Twice more the officiant repeats the question. If anyone accuses himself of a fault, he is permanently expelled (laicized). If silence is maintained, the officiant says, "I take it that the brethren are quite pure in these matters." He proceeds to list thirteen offenses that are punishable by probation to an extent which will be decided later, at a community meeting. There are six more groups of offenses, of decreasing gravity. Some are fairly obvious, such as not slandering or causing dissension, but some may appear rather silly, especially the seventy–five rules of public deportment, which include offenses such as swaying the body while walking, chomping or slurping (making the sounds *chapuchapu* or *surusuru*) while eating, and preaching to someone who is lolling about. However, Buddhism teaches the interdependence of mind and body, that the mind and the body influence each other. How one walks or eats is conditioned by, and conditions, how one thinks. And if one is lolling about when the Dharma is being taught, it probably means one is disinterested and inattentive.

The rule prescribes, in general, that there should be a sufficiency, but not a superfluity, of the Four Requisites (food, clothing, shelter, and medicine); for the holding of all goods in common; celibacy; courtesy and charity within the community; and the recollected comportment of the body. Some of the regulations may be relaxed in case of illness.

The rest of the Vinaya legislates for a wide variety of activities, but quite casuistically, without an *a priori* framework. The Buddha does not hand out a neatly organized rule-book, but waits to be asked about individually disputed points. The institution of the Vassa Retreat grew in this piecemeal way.

At first, apparently, the monks wandered about even during the torrential downpours of the monsoon season. The laypeople protested that this was ridiculous, since even birds and animals took shelter at that time. So, the monks asked the Buddha if they should stay put. "Yes," he said. But he did not say when. So, they asked the Buddha. "During the rains," he said. But he did not say precisely when. So, they asked the Buddha. When this was settled, some monks, having set up residence, moved on again, for they had not been told they shouldn't. The laypeople objected again, so the monks asked the Buddha. He said that once in residence one should stay until the end of the period of residence. This they did, but all they did was reside. It was noticed that non-Buddhist monks held services and discussions. So, the monks asked the Buddha. "Hold services and discussions," he replied.

In this laborious way, familiar to anyone who has tried to buy a bus ticket in India, the monastic rules were gradually built up. There resulted a set of regulations that, having arisen as needed, should have contained nothing adventitious. Minor rules could be dropped after the Buddha's death. However, the monks forgot to ask the Buddha which were the minor rules. So, all had to be kept.

Constitutions, adapting the Vinaya to specific times and places, grew up in each Buddhist country. For example, the Temple of the Tooth in Kandy, Sri Lanka (which contains what is said to be a tooth of the Buddha), has special ordinances established in 1300 c.e.[14] and Po-chang (720–814 c.e.) legislated specific rules for Ch'an (and therefore Zen) monks, including his famous phrase "A day without work is a day without food."[15] Since the Vinaya prohibits manual work, this *requirement* to work was something new.[16]

Monastic Routine

Routine is important as a means of recollection. Time, aging, and death are inescapable. Within samsara we are time–bound beings. Therefore, husbanding our time is a means of waking up to reality. There is a sense of urgency (but not of panic) in Buddhist practice, based upon the Four Foundations of Mindfulness:

1. Our fortunate birth: a human rebirth, especially one in which (a) it is a time when the teaching of a Buddha is known, (b) we actually meet the Dharma, (c) we have the faculties which allow us to understand the Dharma, and (d) we have the leisure to practice the Dharma, is a great and precious rarity (see also footnote 6);

2. The fragility of the human state: we live at most 100 years, and for much of that we are too young, too old, or too sick to practice Dharma;

3. The certainty of death;

4. The uncertainty of the time of death.

Therefore, to avoid triviality and to ensure that whatever time we have is well spent, the monastic day is carefully organized around Dharma activities.

The specifics of the monastic schedule vary from season to season and place to place. Figure 7 attempts to plot the broad limits within which three different types of monasteries might be run, though there is probably no actual monastery which conforms precisely to any one of these schedules.[17]

Rising before dawn, symbolic of the fact that, like the Buddha, they may repose in samadhi (deep meditation), but not actually sleep, the monks prepare their bodies, worship, and meditate. Around dawn, they take a light breakfast, sufficient to maintain their activities. In Theravadin monasteries, this is preceded by the receiving round. Morning worship, study, and work are followed by another meal. This is fairly substantial for those (i.e., Theravadins and some Mahayanists) who observe the original rule not to eat after noon.[18] Work is then resumed until the evening worship. The time between dusk and retiring may be spent in conferences with the Abbot or senior monks, study or free time. In the stricter monasteries, silence is kept as much as

TIME	TYPE		
	Theravada	**Zen**	**Tibetan** *(Gelugpa,* study–type)
4 A.M.	Rise Chanting and meditation Housework	Rise Chanting and meditation	Rise Chanting and meditation Study
7 A.M. *(dawn)*	*RECEIVING ROUND*	Breakfast	Tea
8 A.M.	Breakfast Morning puja	Housework	Study/work/ meditation *DEBATING PRACTICE*
9 A.M.	Study/work/ meditation	Study/work/ meditation	
11 A.M.	*MAIN MEAL* (last meal)		Main meal
12 noon	Rest/study	Main meal	
1 P.M.		Rest	Bath, rest
2 P.M.	Study/work	Study/meditation/ *CONFERENCES*	Study/work/ meditation *DEBATING PRACTICE*
5 P.M.	Bath	Bath (*FORMAL HOT BATH* every other week)	Supper
6 P.M.	Evening puja	"Medicine" (i.e., evening meal)	Puja
7 P.M. *(dusk)*	Study/meditation	*EVENING SERMON* Puja	*MAIN DEBATING SESSION*
9 P.M.	Free time/conferences		
10 P.M.	Chanting and meditation in cell. Retire.	Retire	Retire

Figure 7: SCHEMATIZED MONASTIC SCHEDULES (distinctive features IN CAPITALS)

possible, in order to maintain recollectedness. When a monk has no other duties, he may go off to study, or meditate. Leaving the compound is discouraged, except for the receiving round and official duties. About six hours' sleep is usually allowed, except during intensive retreats, when there is more meditation, less work, and less sleep. At festival time, the normal routine is interrupted, laity come to visit, and meals may be improved.

NOTES
to Chapter Four

1. Strictly, there are no bhikkhunis today, for the Theravadin succession has been lost, but there are those who live according to the spirit of the bhikkhuni rules, observing the eight or ten precepts (see below). The Mahayana lineage of bhikshunis, however, has been preserved in China.

2. Hindu women also become wanderers, but less commonly.

3. For this information I am indebted to Professor Miriam Levering, Department of Religious Studies, University of Tennessee.

4. The destruction is sometimes ascribed to the Muslim invaders of the eleventh century. This must certainly be taken into account, but eyewitness reports indicate that the monasteries in the Subcontinent were already decaying from within before the Muslims arrived.

5. The classic study of initiation rites is Arnold van Gennep, *The Rites of Passage* (Chicago: Phoenix Books, 1961).

6. The candidate should be a human because only in the human realm of rebirth is the web of Karma suitable for the kind of choices necessary to practice Dharma effectively. The candidate is specifically asked if he is a *naga* (snake-god) on account of the curious tradition that a *naga* who had the magic ability to transform himself into a youth once tried to become a bhikkhu. His deception was discovered when he slept, for he was unable to retain his human form except while fully conscious, and the Buddha dismissed him with the admonition to observe a simple fasting practice which would enable him to be reborn as a human and then become a bhikkhu. (Henry Clarke Warren, *Buddhism in Translations*, Harvard University Press, 1896: reprinted by Atheneum, 1962 and subsequently, pp. 401–402.) The requirement of masculinity is apparently an exclusion of those who are biologically hermaphroditic. A bhikshuni candidate, of course, would have to be fully female.

7. For an account of the ceremony for becoming a monk in Sri Lanka, see Henry Clarke Warren, *op. cit.*, pp. 393–401. For a Chinese ceremony, see Holmes Welch, *The Practice of Chinese Buddhism 1900–1950* (Cambridge, MA: Harvard University Press, 1967), pp. 269–275.

8. For a more complete discussion of monastic clothing, see the appendix to this chapter.

9. Vietnamese and Japanese sometimes follow this Chinese custom. They pronounce the character *Shih* as, respectively, *Thich* and *Shaku.*

10. See especially *Monkey* (London: 1942), a readable but greatly abridged and highly interpretive translation by Arthur Waley of an allegorical novel by Wu Ch'eng-en (ca. 1505–ca. 1580) based upon the pilgrimage of Hsüan-tsang between 629 and 645 c.e. and recorded in the

Hsi-yu Chi, "A Record of Travels in the West." A careful and complete translation of the novel has been made by Anthony C. Yu, *The Journey to the West* (University of Chicago Press, 4 vols., 1977–83).

11. Ven. Gesshin Prabhasa Dharma, a woman who is a Zen roshi, has playfully suggested calling such women "nunks." Sandy Boucher, *Turning the Wheel: American Women Creating the New Buddhism* (Harper, 1988), p. 144, note 1.

12. This apparently sexist rule had, when it was composed, a protective function. An Indian woman (even, in many cases, today, and certainly then) must have a male "protector"—her father or other male relative if she is unmarried, her husband if she is married. A woman without a "protector" is in real danger of being regarded as "loose" and sexually available to any man who desires her. Subjugation to the bhikshus was a way of ensuring, in Indian society, the freedom of the bhikshuni to be celibate. The foresight and daring innovation of the Buddha in allowing women to choose a life-style other than that of docile wife is remarkable. It is something with which Indian society is not yet comfortable.

13. Strictly, the Vinaya is set apart from the Patimokkha and the Ten Rules of the samanera, but the word is used loosely to refer to all monastic rules. For an English translation of the Pali Patimokkha, see *Sacred Books of the East,* vol. 13.

14. Text in Richard A. Gard, *Buddhism* (New York: Braziller, 1961), pp. 174–178, quoted from A. M. Hocart, *The Temple of the Tooth in Kandy* (London: 1931), chapter 6, pp. 34–37.

15. D. T. Suzuki, *The Training of the Zen Buddhist Monk* (New York: University Books, 1965), p. 33. See also pp. 148–154.

16. More precisely, the rule is that a full monk (having *upasampada*) may not dig the ground for fear of harming living beings. John Orr (see appendix to this chapter, note 1) told me that in his tradition, if wood were needed, the samaneras would chop the tree down and the bhikkhus could then help to cut it up. Work as such, therefore, is not forbidden in any Buddhist monastic tradition. Chinese monks, however, tended to lapse into dreamy Taoist musings and it was apparently to counter this that Po-chang (sometimes pronounced Pai-chang) wrote his rule making work compulsory.

17. The sources for this chart are various conversations I have had from time to time with present and former monks. Therefore, they should not be taken too literally. The Tibetan schedule is modeled on that of a Gelugpa temple specializing in logic and debate. My informant was Kathy Rogers, who lived in such a temple in South India.

18. After noon, water, tea, or fruit juice may be drunk, and anything not considered "food" (such as plain, but not milk, chocolate) may be eaten.

The rule does not focus on the absence of food but on the attitude of the would-be eater. The body adjusts to a light breakfast and a substantial lunch, and finds that it is quite healthy. Then, as the mind suggests eating after noon, it comes up against the Vinaya saying "no," causing one to reflect on one's progress in the training.

Appendix to Chapter 4

The Monastic Robes

The Theravadin robes are the simplest and may be most like those worn by the Buddha. Following the tradition common for garments in the Indian Subcontinent, the robes are not tailored to fit but consist of lengths of cloth wound around the body. The undergarment is a loin cloth similar to the dhoti or sarong and called the *antaravasaka*. It may be secured with a cloth belt. The upper robe, called the *chivara* or *uttarasanga* goes around the shoulders and is a patchwork of at least five pieces. The pattern of the patchwork and the precise manner of draping the *chivara* is often the subject of lively controversy. An outer robe, the *sanghati*, of thicker material, is worn in cold weather and used as a sleeping blanket. It may also be worn folded over the left shoulder on formal occasions. All three parts of the robe are required to be within three feet of the bhikkhu, or at least in the same room, during the night. Sandals may be worn, though there are times when they must be removed, and "vegetarian" sandals (such as Japanese rubber "flip-flops") are preferred over leather ones. Two cloth shoulder bags, one for the alms-bowl and one for other necessities, may be used, and umbrellas are sometimes carried.[1]

The Tibeto-Mongolian robes are made of thicker material, often flannel, on account of the cold climate. Their basic colors are yellow and maroon. The loin cloth is something like a maroon skirt and the upper robe is like a yellow T-shirt.[2] A long, yellow, patchwork robe resembling the Theravadin *chivara* may be worn during formal teaching sessions, and there is a complicated paraphernalia of colored robes, crowns, and other adornments used during certain Tantric liturgies. The outer garment is a cape. Heavy boots are worn and there are both formal and informal sets of headgear. The design and color of each article of clothing is richly symbolic, constantly reminding the monk of the Dharma in general and his special function in regard to it. For example, the hat is yellow to signify restraint, yellow being the distinctively Buddhist monastic color; the V-neck of the vest symbolizes the jaws of death always ready to close on us; the boots have a special form reminiscent of the general shape of a cock, a snake, and a pig to symbolize the three poisons of attachment, aversion, and confusion that the monk treads underfoot.[3]

Sino-Japanese robes are more strictly tailored and superficially resemble a Catholic priest's cassock. Their basic colors are grey and very dark brown or black. In Japan, the undergarment is a kimono, usually white, over which is worn the "large robe" *(dai-e)*, which is black with wide sleeves and retained by a cincture, and over that again is put the *kesa,* which has a patchwork of vertical strips. The number of strips and the color of the *kesa* indicate rank or formality. An abbreviated *kesa,* called the *rakusu,* resembles a breastplate and is worn on informal occasions and as the minimal garment for sleeping (it being forbidden to sleep naked). Each *rakusu* comes with a *zagu* or bowing mat of identical material. The *kesa* is the most sacred piece of clothing, reminiscent of the scapular of Catholic monasticism, and it must be put on while kneeling, after having been reverently placed, folded, on the head. The combination of the Indian *kesa,* the Chinese *dai-e* and Japanese kimono symbolize the transmission of the Dharma from India through China to Japan. Japanese wooden clogs are worn out of doors, with a special monastic variety of *tabi* (white ankle-socks with separate big-toes). A skull-cap, called *rokkaku,* "six-cornered," after its shape, may be worn informally, and there is a conical mitre, *tatemosu,* for ceremonies.[4]

Shingon (Japanese Tantric Buddhism) has a rich variety of formal robes connected with its elaborate liturgies.

NOTES
to Appendix on Monastic Robes

1. The Theravadin robes are explained in detail, from the standpoint of one of the stricter Thai traditions, in *The Entrance to the Vinaya,* vol. 2, pp. 11–31, by Somdet Phra Maha Samana Chao Krom Phraya Vajirananavarorasa (Bangkok: Mahamakut Rajavidyalaya Press, 2516 B.E./1973 C.E.). I am indebted also to information received from John Orr, the former Bhikkhu Piyavanno, in a personal interview.

2. This "t-shirt" was added to the Tibetan robes under Confucian influence. At a time when the Chinese Imperial court favored Tibeto-Mongolian Buddhism, chanting ceremonies were held in the palace. After one such ceremony, a concubine objected that the custom of leaving the right shoulder and arm exposed allowed more naked flesh to be seen than she thought proper. (For this information I am indebted to Ven. Thubten Pende [James Dougherty] of Nalanda Monastery, Lavaur, France.)

3. *The Life and Teaching of Geshe Rabten,* translated and edited by B. Alan Wallace. (London: Allen and Unwin, 1980) pp. 14–24.

4. This description is a brief summary of the traditions followed by Soto Zen as described to me by Maezumi Roshi of the Zen Center of Los Angeles on June 6, 1984. Roshi graciously brought out for me many treasured *kesas* and *zagus,* not normally allowed to be touched by laymen, and allowed me to handle them while he explained their history and use at length. It is clear that the study of the Buddhist monastic habit is an enormously rich area awaiting to be opened by the serious student. Roshi emphasized that his tradition may not be followed by other lineages of Japanese Buddhists. The Chinese traditions are another matter: I have simply not enquired about them, but superficially they are similar to the Japanese. Diagrams of the *kesa* may be found on p. 179 of *Zen Master Dogen* by Yuho Yokoi and Daizen Victoria (New York: Weatherhill, 1976).

Chapter 5

CONTROVERSIES WITH NON-BUDDHISTS

(Act 7 of the Buddha)

Tolerance does not mean vagueness. Except in a few cases, Buddhism has allowed rival cults to flourish, even when it was politically able to defeat them, but it has never had any doubt about their inferiority. Siddhartha, before finding what he believed to be the answer to the puzzle of existence, tried various forms of meditation and asceticism and rejected them as inadequate.

Criticism of Theism and Atheism:

Buddhism denies both the view that there is a God, a "man upstairs" or "boss" who is finally in control of things, and the view that reality can be explained as merely the chance interaction of material forces. Broadly, that is, it denies the assertions of both the theist and the atheist, and proposes its own viewpoint that is intended to escape the difficulties of both the theistic and atheistic systems.

CRITICISM OF THEISM

The existence of God, of an absolute, controlling Mind, is so commonly accepted by Western religions that those who deny God often call themselves irreligious. To be called "Godless" is tantamount to being called immoral and depraved. God is popularly seen as (1) the final moral arbiter in religious systems, and (2) the logical final term in the majority of pre-modern Western philosophical systems.

God as moral arbiter is a commonplace of American life. "In God We Trust" appears on our money and as a backdrop in many courtrooms. It is sometimes argued that moral laxity is a direct result of an enfeebled theistic belief. When church-going is recommended, it is done in a context that implies that it is the best way to restore America's moral fiber. Buddhism, on the contrary, claims that belief in God leads to moral and spiritual degradation. If I believe that God takes care of everything, it is easy for me either to regard my actions as determined by fate or predestination ("God made me do it") or else to declare that no matter what I do, right or wrong, God will forgive me and make everything turn out all right. Either way, I am not taking responsibility for my actions. But according to the law of karma, I inherit the fruit of my past deeds. If something happens to me by apparent "chance" or "fate," I say that it is the fruiting of karma, and my future happiness or misery will depend on how I act today. In Buddhism, only I can be responsible for what I do or for what happens to me.

God as Ultimate Cause is a standard feature of most pre–modern Western philosophies, and many people who are not philosophers find such a God plausible. The argument goes something like this: nothing can come from nothing (an axiom expressed in the Latin phrase *ex nihilo nihil fit*, "out of nothing, nothing comes"), so the universe must come from something. This something cannot have come from something else, for then we would have an infinite regress, which (according to the presuppositions of the logical system being used) is absurd, so ultimately we see that there must be a Something which caused everything but which was not itself caused. It is the Cause of Itself (Latin: *causa sui*), the Uncaused Cause. This we call God.

This argument, however, is a leg–pull. In a universe understood as the Mystery of Indra's Net (see Chapter 1), everything can be the cause *and* the effect of everything else whether or not time is beginningless.[1] Then again, an Uncaused Cause is a contradiction in terms: it is not only logically inconsistent, but no one has ever met any cause that was not also an effect that was caused by something else. Besides all of which, the Buddha, the Omniscient one, proclaimed the causes of everything, showing that a First Cause was unnecessary, and denied the existence of a Self-Abiding One (God). Thus, the argument may be abandoned.[2]

CRITICISM OF ATHEISM

Buddha never seems to have taken the possibility of God very seriously, and we have to say that his criticisms of God, while excellent psychologically and philosophically, miss the heart of the matter. In his denunciation of atheism, however, he displays a surer touch. His Seventh Act concerns the serious study he undertook under two apparent atheists, and his subsequent announcement of the unsatisfactory nature of their teaching. Then, by practicing extreme self-denial, he tested another atheistic system, and it too he found wanting. These two unsatisfactory systems fall broadly under the headings of Monism and Dualism.

2. Criticism of Monism

The systems taught by Arada Kalama and Udraka Ramaputra apparently proposed that liberation from samsara could be achieved by a meditative technique of extreme enstasis. Suffering, they seemed to say, comes from being entrapped in the multiplicity of things. By withdrawing into ourselves, we shall find peace. Arada identified the state of "nothing whatsoever" with liberation, but Udraka said one had to proceed further into the state of "neither notions nor non-notions" or "neither thinking nor not thinking." This, he said, was the condition of eternal release from rebirth.

Interestingly, the Buddha never denied the existence of these states, nor that one had to be highly skilled in meditation to achieve them. He merely said that they were, although very subtle, still a part of samsara. Buddhism has affirmed the acuity of Arada and Udraka by placing the states which they identified at the top of the Buddhist universe (see chapter 6), but it claims that liberation is *discontinuous* with this series because it is *beyond all afflicted states.*

If I think that liberation is a state of radical enstasis, I will probably come up with an elaborate map of more and more inward states, hierarchically arranged, until I reach the One or the One Point which is behind, or in, everything. What I may not notice is that if the goal is on the same continuum as the path, I may reach the end of the path but I cannot extract myself from the path-goal model. I sit at the end of the path, either doing nothing for ever and ever, or I eventually decide to return along the same path. The Buddha did not want to find the end of the path but the way out of all paths altogether. Thus he went on towards the Bodhi Tree to find another answer.

But many systems are satisfied with this "end of the path" answer. A distinctive teaching of the Upanishads is that there is one universal energy, the Brahman, and that I, at my deepest level, am one with it. *Tat tvam asi,* "You are that," and *Aham brahmasmi,* "I am Brahman," are two slogans of this system which was elaborated as Vedanta. Vedanta became such a popular way for Hindu intelligentsia to explain Hinduism to the West that for many years we thought it was "the Hindu view."[3] According to Vedanta (an elaborate and sophisticated system that deserves better treatment than this one liner),[4] the creation comes out of the One that is called Brahman. Unlike the Biblical God, who must enliven the universe once he has made it, Brahman is the universe itself as inherently alive. It says of Itself, "May I become," and It does. Because of Its creativity and Its oneness with personal as well as impersonal forces, Brahman may also be regarded as a God of some sort, though clearly not of the sort that can exist apart from the world. Sometimes, then, this Monism can be called Pantheism, but in either case Buddhism denies it. Final release is the escape from *all* systems:

> *A monk asked Chao-chou:*
> *"The ten thousand dharmas return to the One; to where does the One return?"*
> *The Master replied, "While I was staying at Ch'ing-chou I made a robe that weighed seven pounds."*[5]

In this koan, the monk is summarizing the monistic cosmology of Taoism, and asking how Buddhism goes further than

Taoism in its explanation of the universe. Chao-chou replies by bringing the monk's mind back into the reality of the present moment. In the NOW, there are no systems. Reality is as it is, and it is unproblematic.

Criticism of Dualism

If I practice radical enstasis, I might decide that the "real me" inside all this is of a different order from the surface me and, especially, my body. I would then propose that matter and spirit were the twin, but finally irreconcilable, forces in the universe, and I would be a Dualist. It may indeed be that Arada and Udraka were Dualists—their techniques would fit with Dualism as well as with Monism. In any case, it is against Dualism that Buddhism has the strongest arguments.

The two most important Dualistic systems in India are Samkhya-Yoga and Jainism. Samkhya is a Hindu system that developed later than the Buddha but which may have had its roots at about the Buddha's time. It has already been summarized in the account of Act Seven of the Buddha in part one. Jainism is a separate religion that arose more or less contemporaneously with Buddhism and was a serious rival to it. In Jainism, the duality between living spirit and dead matter, which is found in disguised or modified forms in many religions, is taught as absolutely correct, and the consequences of this view are carried to their logical conclusion.

The life of Mahavira, known as the Jina, "Conquerer," so that his followers are called Jainas, "they of the Jina," is so close to that of the Buddha, and their teachings are so similar yet so different, that Buddhism and Jainism almost seem like parodies of each other. The extreme self-denial that the Buddha tried and rejected is so much like that which the Jina tried and accepted that the Buddha's rejection seems like a direct attack upon Jainism.[6]

Mahavira was born near present-day Patna about 540 B.C.E.. Born into the Kshatriya caste, he lived in comfort, became dissatisfied with the household life, and left at the age of thirty. He joined a group of monks, but found their way deficient, and wandered on his own. After a while he claimed to have conquered samsara, and was called the Jina. He purposely fasted to death about 468 B.C.E. Although there is, therefore, about a sixty-year overlap between the probable dates of birth and death of the

Buddha and the Jina, and though they traveled in the same general region, it does not seem that they ever met. Controversies between their disciples, however, have been recorded.

Jainism sees suffering as caused by our involvement in activity. Every living being has a soul, called jiva, "living thing," which is, in its true nature, pure and passionless. But the jiva becomes enmeshed in action (karma), which Jainism regards as a subtle form of matter, gets coated with it, and sinks into the phenomenal universe. "Catch 22" then operates: the jiva tries to free itself from karma, but such an attempt is itself karma and, like a fly struggling on flypaper, the harder it tries to escape, the faster it sticks. If the jiva gives up action altogether, the body in which it is encased dies, but because the effects of previous action have not yet worked themselves out, the jiva gets another body, and the process begins again. In order to obtain release, one must simultaneously (1) prevent the build–up of new karma, and (2) destroy old karma. This is done by, respectively, *ahimsa* (non–harming) and *tapas* (asceticism).

Ahimsa is also practiced by Buddhists, with one difference: a Buddhist ascribes much less evil to unintentional harming (e.g., accidentally walking on an insect) than intentional harming, whereas a Jain would ascribe the same amount of evil effect to either case.[7] Jains place ahimsa at the pinnacle of their religion: *ahimsa parama dharma,* "Ahimsa is the supreme piety." Observant laypeople will always be vegetarian, and they tend to seek employment in trading or the jewel business, where the amount of harming *(himsa)* is minimal. The monks are even more strict, wrapped in a single white robe (in contrast to the three robes of the Buddhist monk), carrying a soft broom with which to remove insects gently from themselves and from their path, and speaking in a low voice so as not to harm the air. The most observant monks wear nothing except a face-mask (somewhat like a Western surgical mask), believing that air contains jivas and is harmed even by breathing it. They move slowly and recollectedly, beg all their food (restricting themselves to vegetarian leftovers) and may forego washing, haircuts, finger- and toe-nail trimming, and scratching. As far as possible, nothing whatever must be harmed, even one's own skin, so that the amount of karmic build-up is very small.

At the same time as the Jain restricts his karmic build–up by ahimsa, he must use tapas to remove both the massive accumulation of previous karma and the small amount of new karma that, despite everything, is inevitably produced. *Tapas* literally means "heat": it burns away karma. Sometimes the heat is literal: one may sit naked on a rock fully exposed to the immense heat of the Indian summer sun. Other forms of "heat" are more symbolic: confession of faults, charity to the poor, or the study of Jain doctrine. Abstinence from certain foods, especially delicacies such as the sugary cakes of which India has such an extraordinary variety, is popular, because it unites tapas with ahimsa. When the Jain feels that all but the very tiniest amount of his karma has been burnt away by tapas, he may elect to stop all action: he removes any clothes he may be wearing, refuses all food and drink, refrains from all movement, and composes himself for death.[8] At the very least, the devout Jain should give away all possessions and mentally withdraw from the phenomenal world as he or she feels death approaching. The hope is that, if death has been accomplished properly and at the optimum time, the jiva will shake off the last vestiges of karma and, like a balloon freed from its ballast, rise to the summit of the universe, where it will join other jivas in an eternal but unconscious bliss, like a wonderfully deep sleep, never to be born again.

The Buddhist objection to Jainism is two–fold: practical and doctrinal. In practice, Buddhists oppose any kind of extreme. When Siddhartha lived in his father's palace, he lolled about and frittered away his time on pleasures that were transient, and, so, ultimately unsatisfying. He realized, as did Mahavira, that some withdrawal from sensuality was necessary. But, whereas Mahavira pushed this withdrawal to its limit, Siddhartha complained that excessive fasting only made him weak and sleepy, so that once more he found himself lolling about and frittering away his time. Siddhartha decided that the body should be fed, washed, and clothed just sufficiently to keep it in good running order, but no more: it was like an open wound that must be cared for but not enjoyed.

The doctrinal objection protests that Dualism is simply a mistake. The material world does not exist for me apart from my consciousness. Therefore, any supposedly self-existent, dead matter is in some other universe and of no concern to me. Also, and more seriously, Buddhists claim that Jains, like Monistic Hindus, have just not carried their meditative investigation far enough. When the postulated irreducible jiva is piercingly inspected, it is found to be itself composed of parts, and the parts are changing. Therefore, any attempt to liberate this jiva as if it were ultimate and immortal is doomed to failure.[9]

The Buddhist Response

NON-THEISM

Buddhism responds to theism by downgrading it. It claims that the minor deities (of Hinduism, or of any other religion which Buddhism encountered) are merely more powerful, more beautiful, and longer lived than humans, so that *both we and they* may be deluded into thinking that they are omnipotent, all-beautiful, and eternal. A major deity, or Ruler of the Universe, is not denied by Buddhism, but he (it is always a he!) is also under the control of karma: he does not know this, but thinks that, since there is no being more powerful than he, he created his own power and therefore all things. Buddhism views God as the ultimate megalomaniac. All sentient beings have, time and again, been reborn as God because of the fruiting of their karma. One tradition says that Shakyamuni had been previously born as King of Gods or Universal Ruler thirty-three times, and so, when he became the Buddha, he addressed the present Universal Ruler by a human name that he who is now God had possessed in a former life. A Buddha does not worship God or the gods, they worship him. He is "Teacher of deities and humans." Fortunate and intelligent gods grasp the opportunity to receive instruction from the Buddha.[10] Since this position does not deny God's existence it cannot be called atheism, but it is hardly theism either. I suggest calling the Buddhist position "non-theism."

ABHIDHARMA

The Buddhist response to Atheism, that is, to the viewpoint that reality is controlled by impersonal forces and not by a Big Person who created the forces, is subtle and elegant, with none of the patronizing naivete of its denial of theism. The response developed into a coherent system called Abhidharma.

The word Abhidharma has been subjected to a range of curious translations which have served to confuse generations of students. It is really quite simple. Dharma here means the teaching of the Buddha, i.e., Buddhism. *Abhi* is a prefix meaning "more," cognate with English "upon," i.e., layered or piled up. So, "Advanced Buddhism" is the most straightforward translation of Abhidharma. After one has heard the basics of Dharma, the Four Truths and so forth (See chapter 9), one wishes to go into suffering, its origin, its cure, and the path to its cure in more detail. This is Abhidharma.

Abhidharma explains both Monism and Dualism as mistaken interpretations of how we feel about reality. We all feel a sense of "I." Buddhism does not deny the feeling, and does not make the assertion (which would be unintelligible) "I do not exist." Sometimes we feel that I am a real "me" surrounded by "mine." When we harden that feeling into a philosophy we have Dualism. At other times (especially under the influence of certain drugs) we feel so connected to everything that we do not feel a "me" at all. When we harden *that* feeling into a philosophy, we have Monism. Buddhism takes both of these feelings seriously but, by subjecting them to rigorous analysis, it claims that neither the Dualist nor the Monist has got it right.

The analysis begins with the investigation of "me" and automatically includes the investigation of everything "I" perceive.

When I inspect myself, I am aware, first of all, that I am composed of visible, tangible elements and invisible, intangible elements. I may call these my body and my mind. Buddhism, with more precision, calls them *rupa* and *nama*. *Rupa* is "form" or "color," but its meaning is broader than these English words. Anything that is directly perceptible through the senses of sight, hearing, smell, taste, or touch is said to manifest *rupa*. It is matter, but not in an abstract sense. It is matter *as I experience it:* it is a name for what I see, hear, smell, taste, or touch. *Nama* literally means "name," and refers to those constituents of a person that, while they certainly and indubitably exist, cannot be perceived directly but must be inferred, just as my name "Roger" is undoubtedly mine, but no matter how hard you look at me you cannot see it and even if you subject me to detailed anatomical dissection you will never find it.

It is important to notice that the nama-rupa distinction is *not* a division into mental and physical but into *mental components as I perceive them and physical components as I perceive them. Therefore, mind or consciousness* (chitta) *is a fundamental and irreducible part of the system.* Descartes thought that when he observed an object, the object existed in its own right and so proposed a distinction between mind (the observer) and matter (the observed). He neglected to notice that the object existed in his consciousness and that "I–see–it" is an irreducible and impenetrable operation.

So, Abhidharma is the analysis of the transformations of *chitta*. Thus, it is not materialistic, for it denies, not the existence of matter, but the possibility of investigating anything (even matter) apart from an investigator, i.e., it rejects as nonsensical the question: "Does matter exist apart from mind?" *Chitta*, however, is not Universal Mind, a sort of Emersonian Oversoul or Cosmic Mind-Stuff. *Chitta* is the activity of the perceiving consciousness. It is not a metaphysical principle, it is a fact of everyday experience.

Buddhism takes an interest in metaphysics, but it quickly becomes bored with it, for metaphysics does not help me to live happily. When the Buddha was asked about various metaphysical principles,[11] he did not say he could not answer, he said he would not. "Were I to explain these topics or not, still there would remain suffering, old age, sickness, and death." Buddhism does, however, explain suffering—its cause and its cure—and in doing so it erects what seems like a metaphysic, or a philosophy, or a psychology. But, it is a "soft" philosophy, or, better, it is a therapy whose purpose is to expose the confusion and suffering that makes us construct metaphysical systems into which we then crawl to shelter ourselves from reality just-as-it-is. The Buddha Dharma is *trans*formation manifesting as *in*formation.[12]

The therapy of Abhidharma is a search for the roots of diseased thinking and a method of purifying, or healing, thinking. *Chitta* is not to be destroyed but cleansed and then it will shine with its natural brilliance, omniscience, compassion, and joy. Diseased thinking is analyzed into basic components called dharmas. A single dharma is an irreducible and unique event with a distinct profile called a lakshana (mark, characteristic). Attempts were made to identify a finite set of dharmas, each one characterized whenever it occurred by its own distinctive lakshana. Various lists were drawn up and were the subject of learned debates in the course of which the original dynamism of the system, intended as an analysis of the living flow of mind, was forgotten in favor of scholarly precision over competing tables of "atoms."[13]

In its earlier forms, however, a version of which has been

preserved in Theravada, it deserves respect as a valid path to liberation. Put at its simplest, it goes something like this.

Supposing I see something—a pot is the standard object in such Buddhist discussions. The pot has color, shape, and resistance. That is its *rupa*. How do I know this? Because I use my senses to contact *(sparsha)* it. In order for me to know that the pot is there, certain conditions must be met: the pot must actually be there, there must be sufficient light, I must have at least one eye, the eye must be open and working, it must be properly connected to the brain, and I must be awake. The process of contacting the pot *(sparsha* literally means "touch") forms a continuum but, as a prism divides up white light into its components, so I can divide up the process of contacting the pot into identifiable, but not discrete, moments of coming-into-and-staying-in-consciousness. Since I find that I continue to exist after having slept or fainted (during which time I was not aware of anything), I can assume that there is a basal continuum of mind that is below the level of my conscious attention. This is called *bhavanga,* "becoming-ness," and is like the hidden but undeniable flow of an underground river. When I have a conscious thought or perception, this bhavanga "vibrates" *(chalana)* into consciousness, ordinarily so-called, under the stimulus of the pot's presence.

The process of perception entering through the sense receptors *(vedana,* "feeling") is followed by collating the information into a cluster that can be identified as a something *(samjña,* "notion"). Because I have seen pots before, I have an evaluative reaction to them as nice, nasty, or neutral. This reaction has become habitual. It is called the *samskara* cluster, literally "built up," i.e., something acquired and constructed from previous experience. Finally "I" am conscious of all this process of consciousness and I call this function *vijñana,* "knowing." I do not, however, find an "I" that exists as the eternal, absolute witness behind this process. Descartes said, "I think therefore I am," but Buddhism replies, "Think again."

Each of these factors—the *rupa* of my original contact with the pot and the four subsequent mental operations (or divisions of *nama*) of *vedana, samjña, samskara,* and *vijñana* is a composite or cluster *(skandha)* of *dynamically interacting forces.* Collectively they make up what we call a person and are known as the Five Bundles. They are, then, capable of further analysis into more than two hundred *operationally defined components.* [14]

This division into *nama-rupa,* the five bundles, and so on, has exposed the dharmas, whose interaction we call reality. It is important to notice, however, that the bundles that constitute what we call "me" are not themselves identified with the sense of "I," either individually or together, nor are they, or the other dharmas, reified into components resembling the parts of a machine. They have, of themselves, no "real," autonomous, or particulate existence. Each is dependent on the others for its appearance, its continuance, and its disappearance. This is called their "interdependent arising" *(pratitya-samutpada).* (See "Breaking the Cycle" in chapter 8.) *Continuity,* on this view, is an illusion, similar to the illusion of continuous movement produced by the succession of frames on a film, or (to use a more traditional example) by the illusion of a ring of fire produced by waving a burning brand in a circle.

Reifying the dharmas, seeing them as machine parts, is a great temptation to which untransformed mind is subject. The Sarvastivadin school of Abhidharma (see note 13) apparently fell victim to this temptation. The Sarvastivadins supposed that each dharma not only had a unique profile, but *also* a unique ontology—it had *svabhava,* "own-being" or inherent, autonomous existence. Mahayana (especially Madhyamika) was able to show that this idea is self-contradictory, and it relegated the Sarvastivadin Abhidharma to the status of Inferior Vehicle (Hinayana).[15]

The Theravadin school of Abhidharma (called, in Pali, Abhidhamma) is, on the other hand, an open-ended system.[16] Its dharma (Pali: *dhamma*) lists are many and overlapping (see part two, note 2), indicating an *organic* system, operationally defined, as against the *mechanistic,* atomistically defined Sarvastivadin Abhidharma. Theravada, which has survived as a living system, is not the same as the extinct Hinayana. Theravada understands that the teaching of the Buddha is transformation, and its Abhidhamma is a "soft" philosophy. Hinayana mistook the transformation for information, petrified the operational understanding of reality as interdependent arising into a "hard" philosophy consisting of seventy-five distinct dharma-atoms, and died out.

Theravada Abhidhamma *practice* trains the mind in being

"choicelessly aware" of the appearance, continuance, and disappearance of the dharma-events (see "Meditation: Theravada" in chapter 6). The mind minutely inspects these events and finds no essence, inherent existence, or permanent self in them: *sabbe dhamma anatta'ti*, "all the dharmas are without self," Dhammapada 279. It sees their evanescence, their scintillating procession, their constant newness. It sees their Transparency. Dharma-events are seen to be *conditioned* but *newly arising*, that is, reality is seen to be real but open. Seeing this, the meditator moves from the closed repetitiveness of samsara into the freedom of nirvana.

Abhidharma, the first "soft" philosophy to be developed by Buddhism, presents us with a unified method for understanding and purifying our conduct (ethics), mental states (psychology), and worldview (metaphysics). The two other "soft" philosophies, the Mahayana systems of Madhyamika and Yogachara (to be discussed in, respectively, chapters 9 and 7) are similarly complete in their intent, although the focus of Madhyamika is on metaphysics and the focus of Yogachara is psychology.

Establishing the Truth of Buddhism

LOGIC AND DEBATE

If Buddhism is true, it should be provable. As Mahayana Buddhism grew up in India, it developed both an apologetic (a defense of its own position) and a polemic (a demonstration of the falsity of non-Buddhist views). The general term for the exercise is *Nyaya*, "going into," "going back," i.e., tracing out the causes of things, establishing rules and models of argument. The most representative thinker of this school is Dharmakirti (c. 650 C.E.), whose *Nyayabindu*, "Essentials of Logic," is an elaboration of the foundational work of Dignaga (c. 400–485 C.E.).[17]

As the Mahayana moved into Tibet, it formalized Nyaya into a method of mind training by public debate not unlike the Disputation that was so much a part of Medieval Christian universities.[18] In formal Tibetan debate there is a Defender, who is seated, and a Challenger, who stands. The Challenger puts a proposition, which the Defender accepts, and the Challenger then tries to defeat the position accepted by the Defender by showing its absurd consequences. As the Challenger begins to make a point he stretches out his left arm, keeping his right arm raised, and as he finishes the point he stamps his left foot and brings his right palm down hard on his left palm. A good debate moves swiftly and noisily, the proponents shouting and the audience cheering. For those who can follow the precise thrust and counter-thrust it can be very exciting, but to a casual observer hearing a forum full of young monks practicing debate all at the same time (debate is always conducted in the open air) it seems as if a riot has broken out.

Any argument, if it is to be effective, must be sharp and penetrating, offering no escape to the opponent. If argument is practiced for its own sake, it can generate anger and stimulate pride. However, if I see someone about to eat poison in the mistaken belief that it is food, my strident attempt to convince that person of an error is an exercise of compassion. According to Buddhism, we all eat poison to some extent until we become Buddhas, for our thinking is confused. It is the compassionate purpose of Buddhist logic and debate to remove this confusion and assist the mind to discover its own innate freedom. Since the primary aim of Buddhist debate is the liberation or enlightenment of the mind of both protagonists (trying to convince someone else of a position is the best way to find out if I understand it myself), no distinction is made between *validity* and *truth.* In western logic, an argument is said to be *valid* if it is formally correct, that is, if it follows the abstract rules of proper argument, whether or not it is *true,* i.e., in accordance with reality. In western logic I can say:

> *All men are green.*
> *Socrates is a man.*
> *Therefore, Socrates is green.*

This syllogism is *valid* but *false,* for the major premise "All men are green" is not in fact the case. A clever member of a western debating society can force his opponent to admit to the apparent truth (logical validity) of obvious falsities, and the audience cheers. A Buddhist debater who did this would have shown that his opponent was deficient in an understanding of reality, and that he needed further study. A skilled Tibetan debater forces his opponent to reject all unverifiable views as illogical *and there-*

fore false. Thus the Mahayana view is established and other views are overthrown.

The distinction between validity and truth, which is so important to western logic but apparently lacking in Buddhist logic, points to a major difference in world view between Buddhism and most western philosophies. Until quite recently, western philosophy had assumed rather naively that a word related, more or less directly, to a thing, that words "stood for" things. The correct manipulation of words, then, (i.e., logic), was the correct manipulation of things, and led to a correct understanding of reality. But this produced the curious phenomenon that a correct manipulation (a correct syllogism) might be "valid" yet, sometimes, not "true." It took Wittgenstein to discover that, in fact, words do not relate to things, but only to other words. And this (as he partly suspected) is the Buddhist position. When we manipulate words in order to demonstrate the existence of things (especially those highly philosophical things called essences) we find that all we have is more words. In such a case, Transparency automatically presents itself.

It is important to note that Nyaya is a *logical process* that (eventually) leads to a *logical acceptance* of Emptiness. No more and no less. Since Emptiness or Transparency is the mode of being of everything, it is necessary for correct view to demonstrate that this is the case. If it cannot be demonstrated, the mind becomes stuck in the limiting viewpoint that somehow or somewhere there are inherently existing things. Stuck in this view, it continues to suffer. Once Emptiness has been demonstrated, the mind knows where it is headed. But clearly it does not "know" Emptiness directly at this point.

I may find that the solution to a mathematical equation is a minus quantity or a trans-finite number. The *process* leads me to admit the correctness of the solution, but I can only assent to it as inescapable, I cannot "see" or "feel" it. This shows that my mind can make room for views it regards as correct without having direct perception of them. This is the mechanism of the mind on which Buddhist debate rides. It begins by establishing the rules of correct argument by proving things that are obviously true, and then uses these same rules to prove things that are outside the experience of the observer. The method of demonstrating obvious things works by accepting "for the sake of argument" an obvious *falsehood,* such as "All colors are red." If this (false) premise is accepted, then it follows that "The color of a white conch is red." This is absurd, and it is then shown *why* it is absurd—white and red are mutually exclusive—and thus the Defendant must either retract his proposition that "All colors are red" or persist in a viewpoint now shown to be absurd. If the Defendant then voluntarily withdraws his proposition, the argument is finished, and the viewpoint of the Challenger, although unexpressed, is established.

The logical establishment of the primary colors is an elementary formal exercise whose success or failure can be judged by anyone who is not color blind. Gradually thereafter the method is applied to situations that accord less and less with direct experience until it can be used to establish Emptiness against such views as "All things were created by God."

It will be noted that the statement "All colors are red" is not refuted directly, but by drawing from the statement a consequence *(prasanga)* which is unwanted or unacceptable, i.e., "The color of a white conch is red." If the unwanted consequence is then rejected, it implies the rejection of the first statement without further discussion. Thus, a Buddhist logician would not directly challenge the statement "All things were created by God." He would propose a consequence of holding that view, such as, "All things were created simultaneouly and do not change." This follows from the definition of God as unchanging. Since it is obvious, however, that things are coming into and out of being continuously, and are changing, the statement cannot be accepted. By rejecting that statement, it follows either that God did not create anything or that God changes in order to create continuously. Since neither view is acceptable to the theist, his primary statement "All things were created by God" collapses.[19]

This method of establishing the correct view implicitly in the space left by the demolished consequences of an incorrect view is used by the Gelugpa lineage of Tibetan Buddhism, because of which their school is called *Prasangika-Madhyamika.* It is a tenaciously effective method, for it enters into the incorrect view and appears to accept it as its own, then eats it away from within. It seeks to demonstrate that any view other than those within the scope of a world view of Transparency leads to absurd conse-

quences, whereas if Transparency is maintained, all consequences are shown to be logically correct and in accord with
reality.

BUDDHISM AS THE BEST RELIGION

If Buddhism is true, as Buddhist logic attempts to prove, it
should also be the truest, or best, of all religions. Kukai tells us
how this might be. Kukai, posthumously dubbed Kobo Daishi
(774–835 C.E.), is one of the foremost figures in Japanese Buddhism. He founded the Tantric lineage of Shingon and is traditionally credited with the invention of the *kana*, the syllabery
which enabled Japanese to be written as Japanese rather than as
a weird form of Chinese. His mind was encyclopedic, and in 830
C.E. he completed an enormous work, *The Ten Stages of the
Development of Mind,* that plots the steps of spiritual progress
from unthinking selfishness to final enlightenment. Kukai presented his tome to the Emperor, who sensibly decided that an
abridged edition would be more readable. This appeared shortly
afterwards as *The Precious Key to the Secret Treasury.*[20] It attempts a survey of religions (as far as they were known to Kukai)
and arranges all the systems in an ascending order, with Shingon
Buddhism at the top. Stages one through three discuss non–
Buddhist religions.

Stage One is that of the "goat." Before religion takes hold of
them, people rush about, imagining that they are freely following their desires, but actually being controlled by them, just like
a goat. Food, clothing, sex, and wealth are responded to by reflexes alone. Some of these people are mildly religious, believing
in a Creator God, a vital force, or some kind of predestination.
All such will be reborn in the hells and the lower realms of
existence.

Occasionally, since everything changes, someone will begin to
wonder about the value of controlling his animal-like appetites.
He may then practice virtues and become like a good child:
courteous, but ignorant. This is the second stage, that of the
Confucian Gentleman.

Childish people may increase their liking for self-control until
they loathe anything worldly, and strive for the heavens. Being
born there, powerful and beautiful, they lack all fear; but they
are still so far from final enlightenment that this third stage,

which is occupied by Taoists and Hindus, is called "The Fearless Infant."

After the third stage, the division is according to Buddhist lineages, and is a form of "The Gradual Path and the Division of Teachings" (see chapter 9).

Kukai thus argues that any form of Buddhism is superior to non–Buddhism. Indeed, any religious teaching at all is ultimately attributable to the Buddha:

> Question: Then, are the practices of the various heretics based on the teachings of the Buddha?

> Answer: Both yes and no; yes because they once were, and no because they are not any longer. In the beginning they were the teachings of the Buddha, but, during their transmission from the immemorial past, their original meaning is altogether lost.[21]

Kukai is entirely in accord with the Buddha's rejection of his teachers when he states, of people in the third stage, that:

> Even if they reach the highest heaven, that of absence of thought, they will eventually fall into hell, as an arrow shot into the sky falls when its momentum runs out.[22]

NOTES
to Chapter Five

1. When Buddhism says that samsara is beginningless, it does not wish to say that linear time stretches infinitely backwards. The teaching of samsara is in fact a denial of the reality of linear time. When what we call "the world," i.e., that which we experience as space, time, and suffering, is analyzed, no beginning can be found. What *is* found is circularity, meaningless repetition. Samsara is "endless" in the sense that the outgoing message (OGM) tape of a telephone answering machine is "endless": it just keeps going round and, after a greater or lesser time, we find ourselves in much the same place as we began. Samsara "begins" each time the defilements operate, and it ends when the defilements cease. For more on this see "The Nature of Liberation" at the end of chapter 10.

2. These two criticisms of theism were directed against the kind of theism that the Buddha and early Buddhists knew of in India. They are remarkably effective against many theists, especially unreflective ones, whether they are Hindu, Christian, or whatever, but they do not solve the problem. Western philosophers have seen the difficulty with the Uncaused Cause and have largely given it up. Freud was the great exposer of God as "Fixit Man," showing that he was no more than a projection of our infantile fantasies. So far so good. But the God of the great Jewish, Christian, Muslim, and theistic Hindu mystics seems to be richer than a Fixit Uncaused Cause, and the Buddhist response to such a God has yet to be formulated. Gunapala Dharmasiri, *A Buddhist Critique of the Christian Concept of God*, (Colombo: Lake House, 1974 Revised edition, Antioch CA: Golden Leaves Publishing Company, 1988) is the fullest treatment of the objections, from a Theravada standpoint, to belief in God. A good summary statement is given by K. N. Jayatilleke, "The Buddhist Attitude to God" in *The Message of the Buddha*, edited by Ninian Smart (London: Allen and Unwin, 1975), pp. 104–116. The objections given are almost entirely philosophical and moral (here, especially, concerning what is called Theodicy, the problem of the simultaneous existence of evil and a good, all-powerful God) and have little to do with the God of Biblical revelation and Christian mystical experience. For a sophisticated and detailed modern defense of God's existence from the Christian standpoint, see Hans Küng, *Does God Exist?* (Doubleday, 1980).

3. Because of this (or for other reasons that are not yet clear), western occult systems such as Theosophy are of the Vedanta type. The most lucid modern exponent of this "hierarchical monism" in the United States is Master Da Love Ananda (formerly Da Free John; before that known as Bubba Free John; born as Franklin Jones) who teaches that Buddhism is a non-final system (being stage six of a seven-level hierarchy). Hierarchical Monism was popularized by Aldous Huxley as *The Perennial Philosophy* (Harper, 1945): he carefully selected texts from

rival systems in order to prove that Hierarchical Monism was the underlying, largely esoteric, true teaching of all religions and philosophies whatsoever. The teachings "channeled" (as we now say) by modern western mediums is almost always a form of Hierarchical Monism. An intriguing new development is the marriage of this "perennial philosophy" to the new physics (e.g., "Physics, Mysticism and the New Holographic Paradigm" by Ken Wilber in a volume of essays he has edited entitled *The Holographic Paradigm* (Shambhala, 1982), pp. 157–186.

4. For a selection of texts on Vedanta, see *A Source Book of Advaita Vedanta*, edited by Eliot Deutsch and J. A. B. van Buitenen (Honolulu: University Press of Hawaii, 1971).

5. Heinrich Dumoulin, S.J., *A History of Zen Buddhism,* trans. by Paul Peachey (New York: Random House, 1963) p. 100.

6. For a reliable survey of Jainism, see Padmanabh S. Jaini, *The Jaina Path of Purification* (University of California Press, 1979).

7. Such is the standard explanation, but a Muni (Jain holy man) with whom I talked in Bombay denied this.

8. This form of religious suicide is strikingly similar to the *endura* practiced amongst the Cathars (or Albigensians), a medieval Christian group in Southern France and Northern Italy, which also taught, like Jainism, that the soul was pure but had become entrapped in matter.

9. This criticism of the jiva is also the Buddhist criticism of the atman or permanent self as taught in the Upanishads. However, it seems clear that sophisticated Hinduism has never taught an atman that is separate from Brahman, only one that is *identical with* Brahman. Therefore, the Buddhist criticism of atman should in fact be read as a criticism of the Jain jiva, and the Buddhist criticism of the atman-Brahman identity should be seen as a version of the criticism of the absoluteness of the top two Formless Attainments ("nothing whatever" and "neither thinking nor not thinking"). The confusion on this topic amongst Western Buddhologists is of rococo richness.

10. There is a hilarious story of a monk who wanted to know the answer to a philosophical question and by the power of his meditation, visited the gods to ask it. He is passed up the heavenly hierarchy ("We don't know but our boss is sure to be able to help") until he reaches Brahma, the Universal Ruler. At first Brahma tries to bluff his way out by reciting his magnificent titles, but the monk is not put off, and finally Brahma admits, pulling the monk aside and speaking in a stage whisper, that he does not know, and advises him to ask the Buddha. Henry Clarke Warren, *Buddhism in Translations,* pp. 308–313. For God's mistaken identity of great power and longevity with omnipotence and eternity, see *Sacred Books of the Buddhists,* vol. 4, *Dialogues of the Buddha,* part 3, trans. by T. W. and C. A. F. Rhys Davids (London: Luzac, 1965), pp. 26–27 (*Digha-Nikaya,* 24).

11. These questions are called the Undecided Topics and are dealt with in more detail under "Teaching by Silence" in chapter 9.

12. This is the cardinal Buddhist virtue of Skillful Means, on which see chapter 9.

13. The classic discussion of Abhidharma in English is a small but tenaciously obscure book by the eminent Russian Buddhologist Th. Stcherbatsky, *The Central Conception of Buddhism and the Meaning of the Word "Dharma"* (Petrograd, 1923; Various Indian reprints, e.g., Susil Gupta, 1956; Motilal Banarsidass, 1970). Stcherbatsky describes the Sarvastivadin system of Vasubandhu, for which see *L'Abhidharmakośa de Vasubandhu,* translated into French by Louis de La Vallée Poussin (Paris: Geuthner, 6 vols., 1923–1931). An English translation of the French is being prepared by Leo Pruden. (Asian Humanities Press, 5 volumes, 1988 and subsequently).

14. Henry Clarke Warren, *Buddhism in Translations,* Appendix (pp. 487–496), for a list.

15. Herbert Guenther's study, *Philosophy and Psychology in the Abhidharma,* (Delhi: Banarsidass, 2nd ed., 1974) ably catalogues the intricacies of three Abhidharma systems and does not hesitate to point out the "increasing rigidity and narrowness" (p. 264) which beset the evolution of the systems.

16. The Theravadin Abhidhamma is systematized in the *Abhidhammathasangaha* of Anuruddha. For translations, see *A Manual of Abhidhamma,* Pali text and English translation by Narada Maha Thera (Kandy: Buddhist Publication Society, 1975) and *Compendium of Philosophy,* translated by Shwe Zan Aung (London: Pali Text Society, 1967).

17. This is the subject of Th. Stcherbatsky's classic (but dense, and now outdated) study *Buddhist Logic* (Leningrad, ca. 1930; republished by Dover, New York, 1962, two volumes). A more up-to-date study, concentrating on Dignaga's *Hetuchakra* ("Wheel of Causes," a way of mapping syllogisms) and employing the mathematical symbols common in modern discussions of logic, is *Buddhist Formal Logic* by R.S.Y. Chi (London: Royal Asiatic Society, 1969; reprinted in India by Motilal Banarsidass, 1984).

18. Daniel Perdue, *Introductory Debate in Tibetan Buddhism* (Dharmashala, India: Library of Tibetan Works and Archives, 1976). Distributed by Office of Tibet, 801 Second Avenue, New York, NY 10017. This is, as its title suggests, a good introduction. Some primary texts have been collected in *The Logic and Debate Tradition of India, Tibet and Mongolia: History, Reader, Resources,* by Geshe Lobsang Tharchin and members of the Debate Study Group (Howell, NJ: 1979. Available from Snow Lion, Ithaca, NY). An example of how debate actually goes on is provided by Guy Newland in *Compassion: A Tibetan Analysis* (London: Wisdom, 1984).

19. It is clear that the Theistic opponent in this argument holds to an Uncaused Cause as God. It is rather easy to show that this is a contradiction in terms, and not all theists maintain it. The Rabbinic interpreta-

tion of Genesis 1:1 "In the beginning God *created* . . ." as "constantly *perfected* from moment to moment" (*bara*, the "perfected" mode of the Hebrew verb), and the Christian Process Theology view of God as perfectly "prehending" the fullness of his creation from instant to instant both escape the consequences here deduced.

20. Translated by Yoshito S. Hakeda in *Kukai: Major Works*, (New York: Columbia University Press, 1972) pp. 157–224.

21. Hakeda, p. 171.

22. Hakeda, p. 172.

Chapter 6

THE CENTER

(Act 8 of the Buddha)

"The Middle Way" is a synonym of "Buddhism." In conduct *(shila)* Buddhism strives for the middle between the extremes of fasting and feasting; in knowledge (prajña), it teaches a middle between all possible philosophical viewpoints; and in meditation *(samadhi),* it seeks to establish the centered mind.

In chapter 3, "Buddhism in Family Life," we saw something of the middle way of conduct, and in chapter 9, "Teaching," we will study the middle way of knowledge. In this chapter we will discuss the centered mind. As we experience the world, it has two aspects, an outer reality which we tend to call "the world," and study as cosmology; and an inner reality which we tend to call "the mind," and study as meditation. In Buddhism, both experiences are trained in centering, and are, eventually, seen as aspects of each other. (See 'The Yogachara System" in chapter 7.)

Cosmology: The Centered World

Although Buddhism does not teach the existence of a God who creates an ordered universe, it does not teach, as we have seen, a universe that is merely random. Things arise and decay because of causes and conditions, and those causes and conditions obey laws that are, theoretically, discernible. The picture of the universe is fairly close to that of modern science in this respect. However, the actual picture of the universe that traditional Buddhism draws is not that of modern science. The traditional Buddhist universe is a vast array of plate-shaped world-systems of identical construction, each containing a breathtaking variety of human and non-human beings, some mutually visible and some mutually invisible. The resulting picture is more like science–fiction than science.

An outline diagram of a single world-system is given in figure 8. It is a circular plate made of the element earth and supported successively on layers of the elements water, wind, and space. According to the Abhidharmakosha, which gives the most commonly accepted description of the Buddhist cosmology,[1] each world-system is 1,200,875 *yojanas* in diameter. A *yojana* is one day's march and is normally set at 9 statute miles, thus the system is about 10,807,875 miles across. The rim of a world-system displays a ring of very high mountains made of iron, called *Chakravala.* Because of this ring, a world-system is itself sometimes called a *Chakravala.* It may also be called a *Lokadhatu* or "world-realm."

At the center of a world-system is an enormous mountain, "the king of mountains," known as *Meru* or *Sumeru.* It is like an hour-glass in shape (except that it is square, and has a stepped base) and has four faces made of four different precious materials—gold (or emerald),[2] crystal, sapphire (or lapis lazuli), and ruby. Around Meru are seven concentric squares of golden mountains, decreasing in height towards the outermost, with a calm stretch of ocean between each. The rest of the world-system is filled with the water of the Great Ocean, which is subject to storms. In the Great Ocean are four continents, each of a different shape and color, and each with two satellite continents. Each continent supports anthropoid inhabitants with distinctive life-styles and whose faces are the same shape as their continent.

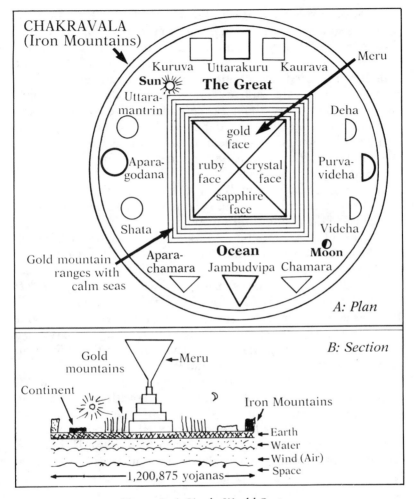

Figure 8: A Single World-System

The northern continent is called Uttarakuru and is square in shape and dark blue or green in color. Its sky appears golden (or perhaps greeny-golden), since its inhabitants, who have square, blue-green faces, look up at the overarching golden or emerald face of Mount Meru. Life is pleasant, relaxed and bucolic. There are no farms or villages, the people are 48 feet tall, and they live for 2,000 years. Birth on Uttarakuru is unfortunate because one becomes so lazy one does not bother to practice Dharma and so delays one's liberation from cyclic existence.

On Aparagodana (also called Godaniya), to the west, life is a little more hurried. The continent is circular and red, the sky is ruby red, there are villages, and the inhabitants, who have round, red faces, are about 24 feet tall and live for 500 years.

Purvavideha (or simply Videha), to the east, is semi-circular and white, its sky is crystal clear, it has towns as well as villages, the inhabitants have white, half-moon shaped faces, are 12 feet tall, and live for 250 years.

The continent of Jambudvipa, to the south of Meru, sounds less like a science fiction fantasy. It is in fact our own world. It is shaped like a triangle with its point towards the south, and is golden (or blue, perhaps blue-gold) in color. It is the most "developed" of the continents and buzzes with activity. One of the principal sufferings of the human realm is having so much to do. Our sky is sapphire or lapis lazuli blue, we are about 5 or 6 feet tall, and we live a maximum of 100 years.[3] In the center of our land is a cosmic *jambu* or rose-apple tree, from which we get our name *Jambu-dvipa*, "Rose-Apple-Tree-Continent." There is also a great lake called Anavatapta, from which flow the four great rivers Ganges, Indus, Vakshu, and Sita.

The picture of Jambudvipa is clearly derived from the actual condition of the Indian subcontinent: it is a south–pointing triangle in a large ocean with a blue sky and inhabitants whose golden or dark, inverted-triangle faces match the shape and color of the earth. The four great rivers rise to the north in the Himalayas, which are of cosmic size, like the gold mountains. Lake Anavatapta may perhaps be identified with Lake Manosarovar which is below Mount Kailas in western Tibet.

The heavenly bodies circle around Mount Meru "as if in a whirlpool," the sun and moon causing the alteration of day and night on each of the continents in turn as they pass behind and in front of the huge central mountain. The slopes of Meru are terraced and inhabited by deities of various degrees of power and accomplishment, and the hells are in the submarine terraces of Meru.

The size of the entire universe is calculated as follows. A "local galaxy-cluster" (as we might call it) of one thousand world-systems like that just described form a group called *chudasahas-*

raradhatu, a small thousand-world-realm or "small chiliocosm." One thousand small chiliocosms form a "distant galaxy-cluster" called a "large chiliocosm." One thousand large chiliocosms make up the universe, which is conventionally caled *trisahas-raradhatavah,* "The Three (Sets of) Thousand Worlds," or simply the Trichiliocosm. In some traditions, however, the universe is said to be infinite.

Many Buddhists believe that this is exactly how the world is and that the Buddha taught it just like that. However, what is called "direct perception" (i.e., scientific observation) is a category in Buddhist logic that cannot be overruled without serious cause, and so the modern view of the earth as a globe and its existence in a solar system and so forth is coming to be accepted. The traditional view, however, still has value as a meditative tool.

The world as we normally experience it is not particularly meaningful. It is, as someone has said, a play without a plot and without heroes or heroines. Scientific cosmology gives us at most a precise account of how billions and billions of worlds go round and round each other. This depressing view of endless repetition is samsara, and it is from this sort of world that we desire release.

Sanskrit has two words that we may translate as "world": *jagat* and *loka. Jagat* means the world as it in itself, before any conscious beings enter it. *Loka* is the world as experienced by conscious beings. When Buddha was asked about *jagat,* he refused to answer, saying that the very idea of a non-experienced reality was nonsense. What we know is what we know, whether it is a fantasy or not. So it is *loka* that is the focus of attention. It is *loka* that is suffering, and it is *loka* that is to be transcended in nirvana.[4]

In order to transcend *loka,* my ordinary hum-drum world, it is helpful at first to see it as an ordered and centered whole, that is, as a mandala. Thus it is that in many Buddhist liturgies one makes gifts to the Buddhas, the Bodhisattvas, and the teacher in the form of a world-mandala having the shape and characteristics of a traditional world-system.[5] This mandala offering can be an elaborate procedure in which a model world-system is actually constructed out of a set of concentric brass rings built up on a mound of rice or other grains, or it can be a brief movement of the mind accompanied by a *mudra* (gesture) in which the fingers are twisted together in special way to symbolize Mount Meru and its four continents.[6]

Such a mandala is a visualization of the world as a *cosmos,* an ordered and joyous place, rather than a *chaos* or hum-drum prison, and the intent is to focus the mind on wonderful, sparkling, fairy-like things that one imagines one owns and then gives to the Buddhas in gratitude for their teaching. It should be noted that this is only *one* meaning of the word mandala. Others will be noted later.

REALMS OF REBIRTH

The realms of rebirth are sometimes said to be infinite and sometimes to be limited to locations mentioned in the description of a world-system. All of the realms are within cyclic existence, but some are more fortunate than others. From the aspect of possible places of rebirth the universe is normally known as the Triple World, that is, as divided into three main levels and many sub–levels. The three main levels are the *kama-dhatu* (the sensuous realm), the *rupa-dhatu* (the realm of forms), and the *arupya-dhatu* (the formless realm).

The sensuous realm is the most complex and it contains most of the realms of which we humans can have any sort of clear comprehension. Its general characteristic is that the inhabitants have a definite shape and bodies of either gross or subtle matter. It is ruled therefore by kama, "sensuality" or "sensuous desire."

The first subdivision of the sensuous realm is into six: *devas* (peaceful deities), *asuras* (wrathful deities), humans, *pretas* (ghosts), animals, and hell-beings.[7] Sometimes the devas and asuras are said to inhabit the same realm, so that only five subdivisions are mentioned. These realms are depicted in the standard Tibetan image of the Wheel of Existence *(bhava-chakra)* in which a monster symbolizing samsara is devouring a wheel containing the beings of the sensuous realm in its five or six segments.[8]

All the realms of rebirth, being within samsara, are states of suffering. The realms of devas and asuras, however, are (relatively) pleasant. They are often called "heavens" since their description resembles that of the Christian heaven, although, unlike the Christian heaven, they are not outside of space and time. Devas are peaceful deities and asuras are wrathful, agitated deities. Although devas have long and relatively untroubled lives they must constantly guard against being robbed by the asuras who, though they have much, are jealous of the superior power, riches, and beauty of the devas. Asuras are never at peace, always fighting and competing, and, because of this, their realm is sometimes called unpleasant rather than pleasant, and ranked with the unfortunate rebirths of animals, pretas, and hell-beings. Rebirth as a deva or asura is the result of pride coupled with fortunate karma. The particular suffering of the deva realm is that known as "falling," that is, losing all the pleasant things one has, and the particular suffering of the asura realm is that of constant quarreling in addition to that of "falling." During life, one is physically delightful, having a wonderful golden body that does not perspire or defecate, and one is rich, powerful, and long-lived beyond any human possibilities. But at death, everything goes and, through one's superior intelligence, one knows one is falling into a relatively stinking and impoverished kind of existence.

The so-called hells[9] are the bottom of the sensuous realm. There are many varieties of hells, very hot, very cold, full of demons, very noisy, full of sword-forests, and so forth. One is reborn there because of anger and hate, and the problem is that the hateful conditions increase one's hate, so it may be millions of years before one escapes to a less horrifying realm, such as that of the animals or the pretas. The suffering in the hells is extreme.

Animals are said to be characterized by confusion—they cannot clearly understand what is happening to them—and indeed they have been reborn as animals just because of such confusion in previous lives. They also suffer the pains of being used as slaves by humans and of being eaten by humans and by each other.

Pretas, sometimes called (from the Chinese translation, *o-kuei*) "hungry ghosts," are characterized by insatiable thirst and hunger. In a previous life they did not control their appetites, and now they cannot. They try to eat and drink everything they can, no matter how revolting it might be. Their particular suffering is that of constant hunger and thirst.

Animals, pretas, and humans inhabit the same realm, but pretas are invisible to most humans and animals. The deities of the sensuous realm live either above Mount Meru in anti-gravity machines called *vimana,* or they inhabit its slopes, with the Palace of Indra at the summit. The deities of form, who have color but no solidity, and the formless deities, who are pure consciousnesses, are said to exist in space, high above Mount Meru. The hells are usually said to be located below Mount Meru, or at least somewhere underground. Each rebirth realm has a distinctive, and non-human, space-time continuum.[10]

This explanation of realms has the effect of locating us, humans, in a comprehensible cosmic place. The human rebirth is the most fortunate because only in it is the fruition of karma sufficiently balanced that we have real choice and so can consciously influence the fruiting of our subsequent karma for better or worse. We have the intelligence to know where we are, enough suffering to make us want to stop it but not so much that we cannot think of anything else, and our lives are long enough to get some real Dharma practice done but not so long that we procrastinate until it is too late. Because we have language, we can receive, understand, and transmit the Dharma. Our main sufferings come from attachment, for we have to guard our possessions, and from aging and death that we, unlike animals, know is going to occur.

It is possible to be born in a certain realm while having a mind more appropriate to another realm. In this way, humans can have the mind of a deva, asura, preta, animal, or hell-being. A dreamy, spacey person to whom nothing really bad happens is like a deva. Someone with the mind of an asura is always quarreling and competing, perhaps following a career in the armed services or in business. An addict who is trapped in the consumption of alcohol or a drug is living like a preta. If one develops a mental disorder one may live in a world of fear and senseless repetition very much like a Buddhist hell. As for "animals," we even say in our ordinary speech, "So-and-so lives like an animal," if all they are concerned with is food, sex, and shelter.

Meditation: The Centered Mind

Having understood that the world may be seen as having a center, we can find its center for us and in us. This is the function of meditation, in which we follow the Buddha's example as he found and entered the bodhi-mandala, the enlightenment space beneath the Bodhi Tree. This is the second meaning of mandala: a space for Dharma pratice.

Meditation is a word so often used today that we need to be clear about its specifically Buddhist meaning. Quite simply it is mind training. The untrained mind is powerful but it is dangerous and stupid. By training it, we can tap into more of its power and make it helpful and clear. At the same time we will find it becoming more compassionate.

Buddhist meditation has two general aspects: stabilization *(shamatha)* and insight *(vipashyana)*. These aspects are distinguishable, but they are not separate. Insight occurs while stabilization is being practiced, and stabilization is not abandoned when insight is being practiced. The distinction is a matter of emphasis: stabilization is the indispensable and enduring foundation upon which insight practice is built. Stabilization is practiced in more or less the same way in all Buddhist meditation systems, indeed it seems to be similar even in non-Buddhist systems. Insight, although always leading to the same result, enlightenment, is practiced differently according to the lineage being followed.

STABILIZATION

The untrained mind is a wanderer, running here and there looking for adventure. Before we can do anything with it, we must calm it down and bring it home. This we do in the practice called *shamatha.*

Shamatha is a Sanskrit word related to *shanti,* peace. It refers to a mind that is calm, peaceful, not restless or fidgeting. Tibetans call it shinay *(zhignas),* "abiding or settled in calm or quiet." Suggested English translations are calming, calm abiding, mental stabilization, or (from the most typical posture employed during shamatha) sitting.

The proper body position is helpful. Put a small, firm cushion under your buttocks and cross your legs so that, if possible, the soles of your feet are upwards and between the crooks of the knees of the opposite legs. This is called the Full Lotus or Vajra Posture. If this is too difficult, lay one bent leg on top of the other. This is the Half Lotus Posture. In either case your knees should touch the floor: adjust the type and thickness of the cushion until your buttocks are high enough to allow this to happen, your knees making a tripod with your buttocks.[11] Make your back

Figure 9: The Wheel of Existence

The wheel of existence *(bhavachakra)* is a visual aid teaching the nature of cyclic existence *(samsara)*.

At the hub of the wheel are three animals, representing the three poisons of attachment, aversion, and confusion, because of which the wheel of existence is kept in motion.

The next circle out from the hub illustrates the paths of deterioration and improvement. On the viewer's right, humans, tied to each other by their defilements, are being dragged downwards by demons. On the left, other humans are moving upwards by practising the Dharma. Laypeople are towards the bottom of the segment and monks are in the upper portion.

The next circle out is divided into six segments. Each segment illustrates one of the realms of rebirth. (See Appendix to this chapter.) The *devas* or peaceful deities are in the top segment, as having the most pleasant rebirth, and the hell-beings, experiencing the most unpleasant rebirth, are in the bottom. Because of the variety of hells, only a few are represented. Note, however, the hot hells to the left and the cold hells to the right.

Shown clockwise from the *deva* realm are the realms of the *asuras* and animals, and anticlockwise we see the realms of humans and the *pretas*.

Around the rim of the wheel are twelve segments with symbolic representations of the twelvefold cycle of interdependent arising (see pages 199–201) beginning with *avidya* (ignorance) at the top and moving in a clockwise direction to *jara-marana* (ageing and death) and so back to avidya.

The entire wheel is held in the grip of a devouring ogre symbolizing that the experience of samsara is the experience of being eaten, that is, of decay and death. The ogre is crowned with five skulls symbolic of the *skandhas*.

The ogre stands firmly rooted on a mountain, that is, on our constructed reality. The Buddha stands in the air to the right of the wheel, unsupported by viewpoints. He holds his hands in the *abhaya* or "bestowing fearlessness" gesture, giving living beings the courage to look for a way of escape from samsara. A Buddha or Bodhisattva is also pictured in each of the realms of rebirth, appearing in a form suitable to that realm.

(Reproduced from *Tibetan Thanka Painting* by David and Janice Jackson, with permission from Snow Lion Publications, Ithaca, New York).

Figure 9: The Wheel of Existence

straight, but not like a ramrod: allow your stomach to drop
forwards so that the spinal curve is natural. Let your shoulders
drop loosely away from your neck. Keep your neck straight,
feeling your head balanced easily on top of it. Pretend that a
string goes up from the top of your head to the ceiling, pulling
your head up gently, then pull your chin in slightly. Restrict your
vision by partly closing your eyes and looking slightly downwards. Let your jaw hang loose but keep your mouth closed.
Allow the face to feel soft and open. Place your tongue behind
the upper teeth and hold it there lightly.

There are various recommendations about what to do with
hands and arms. Theravadins often place their hands palm upwards in their laps, one hand resting in the other. Zen practitioners do something similar but they may arch their thumbs upwards and touch them together, making an oval or circular space
over the palms: maintaining this gesture takes awareness, and
when we find that our thumbs have fallen into our palms, we
realize that our minds have been wandering. Tibetans may hold
their arms diagonally outwards, make a lightly clenched fist with
the thumbs over the middle finger, and rest their fists on their
knees. Finally, it is helpful to "set" our position by smartly contracting and releasing the anal sphincter.

The net effect of all this should be a posture conducive to
relaxed alertness. One teacher has said that, when the proper
position has been attained, there is a feeling of "harmonious
surprise." "Mellowing out" may be necessary at times but it has
nothing to do with Buddhist mind training. Though relaxed, we
want to be alert, like a cat watching a mouse hole.

Having achieved the best posture we can, we may practice
breath observation, first inspecting to see where our breathing is
most noticeable to us (perhaps indirectly in the motion of the
chest, or, more directly, the breath itself as it enters and leaves
the base of the nostrils), and then watching it. We strive just to
be *aware* of the breathing, not to judge it or think about it, and
we do not (as in some forms of Hindu or Taoist meditation) force
or try to control the breath in any way. Counting the breaths
from one to ten and then going back to one again helps in maintaining this bare awareness. We will find this simple task very
difficult at first. Our mind gets bored and wants to go somewhere
and have fun. But we keep calling it home. And after a time, we
find that being at home is fun.

INSIGHT

Having achieved some stability of mind, we are ready to look at reality and see it as it really is. This is *vipashyana,* clear or intense seeing. In Chinese it is called *kuan,* a character meaning "to gaze over the countryside from a high tower, like a watchman," i.e., to open our awareness to everything in general, not judging or selecting, but being very clear about everything that is happening. "Insight" is coming to be accepted as the usual English translation.

There are many varieties of insight training. I will discuss only three.

Theravada

One form of Theravadin meditation which has become popular in the west is that which was at first known as *satipatthana,* literally "remembering," "being aware," or "recollectedness." Today, it generally goes under the name of *Vipassana* (the Pali form of the Sanskrit word *vipashyana*) or Insight Meditation.[12] This name is somewhat misleading, for it is far from being "the" Buddhist form of insight training.

The method is simple to describe but difficult to do. In whatever activity we are engaged, sitting, standing, walking, eating, or whatever, we simply observe *that it is going on.* The practice arises naturally out of the breath-awareness just described. By observing the simple, bald, and unadorned fact that *there is breathing* without jumping to the (common but unwarranted) theoretical conclusion that "I" am breathing, we pay attention to the process and we do not allow any other type of mind—analytic, discursive, or whatever—to distract us. Having practiced insight while sitting, we try it while standing. Just standing, noticing how the floor feels (we will be able to feel the floor because we have taken our shoes off in order to be able to get into the best sitting position) and how our body rises in relation to gravity. Then, we try to maintain insight while walking. We walk as slowly as possible, observing merely that there is a lifting, a stretching out and a putting down of one leg and then the other leg, a touching, rising, and touching of feet to the floor. Since we are walking merely in order to observe walking, to gain insight into it, we do not walk *to* anywhere. We either walk around the room in a circle, or back and forth along a predetermined path a dozen or two paces in length. We can then extend our insightful awareness into all other activities until, ideally, it becomes natural, and we are meditating all the time.

The aim of this particular insight practice is *choiceless awareness,* allowing us to experience directly the appearance, continuance, and disappearance of the dharma events of which we gained a theoretical understanding (see section on Abhidharma in chapter 5). There are many other meditation practices in Theravada, but I have chosen to deal only with this one because it is basic, and is the one most often taught by Theravadin groups in the United States.

Zen

Zen has also become very popular in the west. It has many features similar to Theravadin Insight Meditation. The basic practice of Zen is called *zazen,* "sitting-meditating."

The Soto Zen Master Dogen especially emphasized zazen and used the term *shikandaza,* "striking just at sitting."[13] While sitting in the proper posture one strives *just to sit.* Even observing the breath is not necessary. If a thought arises, it is allowed to disappear. The mind is like the sky, the thoughts are like passing clouds. We might imagine ourselves watching boats pass beneath a bridge on which we are standing. Various boats, full and empty, interesting, frightening, or boring, pass beneath, and we let them go. We do not jump into any of them to find out where they are going.

The mind is not made a blank. If we blanked the mind (which we probably could not, anyway) we would destroy consciousness, and become like a stone. A stone, however, is not a liberated being.

We just sit. Why do we sit? Because we sit. What are we doing? Sitting. What shall we do next? Sit.

As a matter of fact, *all we ever really do is sit.* Wandering mind wishes to go somewhere—tomorrow, yesterday, Hawaii, New York—anywhere. But, when we get "there," we find we are here. So we try and go to another "there." Disneyland promises, in a bronze plaque above its entrance, that we can leave today behind and enter the worlds of yesterday, tomorrow, and fantasy. However, with all due respect to dear old Walt and his millions of admirers, this only increases our suffering. We are trying to escape from wandering about in samsara by wandering about in it. The problem is precisely this: our mind does, in any case, leave today behind and enter the worlds of yesterday, tomorrow, and fantasy. In meditation we strive to do the opposite: to *leave* the worlds of yesterday and its regrets, of tomorrow and its fears and apprehensions, and of dreamy fantasy, and *enter* the world of NOW, which is the only real world.

When we give up wandering and come home to the dimensionless present, samsara momentarily disappears. This is called *satori,* "awakening," or *kensho,* "seeing the essential" (i.e., seeing the essential transparency of self, other, and their connection). It is the purpose of Zen to permit satori experiences (caution: one satori does not make you a Buddha; it means you have begun to see what Buddhism is all about), cultivate them, and allow their frequency and depth to increase.

Tibetan

Tibetan meditation may seem strange at first, since it superficially differs so markedly from zazen and insight meditation. A Tibetan shrine room is full of images, statues, posters, candles, tables of offerings, ritual implements, incense, and what-have-you. In a word, it is full of symbols.

At the elementary level Tibetan meditation is similar to Insight Meditation, and at the very highest levels, where the mind is observed directly with the mind, it is similar to Zen. But in the middle, it looks like Mexican Catholicism gone mad. The purpose, however, is still the same. Rather than avoiding mental images like Theravada, or seeking to transcend them like Zen, it uses symbols to go beyond symbols.

The characteristic technique of Tibetan meditation is visualization.[14] An entity of purified mind, such as a Buddha or Bodhisattva, is seen as present, and the meditator interacts with the entity.

Seated in the proper posture, we might visualize such a being as the Bodhisattva Avalokiteshvara appearing before us. He will be crystal clear white in color, a handsome young man about sixteen years old, smiling graciously at us, richly clothed, sitting cross-legged on a lotus throne, his hands in the particular gestures which signify compassion and purity. We try to see him as clearly as we can, and feel his compassionate presence. Then we commune with him, offering him gifts and praying to him for ourselves and all sentient beings, according to the direction of whichever liturgical text *(sadhana)* we are following. When we are finished, we dismiss the visualization by dissolving it into light and then into space.

Tibetans can do this sort of thing quite naturally, and are surprised and bemused by the westerner who protests, "But is Avalokiteshvara *really there?*"

The answer is, quite simply, he is there as much as, and in some ways more than, anything is there. Nothing has inherent existence (and so, at the end of the practice, the visualization is dissolved into space to remind us that it, like everything else, is empty or transparent to analysis), but my reality of samsara as suffering is a mistake produced by my confused mind, whereas Avalokiteshvara is an aspect of clear mind, and is beyond suffering. The question should rather be "But is samsara *really there?*" Avalokiteshvara is not a daydream or an imagined being. It is, on the contrary, samsara that is the dream.[15]

The Need for the Samgha

Practicing meditation without a teacher is generally futile or dangerous. When we turn towards Buddhism to practice it, we are, whether formally or informally, taking refuge in the Buddha and his Dharma. The third part of the refuge is the Samgha, and it is essential for most of us. By linking oneself with a teacher and fellow students, we will obtain authentic and personalized instruction, the support and encouragement of a group, and something intangible, which I cannot explain but seems to come along with all of this: the Buddhas start to become real for us.

However, it is not helpful to rush out and throw oneself at the feet of the first guru one happens to find. That way, even more confusion is likely to result. In Buddhism it is not only recommended, it is *required*, to test any potential teacher as much as one wishes before taking him or her as one's own. Critical observation is linked to insight. You should enter a practice group cautiously, with a receptive but alert mind, and ask as many penetrating and embarrassing questions as you want. When you have found a group which is genuinely helpful to your progress in the Dharma, give yourself to it and the teacher wholeheartedly. You have found something very precious.[16]

NOTES
to Chapter Six

1. A summary of the scheme given in the Abhidharmakosha is in the article "Cosmogony and Cosmology (Buddhist)" by Louis de La Vallée Poussin, *Encyclopaedia of Religion and Ethics*, volume 4, pp. 129–138.

2. The precise identification, in English, of the precious materials and their colors, is difficult.

3. Note that a peculiarity of Jambudvipa is the variation in the height of its inhabitants, and the uncertainty of their life-span.

4. Nathan Katz, *Buddhist Images of Human Perfection* (Delhi: Banarsidass, 1982), pp. 147–151.

5. The mandala offering is described in *The Torch of Certainty* by Jamgon Kongtrul (translated by Judith Hanson) (Boulder: Shambhala, 1977), pp. 92–117.

6. See Stephen Beyer, *The Cult of Tara* (University of California Press, 1973), figure 20 (on p. 168) and plate 3 (between pp. 260 and 261).

7. Devas, asuras, and pretas are beings with no exact equivalent in English. I will use their Sanskrit names and ask you to stretch your minds to accomodate them, as if you were reading about alien creatures in a science fiction story.

8. For a description and commentary see Sermey Geshe Lobsang Tharchin, *et al.*, *King Udrayana and the Wheel of Life* (Howell, NJ: Mahayana Sutra and Tantra Press, 1984). See Figure 9.

9. They are called hells because of, once again, their resemblance to descriptions of the Christian hell. But, in Buddhism, all of samsara is a sort of hell.

10. For a more detailed description of the realms of rebirth, see the appendix to this chapter.

11. A competent meditation teacher will suggest another posture to practitioners who cannot, for whatever reason, adopt the full or half lotus positions.

12. A good introductory book is *The Experience of Insight* by Joseph Goldstein (Boulder: Shambhala, 1983).

13. My favorite book on *shikandaza* is *To Forget the Self* by John Daishin Buksbazen (Zen Center of Los Angeles, 1977). It is out of print, but worth searching for.

14. See, for example, *The Diamond Light* by Janice Dean Willis (New York: Simon and Schuster, 1972). Many recently published

books on Tibetan Buddhism contain examples of visualization meditations.

15. The ontological status of such beings may become clearer after the discussion of the Yogachara and Tantric systems in chapters 7 and 10.

Appendix to Chapter 6

The Triple World

All Buddhist traditions accept a cosmology of the Triple World *(trailokadhatavah)* along the general lines sketched in this chapter. Within this general scheme there are many variations. The reader who embarks on a detailed study of Buddhist cosmology will find plenty of material, and will very soon become confused trying to reconcile the traditions with each other. Most explanations remind me of Dylan Thomas's complaint, in *A Child's Christmas in Wales,* against books that told him "everything about the wasp, except why." The following explanation attempts to go deeper than a general sketch, but not so deep as to produce merely a mass of facts without any notion of "why."

GENERAL PRINCIPLES:

In figure 8 I have represented how a single world-system looks from the physical perspective. In figure 9 I attempt a schematic representation according to certain fundamental *organizational principles.* The levels of the pyramid in figure 9 sometimes correspond to physical levels, but this is coincidental. Each level of the pyramid is a rebirth. Some rebirths occur on the same physical

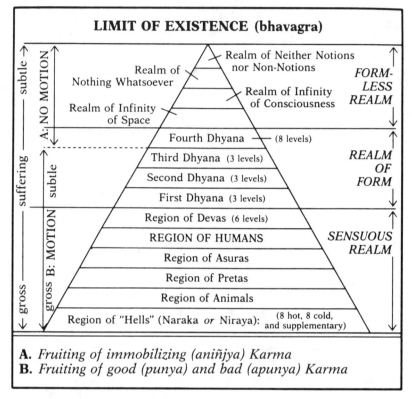

Figure 10: Schematic Representation of The Triple World.

plane, but are distinct rebirths: for example, animals and humans may occupy similar spaces and be mutually visible, yet
beings are born either as animals or as humans. Again, some
rebirths, such as those in the formless realm, are by definition
non-physical (or, according to another tradition, so subtly physical that they are to all intents and purposes non-physical) and
cannot be "placed" anywhere.

The most important organizational principle of the pyramid in
figure 9 is the *spectrum of suffering*. All of samsara is suffering,
but the amount of suffering varies. The diagram represents a
spectrum of extreme suffering in the hell realms at the bottom,
through extremely pleasurable deity states in the middle, to
heavens of unconscious bliss at the top. The topmost regions do
not contain any suffering perceptible to the beings who inhabit

them: the suffering is extremely subtle and only becomes manifest when the karma of those beings fruits and they leave that
realm for another, less pleasant realm.

The next organizational principle is the *spectrum of motion.*
All of samsara is in motion: the word itself means always moving, always changing, always having things to do. But the motion
in the top five regions (the formless realm and the top part of the
realm of form) is so subtle that it manifests as immobility *(aniñjya).* While beings inhabit the aniñjya realms, nothing happens
for them. They appear to have arrived at a condition of eternal
rest. Jainism (see chapter 5) does in fact teach that the top of the
universe is the place of permanent stability, and that, when the
jiva reaches it, it has escaped from samsara. Buddhism teaches,
on the contrary, that the stability of the topmost region is very
extended (surviving the disappearance and reappearance of
many universes) but finite. During a being's residence in the
aniñjya realms, karma continues to fruit (so that there is, in fact,
some movement, or at least change, but it is so subtle that it is
perceived as no movement at all) and, eventually, rebirth occurs
in another realm. Buddhists prove this point by referring to
Shakyamuni's experience under his two non-Buddhist teachers
(Act 7), in which he went to the limit of existence *(bhavagra)* but,
returning to normal consciousness, proclaimed that it was not
the end of desire and suffering.

A third organizational principle, which is however not entirely
consistent, is the *mental-physical spectrum.* Beings in the sensuous realm have bodies, those in the realm of form have shapes
only, and those in the formless realm are purely mental. Or,
perhaps not. Some traditions are wary of calling anything purely
mental, for fear of implying an inherent existence of body and
mind apart from each other. They therefore say that the upper
realms are predominantly mental, but that the mind rides on a
subtle body something like a very fine wind. Also, the bodies of
hell beings are not physical in the ordinary sense, for they are
able to survive tortures like being torn apart and reconstituted
many times, until their inauspicious karma is used up. So, the
bodies of hell-beings are sometimes called mind or dream bodies. We can have a dream that, for example, we are eating, but
when we wake up we still feel hungry. This is taken as proof that
physical feelings do not require a physical, or at least a gross
physical, body.

Another organizational principle, which is not represented as such in the chart, is *time dilation*. Time in Buddhism does not exist inherently, as an absolute, but in relation to the perceiver. When the Triple World is explained in terms of time, human time is taken as the temporal base-line. As we move away from the human realm, whether upwards or downwards in the diagram, time dilates. For example, one day in the topmost hell and in the lowest deva realm is equal to 50 human years, and the lifespan of beings in those realms is 500 years of such days. In the next highest deva realm, and the next lowest hell, one day is equivalent to 100 human years, the lifespan of beings is 1,000 years of such days—and so on in geometrical progression. The time dilation is symmetrical for the progress down through the hells and up through the deva realms, but otherwise it is not entirely consistent (the lifespan of animals, for example, is quite varied—and it is interesting to speculate whether time goes differently for a mayfly and a giant tortoise), but it is, in general, progressive, the lengths of time associated with the realms at the top and bottom of the chart being quite unimaginable in human terms.

The enormous stretches of time proper to many of the non-human realms are counted in units called *kalpa*. The length of a kalpa (and, note, Buddhist kalpas should not be confused with the related, but different, Hindu kalpas) is expressed by means of mind-expanding analogies. Three popular ones are the blind turtle, the cosmic mountain, and the warehouse of sesame seeds:

> *1. On the surface of the Great Ocean (i.e., that in which are the four continents—see figure 8) is a yoke, moving about at random with the winds and the waves. In the ocean there is a blind turtle, swimming about at will. Once every hundred (human) years, the turtle surfaces at random. How long will it be before the neck of the turtle passes through the hole in the yoke?*

> *2. There is a mountain as large as Mount Sumeru. It is smooth and without fissures or loose boulders. Once every hundred years a being strokes its peak once, lightly, with a piece of the finest Benares silk. How long will it take to reduce the mountain to dust by this method?*

3. A warehouse as large as a world is full of sesame seeds. Once every hundred years, a single sesame seed is removed. How long will it take to empty the warehouse completely?

The answers to the three problems above are variously given as one kalpa or *less than* one kalpa. Then, that is sometimes said to be a micro-kalpa *(kshudra-kalpa)*, in which case there are also meso-kalpas *(antarah-kalpa)*, macro-kalpas *(maha-kalpa)* and, finally, the unimaginably long "incalculable kalpa" *(asam-khyeya-kalpa)*. In this schema, it may then be said that the inhabitants of the top level of rebirth, the realm of neither notions nor non-notions, live for 80,000 micro-kalpas, or perhaps even 80,000 incalculable kalpas.

There is an analogy to this time dilation in our human experience. One hour of clock time while we are having wonderful sex with the perfect partner may seem like a minute, whereas one hour of clock time when we are in great pain seems like days. So we might be able to understand why it is said that time in the hells is perceived as longer the more exquisite the suffering, (i.e., the lower the hell, the longer the lifetime) and that the more pleasant the realm, the longer the lifetime but the shorter it seems.

A story from the sutras illustrates the difference between human and deva time. A certain goddess was sporting with her retinue in one of the heavens when the fruiting of her karma caused her to die from there and be born as a human woman. Because of her merit, she became a great queen and ruled wisely and long, dying from the human realm at a ripe old age and, again because of her merit, being reborn in the same heaven she had left eighty or so human years before. Those in that heaven, however, had not noticed her absence, for it had only been, from their perspective, a few moments.

Special Characteristics

Traditional accounts of the realms start at the hells and move up, describing each realm in great detail, but this method loses the "why" and makes it seem that the cosmology is an exercise in biology, anthropology, or astronomy. The primary point of the description is to emphasize the great value of the human rebirth by showing how many other realms there are, how long we might get stuck in them, and how rare, therefore, is a rebirth which is not only human but possessed of the advantages connected with hearing and practicing the Dharma. Secondarily, it serves to open the mind to the many sorts of beings (which we might call spirits) in the universe which might wish to help or hinder humans, and to show them as, finally, less important than the Buddha, for they are intra-samsaric, relatively ignorant, and bound by their passions. A Buddhist can, for example, accept a phenomenon like mediumship (which now, apparently, we call channeling) matter-of-factly, judging the worth of each entity's reported messages against the superior word of the Dharma.

In order to make the point of the cosmological descriptions clear, then, I will start at the human level and move away from it, first downwards and then upwards, and, for additional clarity, will only mention some of the details of some of the realms.

Moving down the spectrum of suffering from the human realm, we encounter the realms of asuras, pretas, and animals. These realms have been sufficiently discussed in the body of the chapter.

At the bottom of the spectrum of suffering is the realm called *Naraka* or *Niraya*, words of uncertain etymology but generally interpreted to mean "joyless" and usually called hells in English. The Chinese translation is *ti-yü*, literally "earth prison," referring to Naraka's location underground or under the base of Mount Sumeru. There are normally said to be eight hot hells, eight cold hells (so that a Buddhist cannot say, "It'll be a cold day in hell before I . . .") with supplementary hells located at the corners of the main hells, and "occasional" hells found in various places such as deserts or dense forests as well as underground. The precise number and location of hells does not seem to have been finally decided.

The cold and hot hells are the focus of the traditional descriptions, which are long, juicy, and worthy of Dante at his most lurid. They are stacked on top of each other, and given names appropriate to their particular suffering, e.g., *Tapana* (Heating Hell), *Pratapana* (Great Heating Hell), *Raurava* (Howling Hell, from the cries of the denizens), *Atata, Hahava,* and *Huhuva* (three hells where the denizens repeat these sounds due to the intense cold). The bottom hell is called *Avichi,* usually interpreted to mean "waveless," i.e., where the suffering is, unlike the more pleasant hells, entirely without intermission. It also goes on for an unimaginably long time. Below Avichi there is sometimes said to be the Vajra Hell, an especially unpleasant rebirth for those who break their Tantric vows.

Above the realm of humans, both physically and along the spectrum of suffering, are the realms of the devas, often called, in English, the heavens. There are six deva realms. The first level contains the Four Divine Kings, whom we met in chapter two. The next level is called *Trayastrimsha*, literally "Thirty-three," which is said to contain thirty-three devas, or 33,303, or an indeterminate number of devas ruled by a committee of thirty-three. It is located on the flat summit of Mount Sumeru in the city (or palace) of Vishnu (or Indra, or Brahma) and functions as the realm of the "king of the gods" in the Buddhist cosmology.

There are four deva levels above Sumeru. The devas who live there have flying or anti-gravity machines called *vimana*. The most important levels are the fourth and the sixth deva realms (the second and the fourth anti-gravity machine levels). The fourth level is Tushita in which, as we learned in chapter 1, the entity which is to be the next Buddha resides. The sixth level rejoices in the title of *Paranirmitavashavartin*, meaning that the inhabitants do not even (as do the devas next below them) have to create what they need just by thinking about it: delights come to them automatically, and they rearrange them at will. Mara, the deity who tried to prevent Shakyamuni from becoming a Buddha, and continues to block the practice of the Dharma, lives here. We shall learn more about him in chapter 7.

Leaving the regions of the devas, we enter the realm of form. Here, bodily contact is not possible and the inhabitants live in worlds of shapes and colors (and, possibly, tastes and smells). There are four main divisions, associated with four states of progressively focused mind called dhyana. They are simply called the first, second, third, and fourth dhyanas. Each dhyana level has subdivisions, usually three each for the first three dhyanas and eight for the fourth dhyana.

Discussions of Buddhist meditation usually go into great detail on the dhyanas. I have chosen to ignore them since they appear to be only of theoretical importance. In some years of receiving teachings in various Buddhist traditions, I have never once encountered any *practical* instruction on the dhyanas. They are, however, said to be attained when one progressively drops off the mental functions of discursive thinking and the emotions connected with ratiocination. The fourth dhyana is the state of totally focused mind (*chittaikagrata*, "mental one-pointedness") with no movement or emotional reflex. As a part of the Triple World, the fourth dhyana is the first of the aniñjya or immovable states. Below the fourth dhyana, rebirth is the fruit of good (punya) or bad (apunya) karma. Rebirth into the fourth dhyana level and above is the fruit of a special karma called, from its result, *aniñjya-karma* or immobilizing karma. These appear to be the levels to which, according to Buddhism, some non-Buddhist systems such as Yoga and Jainism aspire.

Above the fourth dhyana level we enter the formless realm, which is, either actually or virtually, purely mental or abstract. Since the word *arupya,* normally translated "formless," more nearly means "non-sensate," i.e., beyond the realm of anything that could be called sense data, the formless realm might, in fact, be identified with what Plato called the realm of the Forms (i.e., the Ideas). The formless realm is also associated with meditative states (also, apparently, of theoretical importance only) called the *arupya-samapatti* or "formless attainments." Shakyamuni is said to have attained the top two, the realms of nothing whatsoever and neither notions nor non-notions, under his first ("heretical") teachers. Below these realms are the realms of infinite consciousness (the feeling that the mind is boundless) and infinite space (the feeling that space goes on for ever). At the top is the *bhavagra,* the pinnacle or limit of existence, the border of samsara. Nirvana, it should be noted, is not *beyond* the bhavagra, for there is no such "beyond" (if there were, it would not be the end of the universe!); nirvana is *outside of* samsara or, finally, the *disappearance* of samsara.

Further Reading

If you are still with me you will at least have realized how rare and precious, from the Buddhist point of view, is the human rebirth, which you presently have, and you will seek to preserve it and use it fruitfully, for your own freedom and that of all sentient beings. If you want still more information, there is a brief account from the Pali sources in Henry Clarke Warren, *Buddhism in Translations,* pages 289–291. A longer account, mostly from Japanese sources (with, let the reader beware, a heavy dose of psychologizing interpretation), is in Alicia Matsunaga, *The Buddhist Philosophy of Assimilation,* pages 48–59. For a Tibetan account, see Herbert Guenther's translation of Gampopa's *The Jewel Ornament of Liberation,* chapter 5. Randy Kloetzli, *Buddhist Cosmology* (Delhi: Banarsidass, 1983) studies the whole question from the standpoint of western Buddhology and his book is an excellent place from which to launch into the detailed classical treatments in (mostly) French and German (see his bibliography).

Chapter 7

REMOVING OBSTACLES

(Act 9 of the Buddha)

When the Bodhisattva Shakyamuni sat down beneath the Bodhi Tree and determined not to arise until he had reached final and complete enlightenment, he was attacked by enemies. They were non-human, but anthropoid, and they were led by a being called Mara. Mara has sometimes been compared to the Devil in Christianity,[1] but in Buddhism he is chiefly the manifestation of, and the symbol for, any obstacle to enlightenment. These obstacles are both external and internal. The Buddhist practitioner must overcome these obstacles, just as the Bodhisattva Shakyamuni overcame Mara and so became the Buddha.

Mara and External Obstacles

At the grossest and most obvious level, Mara is a being who is the embodiment of evil.[2] Buddhism recognizes the existence of many demons, both those derived from its origin in the Indian subcontinent and those discovered in the countries to which Buddhism spread. They are, like the demons who haunt American horror movies, characterized by having a terrifying appearance, making loud noises, being active mainly at night, and causing physical and mental harm. More importantly, however, they are credited with blocking the path to final liberation and perfect enlightenment. Sometimes they do this, as it were, for mere devilment, but at other times they do it for self-preservation. For instance, Mara is said to feed on the negative energies of the passions. If one is calm, loving, and so forth, one deprives him of food. Understandably, when Mara is starving, he becomes annoyed and tries to stir up hate, lust, and confusion. A bhikshu is sometimes called "he who causes Mara to tremble" because the bhikshu has made a formal, public decision to forego his negative thoughts, words, and deeds.

Mara may thus be regarded as a powerful deva. In some texts he is called the chief of the deities of the sensuous realm *(kama-dhatu)*, living in the Paranirmitavashavartin realm (see appendix to chapter 6), and it is from that exalted position that he feeds upon the passions of weaker beings such as humans. In other Buddhist traditions, however, the precise location of Mara within the triple-world is unclear. A Tibetan lama whom I asked about this laughed and said that the question had never come up before, but possibly Mara lived somewhere in the great ocean out towards the ring of iron mountains *(chakravala)*. The existence of Mara, however, and his propensity to obstruct the Dharma, is accepted by all Buddhist traditions.

Mara obstructs chiefly by deceiving and confusing. He is a shape–shifter, often appearing in anything but his true form. By causing, or exacerbating, confusion, he keeps sentient beings wallowing in the passions, so that they bind themselves to the sufferings of cyclic existence. His name is related to the word for death (from the root *mr*, "die") because the realm of rebirth is the realm of re-death, and it is, finally, the realm of Mara.

Mara is attended by his army and his daughters. His army

obstructs by means of hate and fear, while his daughters obstruct by means of lust. Both the army and the daughters came to hinder Shakyamuni from attaining enlightenment. They are sometimes collectively known as "the host of maras," and it is at this point that the word "mara" can be seen to refer to internal as well as external obstacles. Because the absolute distinction between object and subject is, according to Buddhism, an error made by ignorant mind, both the external and internal maras can be said to be, in effect, one mara, or aspects of Mara.

The ambiguity of Mara's ontological status, that is, whether he is inside or outside, is clearest in the Zen teaching on *makyo*. Makyo literally means "Mara's Images" and is the name for a certain type of hallucination that occasionally disturbs the Zen practitioner.

Zazen tries, as we have seen, to awaken in the practitioner an experience of Emptiness directly, without any intermediary, particularly without the aid of any images. Because of this, the consciousness is peculiarly vulnerable to images that may occur spontaneously, that is, through the fruiting of previous karma, and at the time that the image appears it may be uncertain whether it "really exists" or not.

A story is told of a Zen practitioner who, while sitting in meditation, saw a large black spider in front of him. Frightened, he was going to stab it to death, but he refrained until he had asked the advice of his teacher. The teacher told him that, instead, he should mark a chalk "X" on the back of the spider the next time he saw it. The monk did so, and when next he went for his interview, the teacher said, "Lift up your robe and look at your stomach. What do you see?" The monk saw a chalked "X."

Mara and Internal Obstacles

When Mara is seen as the negative tendencies within the defiled minds of sentient beings, the obstacles to enlightenment can be spoken of as the Three Poisons: *raga* (attachment), *dvesha* (aversion), and *moha* (confusion). The poisons are divided into five hindrances *(nivarana)* because they block or hinder the natural functioning of pure mind *(chitta-prabhasa)*, acting like a shade obscuring the light of a lamp; and ten "troublings" (*klesha*, normally translated as "passions") that cloud pure mind like the agitations of waves and mud clouding the water of a lake. The three poisons are symbolized, at the center of the Tibetan Wheel of Existence,[3] as a cock, a pig, and a snake chasing and attempting to eat each other.

The basic poison, or root negative tendency of the minds of suffering beings, is confusion, symbolized by the pig, an animal regarded as very stupid. Arising from this confusion, the defiled mind tries to get certain things and avoid others. These are the activities of attachment (symbolized by the cock, a famously lustful animal, whose very name, in English slang, signifies lust) and aversion (symbolized by the snake, an animal regarded as full of hate and anger). The strong but mistaken feeling called attachment is that a certain thing, person, or place must be had to make us happy. Aversion is its opposite: a certain thing, person, or place must be avoided. It is this passionate or addictive behavior (see chapter 3, "A Note on Samsara and Addiction") that is called attachment and aversion. It is not the choice between one thing and another in itself. Such a choice may be made on the basis of compassion for all sentient beings, when it would be a manifestation of the bodhisattva resolve. But if the choice is felt as an overpowering, addictive "must have" or "must avoid," it is the poison of Mara. Its addictive nature can be discovered by asking ourselves: "Does it really satisfy?" Buying one new car after another, or getting into one relationship after another, without any sense of having got what one was really looking for, is a mark of addictive behavior.

These internal maras can be related to the external maras as follows: confusion, the root poison, is Mara himself; attachment is the troupe of Mara's seductive daughters; and aversion is Mara's terrifying army.

In order to defeat the internal maras, it is necessary to identify them and apply the specific antidote (*pratipaksha*, literally "opposite wing"). There are many traditions on how to do this. A well-known one is found in chapter two of the Visuddhimagga (The Pure Path), a systematization of the Pali scriptures and commentaries, composed by Buddhaghosa (fourth or fifth century c.e.), which has become a standard compendium of Theravada doctrine and practice.[4]

Buddhaghosa begins by saying that there is nothing directly on this subject in the scriptures. All the traditions have been passed down orally. By this, he seems to mean that the identification of different personalities is something that has been built up over time by meditation teachers observing their students. It is a practical analysis, not a dogma.

After considering a number of schemes he knows, Buddhaghosa adopts the one that classifies personalities into six, subdivided into three unwholesome and three wholesome, related to the three poisons.

The three unwholesome personality types are related to the three poisons directly. They are the sensuous type, characterized by attachment; the aggressive type, characterized by aversion; and the muddled type, characterized by confusion. The three wholesome personality types are the trusting *(saddha)*, intellectual *(buddhi)*, and discursive *(vitakka)*. They are indirectly related to the three poisons. A trusting type manifests wholesome attachment, an intellectual type manifests wholesome aversion, and a discursive type manifests wholesome confusion. "Wholesome" does not mean *completely* wholesome, since all six types are intra-samsaric, but rather "less unwholesome."

No actual human being can be completely identified with his or her personality type. All humans (in fact, all sentient beings) are afflicted by all three poisons, but one or the other is dominant and needs to be given special attention. When the dominant poison has been removed, the others will follow.

The dominant type can be recognized by the manner in which a person performs ordinary activities such as walking, eating and sleeping. Thus, the types are called, literally, "ways of carrying oneself" *(chariya)*.

A sensuous or trusting type walks carefully and correctly, eats slowly and with relish, goes to bed methodically, sleeps curled up, and in general is precise and neat, seeking out pleasant things and overlooking faults. An aggressive or intellectual (critical) type, on the other hand, stomps around, eats quickly and disinterestedly ("food is food"), throws himself into bed, sleeps prone, and in general is aggressive, avoiding unpleasant things and overlooking virtues. A muddled or discursive type walks in a vague sort of way, tripping over his feet, eats sloppily, getting food all over the place, gets into bed uncertainly, sleeps supine, and is generally uncoordinated.

The connection between the three wholesome and three unwholesome types is as follows. A trusting type is like a sensuous one in that there is attachment to persons or viewpoints. This is good when the object of attachment is the Dharma, but it is bad when it is an uncritical attachment to "my teacher" (or country) "right or wrong." An intellectual or critical type certainly does not take anything on faith, and may feel superior to a trusting type, but the danger here is that the intellectualizing or the critical appraisal will never end, and no committment will be made. The energy of intellectualizing or critically judging is, also, very close to aversion, as anyone can testify who has seen learned academics hotly debating. A discursive type is like a muddled one in that any topic that is brought up is earnestly followed. Both the discursive and muddled types seem to have no opinion of their own. They react to whatever is at hand, and can easily be distracted.

The antidotes appropriate for the six types are:

1. Sensuous type: *meditation on the repulsive aspects of the physical body, to offset attachment to it as something intrinsically attractive. The body is observed to be "a skin bag of bones, oozing excrement from its nine openings." The most colorful meditation for the sensuous type is the studied observation of the stages of decomposition of a corpse, known as the contemplation of "the unlovely"* (asubha). *It should be carefully noted that the observation of the repulsiveness of the body is an antidote to attachment to its beauty. If the meditator begins to hate the body, the antidote has been overused. This warning applies to all the antidotes: they are like medicines, to be given up at the proper time.*

2. Aggressive type: *meditation on the four pure abidings (see chapter 3). The pure abidings offset the general pessimism of the aggressive type.*

3. Muddled *and* Discursive types: *the observation of the breathing, to offset the tendency (which the mind has in general but which this type has more than other types) to wander, and the difficulty of seeing that the universe is not haphazard, but that some things follow other things.*

4. Trusting type: *meditation on the excellent qualities of the Buddha, the Dhamma, and the Sangha. Since the trusting type will tend to give itself wholeheartedly to something or another, the Triple Jewel is suggested as a worthy object of attachment.*

5. Intellectual type: *meditation on the four elements, earth, air, fire, and water (in more modern terminology: solids, gases, heat, and fluids—in effect, physical science, a worthwhile subject of critical investigation), and on peace (presumably to calm the tendency of this type to aggressive critical attack).*

This classification of the personality types, their impediments and their antidotes, is offered by Buddhaghosa as an aid to the meditation teacher in understanding the differences between students and the best way to advise each of them individually. It is the fruit of the experience of past teachers and is not supposed to be a rigid classification, to be applied without proper judgment or compassion. Indeed, says Buddhaghosa, if the teacher has true insight (*dibba-chakkhu*, "divine eye") this scheme will not be needed. The teacher will know immediately and directly, just by looking at the disciple, what is best.

Buddhaghosa recommends dealing with impediments to enlightenment by replacing them with aids to enlightenment. Another way of dealing with impediments is to transform the impediment itself into an aid. This is the method of the *lojong (blo sbyong)*, "thought transformation," tradition of Tibetan Buddhism. Buddhaghosa, we might say, recommends replacing a stumbling block with a stepping stone. In lojong, the stumbling block itself becomes a stepping stone.

Lojong is traced back to Atisha (982–1054 C.E.), an Indian teacher who studied for some time in Sumatra (which was Buddhist at the time) before returning to India and then being summoned to Tibet by King Yeshe O. His method was passed down orally until Geshe Chekawa (1102–1176 C.E.) of the Kadampa lineage wrote a summary of it as the Seven Point Thought Transformation (Blo Sbyong Don Bdun Ma). Through this text, the lojong tradition, sometimes called "Atisha's Seven Points of Mind Training," has passed into all lineages of Tibetan Buddhism[5].

The distinctive lojong approach to adversity is found in the third of the seven points, "changing adverse circumstances into the Path."[6] Instead of trying to escape from suffering, or treat it with an antidote, the suffering itself is used as a means of advancing along the path to enlightenment. Geshe Chekawa advises:

> *When the container and its contents are filled with evil,*
> *change this adverse circumstance into the path to full*
> *awakening.*[7]

That is, if someone gets angry with us, we do not react with anger, but we "inwardly thank him for such kind teachings because now we shall know we must be careful not to create any further causes for such results."[8]

The method is founded on an understanding of the working of karma. If someone expresses hatred for me, it is because I have been angry at that being, either in this life and in this form or in a previous life in another form, and now the anger is coming back to me. The other being's anger is not without cause, even though at the moment it might seem so. It is as if I were to scowl into a mirror and then see a face scowling back at me. The anger of others at me is my anger at them, which has now fruited. Thus, I am asked to regard the angry being as my kind spiritual friend who is teaching me about the fruiting of karma and giving me an opportunity to redress my past anger with present compassion.

This can work for any adverse circumstance in which I might find myself. If I meet a relatively minor adversity, such as finding myself stuck in a traffic jam, I can think, "How kind and good are the other motorists, who have so generously granted me an opportunity for cultivating patience; if no one ever gave me such an opportunity, I could never develop this virtue!" And even if the adversity is grave, such as being born with a severe deformity, or meeting with a terrible accident, it is still possible for me to "bring it into the path" by understanding it as the fruiting of karma and being grateful that it has fruited now, in this life when I am a human who practices Dharma and so can deal with the negative effects. Then, in whatever I do, I shall be meditating, and cultivating virtue.

Removing Confused Perception

Mara's chief weapon is confusion. The root poison, *moha,* is
the confusion of befuddlement or drunkenness. Just as a drunk-
ard takes reality to be something other than that which is perceived by a sober person, so the mind of an unliberated being
misperceives reality, while the mind of a Buddha sees reality as
it truly is.

The Buddhist investigation of misperception has two aspects:
various misperceptions *within* samsara, or *illusion;* and the misperception *of* samsara, or *delusion.* The examination of illusion
is a branch of Buddhist logic. The Mahayana system called Yogachara concerns itself with the investigation of delusion.

ILLUSION

The Buddhist understanding of illusion is more or less com-
monsensical. The standard of reality is that which is seen by any
ordinary person, free of gross physical or mental defects, while
in the state of consciousness, which we call, in everyday terms,
fully awake. In this state, it is observed that various mistakes can
be made. These mistakes are classified by means of a number of
standard, and sometimes quite colorful, similes.

One of the commonest similes is that of mistaking a coil of
rope, seen in poor light, for a snake. Mistaking a rope for a snake
is what we would call a visual distortion. Something is really
there, but what is seen by the person who is in error is not what
is there for a person whom we call normal. Visual distortions are
sometimes a feature of withdrawal from certain drugs and alcohol. Their connection with the root poison of confusion *(moha)*
is thus rather direct.

Almost equally common is the simile of the "hairnet." Some
monks, it is said, see hairs in their almsbowls and try to scrape
them out, but they are unsuccessful since the hairs are an illusion produced by "eye disease." It is uncertain what kind of eye
disease is in question. Sometimes it is explained as cataracts, and
one scholar tells us, as if it were obvious, that the hairnet (or
"hairtuft" as he calls it) is due to color blindness.[9] But neither of
these conditions would seem to produce the reported effect. It is
perhaps due to retinal breaks, which can produce "floaters,"
translucent wormlike objects which drift across the field of vi-

sion, or an appearance like wispy smoke or cobwebs.[10]

Seeing a hairnet due to eye disease is an illusion caused by a defect of the organ of perception. Seeing a rope as a snake is a defect of the mind that is processing the perception, that is, of the particular mental functions associated with seeing (*chakshuh-vijñana*, "eye-consciousness").[11] If the defect of the eye-consciousness is more severe, we experience a hallucination. A hallucination is something that is seen only by the person experiencing it. Nobody else sees anything there at all. The Buddhist simile for this is the sight of a "fairy castle" *(gandharva-nagaram)* in the sky. The aerial beings, known as *gandharvas,* live in castles, or cities (*nagaram* is a fortified city), which they create by their magic. Such deceptive dwellings are similar to the fairy grottoes of indigenous western religion.

Another form of illusion is dreaming. When we are dreaming, we think we are awake. That is, we mistake the dream's reality for the more solid reality of waking consciousness. A dream is an example of how the mind can see subjective reality as apparently objective reality. It is, we might say, a simile of a "philosophical" mistake, whereas the illusions discussed so far have been "commonsense" mistakes. Another example of a "philosophical" mistake is the plantain or banana tree. It has a massive trunk, but it is hollow. Its apparent solidity, but its actual insubstantiality, is an analogy of how we mistake entities to have inherent existence *(svabhava).* The mistake comes from superficial examination. On more profound investigation, the deception of solidity or substantiality is exposed.

The funniest similes are "rabbit horns" and "turtle fur." Rabbits do not have horns (except on the postcards sold to tourists in the American west) and turtles do not have fur. To say they do is a mistake of fact. These examples are used to characterize errors in the premises of a syllogism. The valid but false syllogism given above (chapter 5), which produced the conclusion that Socrates is green, can be disproved by showing that the premise "All men are green" is as false as saying "Rabbits have horns" or "Turtles have fur."

Two important points emerge from this discussion of illusion. First, commonsense reality is not dismissed *in toto.* Samsara is real, and within its reality mistakes can be made. These mistakes can be uncovered by physical or logical investigation. There is nothing very mysterious about this kind of illusion. However, secondly, samsara, although real, is not *ultimately* real. It is the product of causes and conditions. This *conditional* reality (or unreality) can be *symbolized* by such things as a dream or the trunk of a banana tree. It is important to note that Buddhism does not say, as do some other systems (e.g., some forms of Hinduism) that reality *is* a dream, or that reality itself is an illusion. Buddhism teaches that *reality is misperceived.* It is dream*like* in the sense that a dream disappears upon waking, that is, upon its causes and conditions being removed, but it is not in and of itself a dream. Samsaric reality, or the experience of suffering, is a *real delusion* within which there are unreal events, or illusions.

How this real delusion comes to be, and how it is dispelled, is explained by the Yogachara system, to which we now turn.

DELUSION: THE YOGACHARA SYSTEM

The main contention of Yogachara is that objects exist in dependence upon consciousness. Western scholars have often regarded it as a form of philosophical Idealism, a system that maintains that no external objects exist. That this is not the Yogachara position should become clear.

Yogachara begins its analysis of perception by investigating illusions. The fact that consciousness *(vijñana)* can make mistakes, such as seeing a coil of rope as a snake, throws suspicion on its ability to perceive reality correctly, and the fact that we dream indicates that we can perceive what we believe to be external objects without there necessarily having to be an external object at all. It then moves to the observation that what is perceived is dependent upon the state of mind of the perceiver. The standard example is that of beings from different levels of rebirth perceiving a fluid.

> *Hell-beings see a bowl of fluid as molten bronze. Hungry ghosts see it as pus and blood; animals such as fish, as an abode; humans, as water for drinking; gods, as ambrosia.* [12]

We can understand this from our experience as humans. Suppose it is a bright spring morning, the birds are singing, the air is brisk and tangy. Is it a good morning? For Mary, who has just fallen in love and has also won the state lottery, it is a *fantastic* morning! For Joe, however, whose girlfriend told him last night that she was through, so that he went out, got drunk, totaled his car, and has woken up in jail with a hangover, the morning is definitely a bad one. What is the difference? The consciousness of Mary and the consciousness of Joe.

We might want to say, perhaps, that Joe and Mary see the same objectively and independently existing morning and interpret it differently; but, who is to report on this "same" morning and tell us what it really is? Is it the morning the way Jane sees it? She is a scientist, and has been trained to look at things impartially and dispassionately, but she is stuck in a job that, though it pays the bills, is no longer exciting, and she really doesn't care what sort of a morning it is. If the morning is observed at all, it must be observed by some consciousness, and there is no independent way of judging between the reports of these consciousnesses.

The claim that there is a real morning that exists absolutely, objectively, and independently (or, as Yogachara puts it, "from its own side") and is seen differently by different observing consciousnesses is the position of the Realist. The difficulty with the Realist position is that it is an assumption. The Realist collects a mass of data until he thinks he has enough to be statistically significant, and then extrapolates to a real object that he claims to know is there. In another words, the Realist has already decided that objects exist independently, even before making any observations, and then uses the data to prove that they do. The logical circle is too small to be convincing.

So, if we cannot find one externally and independently existing morning, we might decide that in fact there are three mornings: Mary's fantastic one, Joe's miserable one, and Jane's neutral one, and that these exist separately in the consciousnesses of Mary, Joe, and Jane. On this view, "morning" is just a subjective concept and it just so happens that three consciousnesses have perceived a morning. They might, instead, have perceived an evening.

The claim that "morning" is merely an idea that I happen to have is the Idealist position. The problem with Idealism is that it does not explain why it certainly seems, to everyone except the Idealist philosopher, that mornings are the sort of thing that exist more or less independently of anyone thinking them up. Idealist philosophies tend to produce the conundrum called solipsism; that is, I know what I see but I can't be sure anyone else sees it, or even that anyone else *exists,* since all of you may just be a part of my subjective fantasy. That is, for the Idealist, reality is *in fact* a dream, and it is not clear how ones wakes up from it.

Some Idealists have found ingenious ways out of the solipsist cul-de-sac. For instance, Bishop Berkeley, perhaps the most famous exponent of Idealism in the west, said that things are more or less the same for everybody, and they stay around even when no one is looking at them, because they are observed by the Mind of God, who observes everything all at once and never goes to sleep. Since Buddhists deny the existence of such a cosmic workaholic, they cannot make sense of Berkeley's solution.

The answer given by Yogachara to all this perplexity is that the data compel us to admit that an object, and *that same object in consciousness,* together constitute a *single entity.* That is, what I perceive is what I perceive. I see a good, bad, or neutral morning depending upon my state of consciouness or, what is the same thing, dependent upon the fruiting of my karma. A thing and the observation of that thing *arise simultaneously,* dependent upon each other. If the object were to exist, in the way that we now see it, *before* the observing consciousness came into being to observe it, we would not have perceived it. If the object were to arise *subsequent* to the observing consciousness, then it seems that I created it. But I find that I cannot make things appear just by thinking of them.

What I *can* do, however, is think of a thing and then notice that the thing I have thought of (which is a mental, not a physical object, but an object nevertheless) and my consciousness of that thing came into being simultaneously. I do not notice any temporal gap between, say, thinking of a violin and the appearance of an image of a violin; that is to say, I do not observe that my thought of a violin was the cause of an image of a violin appearing. The thought and the image arose together, dependent upon each other. Therefore, a thing and my consciousness of that same thing are only mentally divisible, into what Yogachara calls the grasper *(grahaka)* and the grasped *(grahya);* that is, the perceiving consciousness and the thing perceived by that consciousness.

There is no mention here, be it noted, of a universal consciousness or Cosmic Mind. Yogachara focusses on a particular moment of perception of a particular thing by a particular consciousness, and concludes that it is observably the case that, at that moment, perceiving and perceived are neither different nor the same. That is, the connection between them is empty. This is the Yogachara demonstration of Transparency.

Yogachara then analyzes this situation in two ways. First, it describes the functioning of consciousness as self-referencing, and secondly, it shows how reality can be misperceived as manifesting duality although it is in itself empty of duality.

All Buddhist traditions accept the existence of a mental function called vijñana, which has something to do with awareness and is normally translated as consciousness. It occurs in the Abhidharma system (see chapter 5) as the cluster *(skandha)* which produces self-consciousness. In addition, most Buddhist traditions say there are five consciousnesses, one for each of the senses: a visual, an auditory, an olfactory, a gustatory, and a tactile consciousness. To this they add a sixth, the mental consciousness *(mano-vijñana)*. As the eye is aware of sights, the ear of sounds, and so forth, so the mental consciousness is aware of thoughts, ideas, or concepts. In effect, it is a sense organ. The existence of the mental consciousness explains how it is that, for example, by seeing marks on a page or hearing noises we report the reception of ideas. They are transmitted by our eye and ear consciousnesses to our mental consciousness, where they are decoded into meaning.

One branch of Yogachara, attributed to Dharmakirti (7th century C.E.), stops there. It is accepted by Tibetan Buddhism, but only provisionally, as a non-final system that needs to be understood in the light of Madhyamika (see chapter 9). Another branch, attributed to Asanga, a fourth-century monk from the area that is now Pakistan, teaches that there are two more consciousnesses. The Asanga branch has been fully incorporated into Chinese, Korean, and Japanese Buddhism. Because of its importance to the living tradition, the eight consciousness system will be described here.

The functioning of the eight consciousnesses is diagrammed in figure 10. Sense data coming in from the five consciousnesses associated with the five physical senses are processed by the mental consciousness, where it is named and becomes a concept. Suppose that a certain object is examined for shape, color, texture, and so forth, and it is determined that it is a chocolate chip cookie. This coherent piece of information is passed down

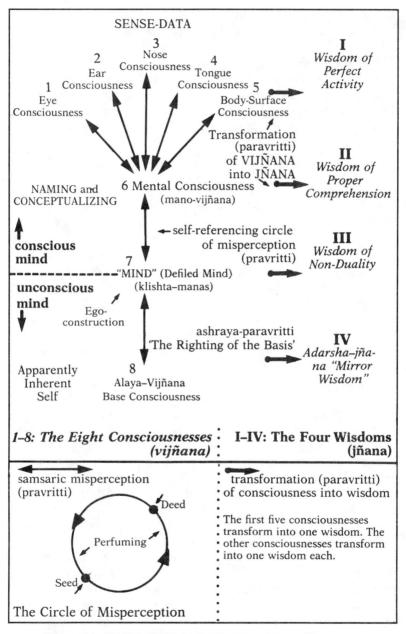

Figure 11: IGNORANCE AND WISDOM ACCORDING TO
YOGACHARA (Asanga Branch)

through the "defiled mind" (*klishta-manas*, sometimes just called the mind, manas) and placed in the "foundation" or "base" consciousness *(alaya-vijñana)* (called by the Chinese the receptacle or store consciousness, *tsang-shih*). When another object is perceived, let us say a photograph of a chocolate chip cookie, its data is compared with the data on the chocolate chip cookie, and with previously stored data on photographs, the object is identified as a photograph of a chocolate chip cookie, and the decision is made not to eat it.

The process never goes only one way, but both ways at once, simultaneously. Perception, storage, checking, and action all occur in a self-sustaining, or self-reflecting, circle. I know whether or not I am dealing with an edible chocolate chip cookie because I have previously programmed myself to recognize chocolate chip cookies, and since I happen to like chocolate chip cookies, I react by eating one. The system is a closed or endless circle, for it is samsaric, and it is a process of re-cognition rather than cognition. The Chinese invented a short mnemonic verse to express the self-reflective workings of consciousness:

A seed gives rise to a deed;
A deed perfumes a seed;
These three factors circle around
Simultaneously being cause and
    effect.[13]

The "seed" in this verse is the stored data in the alaya-vijnana. The data is called a seed *(bija)* because it is concerned with the fruiting of karma. It is not an unchanging "thing" like a computer bit. At the proper time, it grows and fruits. This fruit is the "deed" *(karma)*, which produces a new seed by what is called "perfuming" *(vasana)*. These three factors, seed, deed, and perfuming, arise simultaneously and interdependently.

This model is offered as an explanation of the observed simultaneity of perceiving and perception. The special features of the model are the *manas* and the alaya-vijñana. Manas is identified as the source of the sense of "I." It exists astride the conscious and unconscious sectors of mind in general and, seeing the seeds it has stored in the alaya-vijñana, mistakes the alaya for an inherently existing self. What it fails to understand is that the *alaya* is not a static entity, but a river *(ogha,* "flood") that is constantly in motion. The *alaya* is indeed a self, just as a river is indeed a river, but it is not an eternal, unchanging, or inherently existing self any more than a river is eternal, unchanging, or inherently existing. The alaya exists below the level of conscious mind, which accounts for the feeling that the real "me" is somewhere deep inside, and the fact that I continue to exist even when asleep or unconscious. The alaya is also the receptacle of the seeds of rebirth, that is, it is the transmigrating entity, though it is not an inherently existing transmigrating entity.

When these eight consciousnesses are purified upon enlightenment, they are said to be "turned around" *(paravritti)*, or turned upside down (or, rather, right side up), to become the four wisdoms (jñana) of perfect activity, proper comprehension, non-arising (i.e., the wisdom which understands non-duality), and Mirror Wisdom *(adarsha-jñana)*. Since Mirror Wisdom arises when the *alaya-vijñana*, or base consciousness, is purified, it is called *ashraya-paravritti*, "the righting of the basis." Mirror Wisdom sees reality as it truly is because it simply reflects, it does not project *(pravritti)* any notions of its own onto it.

Case 14 of The Gateless Gate, a collection of Zen koans, reads:

> *Once the monks of the eastern and western Zen halls were quarreling about a cat. Nansen held up the cat and said, "You monks! If one of you can say a word, I will spare the cat. If you can't say anything, I will put it to the sword." No one could answer, so Nansen finally slew it. In the evening when Joshu returned, Nansen told him what had happened. Joshu, thereupon, took off his sandals, put them on his head and walked off. Nansen said, "If you had been there, I could have spared the cat."[14]*

The cat represents duality. We are all walking upside down. When someone acts with Mirror Wisdom, he appears to have his shoes on his head.

We have seen how self-referencing consciousness functions according to Yogachara. Now we will look at how it shows that reality can be misperceived as manifesting duality. This aspect of Yogachara is called the Three Reality *(trisvabhava)* model.

Reality is said to exist in three ways. The first is reality as we ordinarily perceive it, with its independently existing subjects and objects. This is called cognized reality *(parikalpita-sv-abhava)*, the imagined reality that is produced by the activity of *vikalpa*, "judging or classifying mind." This is reality as we ordinarily cognize it, but, however ultimately real it may seem, it is found on analysis to be pure fiction. It is like rabbit horns or turtle fur.

When we examine reality more closely, we find that subjects and objects arise simultaneously and codependently. This is called conditioned reality *(paratantra-svabhava)*, reality seen according to *(para)* its connectedness *(tantra)*. This is like a sophisticated observer looking at a plantain tree. Its apparent solidity, which is its cognized reality, is known to be a fiction, and its actual hollowness is understood to be the case.

Reality as it truly is, however, does not even manifest connectedness. When this view is directly experienced, it is called finally established reality. The Sanskrit term is *parinishpanna-sv-abhava*, literally "the reality that is fully perfected"; that is, reality when it is finally understood as it truly is, when it is seen with Mirror Wisdom after "the righting of the basis."

These three realities are called *svabhava*, a word that usually means inherent existence. However, it cannot mean that here, since all three are said to be *nihsvabhava*, without inherent existence. This means that the three realities *appear* as three separate, autonomous realities, but *in fact* they are all aspects *of each other*. They are not three aspects of a fourth "real" reality.

A simile of this is given in a text called The Teaching on the Three Realities (Trisvabhavanirdesha).[15] In elegant but somewhat obscure Sanskrit couplets, the author tells us that the three realities are non-dual, because the first (cognized reality) does not exist at all, the second (conditioned reality) does not exist as such, and the third (finally established reality) is merely the absence of the first.

In case we might not have grasped his meaning, he gives us a simile. Suppose a magician were to produce the appearance of an elephant by using a piece of wood and a spell. A naive observer would see an elephant, and believe that there really was an elephant there. A sophisticated observer, however, would see the form of an elephant, but would know that it was a trick. A very sophisticated observer would say, "Such an elephant is non-existent." The apparently solid elephant is like cognized reality, the elephant known to be a trick is like conditioned reality, and the absence of an elephant is like finally established reality. Then, the spell is like the base consciousness *(alaya-vijñana)*, the piece of wood is like Suchness *(tathata,* "reality as it truly is"), and the apparent elephant is like judging or classifying mind *(vikalpa)*. Base consciousness, once it has been purified or turned right side up, does not see any duality.

This sounds like a very important explanation, and we get the impression that the author is delighted to have come up with such a satisfyingly clear simile. However, most of us are left feeling as if we have missed the punch line of a very good joke. Our frustration is perhaps largely due to never having observed a magician produce an elephant out of a piece of wood, so that the analogy is unhelpful.

The innovative suggestion has been made that we should change the simile from a magically produced elephant to a physically produced hologram.[16] A hologram is generated by shining a light or laser beam onto a specially prepared photographic plate so that a three-dimensional image, suspended in space, is produced. The secret is in the photographic plate, which contains information from all sides of the original object. This information, which to our ordinary sight contains no image at all, is called the interference pattern, since it is composed of all the light waves carrying information about the object's surface spread across the entire surface of the plate so that they "interfere" with each other. When the interference pattern is read by the proper equipment, all the surfaces of the object reappear in the image. A very good hologram is difficult to distinguish from a solid object.

So, we can say that the hologram itself, which appears as a solid object, is a simile of cognized reality. However, we know that a hologram is the product of the laser, the interference pattern, the rest of the device, and the observer. This is like conditioned reality. The image seems to exist "from its own side," but we know that it is the product of causes and conditions.

Now, when we see one hologram, we are seeing one image read out of the interference pattern. It is possible, however, for many interference patterns to be encoded (or "enfolded") onto one plate. When this is done, the surface is called the implicate domain. An implicate domain has the potential of producing many apparently solid images, but when we look at the implicate domain directly, all we see is a blur. There is neither an object nor a subject. This is a simile of finally established reality, which is not itself anything but is the basis upon which judging or classifying mind *(vikalpa)* produces the dualisms of cognized reality.

All three aspects of the holographic process—the image, the functioning device together with the conscious observer, and the implicate domain, can be described as if they were separate entities, yet they are in fact aspects of each other. This is a simile of the three realities or "natures" *(svabhava)* being empty or "natureless" *(nihsvabhava)*.

The hologram analogy also helps us to understand the "rainbow body" and Indra's Net.

In Tibetan Buddhism it is taught that the Enjoyment Body or Sambhogakaya (see chapter 1) is like a rainbow, for it exists, it shines as if made of light, and yet, since it is of the nature of Emptiness or Transparency, it has no solidity and cannot be grasped. High lamas are said to "attain the rainbow body" at death, and it is customary to look for a rainbow during their cremation ceremony.[17] A rainbow is similar to a hologram in that it appears to exist in space, yet we cannot touch it.

A curious feature of the information encoded onto a holographic plate is that the entire image can be generated from any part of it. Because the interference pattern is spread across the whole plate, the image is implicitly (or implicatively) everywhere on the plate. The part is in the whole and the whole is in the part. This is the way reality is described as the Realm of Indra's Net in Fa-tsang's *Essay on the Golden Lion* (see chapter 1). Fa-tsang was, it seems, trying to describe how reality appears when it is seen in its finally established nature.

To sum up. Yogachara recognizes that consciousness is subject to *illusion.* It uses illusion as the gateway to understanding that reality as a whole is experienced by unliberated beings as a grand *delusion* called samsara. This delusion is explained as a closed circle in which an object, and that same object as it exists in a particular consciousness, arise simultaneously and codependently, such that delusions perpetuate themselves. The way out of this circle is the purification of the consciousness, part by part, until the absolute openness to reality known as Mirror Wisdom is attained. The possibility of breaking out of the circle is demonstrated by the explanation of reality's three aspects, the cognized, the conditioned, and the finally established, none of which is ultimately different from the other. Reality as it truly is, is not different from delusory reality. Delusory reality and reality as it truly is are alike empty. The circle of delusion is therefore not finally closed. Its perpetual samsaric circling is the result of causes and conditions. When these causes and conditions are removed, we wake up from our dreamlike delusion.

NOTES
to Chapter Seven

1. James W. Boyd, *Satan and Mara: Christian and Buddhist Symbols of Evil* (Leiden: Brill), 1975.

2. This section is heavily indebted to *Buddhism and the Mythology of Evil* by T. O. Ling (London: Allen and Unwin, 1962), especially chapter 3, "The Buddhist Symbol of the Evil One."

3. See chapter 6, note 7, and figure 9.

4. *The Path of Purity,* translated by Pe Maung Tin (London: Pali Text Society, 1923–1931, in three volumes; reprinted as one volume, 1971; one volume version distributed in the U.S.A. by Routledge; three volume edition reprinted in the United States by AMS Press), pp. 118–129 (of the one volume edition). An alternative English translation is *The Path of Purification,* by Bhikkkhu Ñānamoli (3rd edition, Kandy, Sri Lanka: Buddhist Publication Society, 1975; reprinted in the U.S.A. by Shambhala, 1976).

5. A number of commentaries are now available in English, for example, *Advice from a Spiritual Friend* by Geshe Rabten and Geshe Dhargyey, translated and edited by Brian Beresford *et al.* (London: Wisdom, 1984), written from the Gelugpa standpoint, and *The Great Path of Awakening* by Jamgon Kongtrul, trans. by Ken McLeod (Boston: Shambala, 1987). from the Karma Kagyupa standpoint. The fact that these commentaries, although from different lineages, show little variation in substance is an indication of the unity of Tibetan Buddhism in regard to the lojong tradition.

6. *Advice from a Spiritual Friend,* pp. 65–69.

7. Root text quoted from *Advice,* p. 65.

8. Commentary quoted from *Advice,* p. 66.

9. Chhote Lal Tripathi, *The Problem of Knowledge in Yogacara Buddhism* (Varanasi: Bharat-Bharati, 1972), p. 58. This is one of the best books on Yogachara in English, and Dr. Tripathi can be readily excused this small slip.

10. Conversation with my colleague and (unrelated) namesake Dr. Joseph M. Corless of the Departments of Anatomy and Ophthalmology at Duke University, November 1986. Dr Corless's suggestion is, however, a physical one, but there may also be a chemical cause. Dr Jeffrey Hopkins tells me that his mother saw "hairnets" and the symptoms were traced to a vitamin deficiency. Perhaps we are not here dealing with a single disease, but a family of similar symptoms.

11. For the place of vijñana in the Abhidharma system, see above, chapter 5.

12. Jeffrey Hopkins, *Meditation on Emptiness* (London: Wisdom, 1983), p. 372. Pages 365 to 397 of this book present an authoritative and detailed account of Yogachara (called there Chittamatra) from the standpoint of the Gelugpa lineage of Tibetan Buddhism. The beginning student should note that although Hopkins describes both the Dharmakirti and Asanga branches of Yogachara, he emphasizes, in accordance with Gelugpa tradition, the Dharmakirti branch. This branch rejects the *alaya-vijñana* as it is taught by the Asanga branch. As noted below, I have chosen to discuss the Asanga branch, as it is accepted by East Asian Buddhism.

13. My translation of the Chinese in *The Essentials of Buddhist Philosophy* by Junjiro Takakusu (Honolulu: Office Appliance Company, 1956), p. 90, note 104.

14. *Gateless Gate,* translation and commentary by Zen Master Koun Yamada (Los Angeles: Center Publications, 1979), p. 76. The interpretation of the koan is my own and should not be attributed to Yamada Roshi.

15. I have used the text (given in Tibetan and Sanskrit recensions) and French translation of Louis de La Vallée Poussin, "Le petit traité de Vasubandhu-Nāgārjuna sur les trois natures" in *Mélanges chinois et bouddhiques,* vol. 2 (1932–1933), pp. 147–161. Stephen Kaplan (see following note) refers to an edition of the Sanskrit in *Journal of Indian Philosophy* 11 (1983), pp. 225–266, "The Trisvabhāvakārikā of Vasubandhu," by Fernando Tola and Carmen Dragonetti.

16. Stephen Kaplan, "A Holographic Alternative to a Traditional Yogācāra Simile: An Analysis of Vasubandhu's Trisvabhāva Doctrine," paper presented at the Eighth Conference of the International Association of Buddhist Studies, Berkeley, California, August 8–10, 1987. This section is heavily indebted to Professor Kaplan's paper, although I have modified his ideas at several points and my discussion does not necessarily represent Professor Kaplan's opinion.

17. A sudden clearing of clouds and the appearance of a "rainbow" around the sun was reported by those who attended the cremation of Ven. Chögyam Trungpa, Rinpoche at Barnet, Vermont, on May 26, 1987. According to Laura M. Roth ("A Halo for the Vidyadhara," letter in *The Vajradhatu Sun,* 8:6 (August/September 1987)) what actually appeared was a solar halo.

Chapter 8

THE PINNACLE

(Act 10 of the Buddha)

The tenth act of the Buddha is bodhi, the awakening or, as it is usually called in English, the Enlightenment. Enlightenment, however, is a rather weak word. It generally means the gaining of knowledge or information, and it is also used to refer to a movement in European philosophy which emphasized what it regarded as reason. Bodhi is much more than this. It is the perfect liberation of body, speech, and mind. Tibetans call a Buddha *Sangye (sangs rgyas). Sang* means to come to one's senses after having been asleep or drunk, and *gye* means broad, wide, or fully developed. Thus, *Sangye* means fully awake, having one's potential fully developed.

In this state of full awareness, a Buddha sees reality as it truly is, but even before he has become a Buddha he has developed such mental powers that he can see and do things that are, to the rest of us, extraordinary.

In this chapter we will, first, look at these extraordinary powers and see how they have been used in the service of the
Dharma, and secondly, investigate the content of enlightenment
itself.

Psychic Powers and Magic

THE ABHIJÑAS

A considerable amount of Buddhist literature and practice is
concerned with what is called *abhijña.* This is a Sanskrit word
with no exact English equivalent. Literally, it means "further
knowledge" or "extra knowledge." It has been translated as
higher knowledge, super-knowledge, higher power, and super-
power. Since the knowledge in question is know-*how* rather
than know-*what,* I suggest the translation "supernormal skill."
It includes what we generally call, in English, psychic powers
and magic.

To call something a psychical or magical phenomenon is, in
modern America, a way of belittling it so that we do not have to
investigate it. Only deluded or unscientific people, we may say,
take such things seriously. Anthropologists are allowed to take
them seriously, but only if they are happening somewhere else.
That is, they are allowed to report that magic is said to occur, but
they are not supposed to believe that it actually did occur.

There are certain presuppositions behind our cultural discomfort with psychic and magical phenomena. They need to be examined here, since they are thoroughly un-Buddhist. Generally,
it seems that a materialist cr Realist attitude is being implicitly
adopted. Physical reality is regarded as the only real reality, and
mental reality is regarded as an epiphenomenon of it. Therefore,
psychical reality must be explicable in terms of some, perhaps
as yet not understood, but anyhow quite definite, physical reality. Physical reality also, it is assumed, operates according to
Newtonian laws, so that magic, or miracles, must be some kind
of trick, illusion, or delusion.

The Buddhist objection to this view should by now be fairly
clear. It is the Realist position of classical physics that is, for
Buddhism, the delusion. It must be taken seriously, but it cannot
be taken seriously just as it is. It is a serious disease, but it is not
a serious truth.

It should also be noticed that a scientific law is not an absolute condition that exists prior to the data. A scientist amasses data and, when some significant consistency seems to be emerging, formulates a hypothesis. With more data and increasing consistency, the hypothesis is upgraded to a theory. Finally, it becomes a law, meaning only that the statistical probability of things occurring that way is so great that contrary instances may, for all practical purposes, be ignored. A single verifiable instance of a contrary instance is, however, enough to throw the law into doubt and perhaps eventually to change it. This is the way "paradigm shifts" occur in the development of science.[1] Therefore, if the data from Buddhism is contrary to received scientific laws, but is found to be verifiable, the laws will have to be changed. There are some signs that this may be occurring. Following on the observed success of acupuncture, a supposedly magical practice in Chinese medicine, physicians are cautiously investigating Tibetan Buddhist medicine, to see if it might not be as superstitious as they thought it was.

Some westerners are all too ready to admit the defeat of classical physics, and indeed the whole of science. They propose, instead, various occult systems in which, they say, mind alone is real and matter is an illusion. This is merely the reverse of the view they are opposing, and Buddhism finds it no more coherent.

When the Buddhist position of the interrelatedness of mind and matter is accepted, then it becomes reasonable to suppose that there might be a certain fluidity in their interrelatedness, that is, that psychical or magical phenomena might in fact occur.

The supernormal skills are commonly listed, by both Theravada (Pali: *abhiñña*) and Mahayana, as six. The first five are termed mundane (Sanskrit: *laukika;* Pali: *lokiya;* literally "of the *loka*," i.e., intra-samsaric) and the last is supramundane or extra-samsaric (Sanskrit: *lokottara;* Pali: *lokuttara;* literally "outside of the *loka*"). *Loka* is "world" (the world as experienced, not *jagat,* the world as it is in itself; see the discussion of this in chapter 6) and it is cognate with the English word "location." So, we might call the intra-samsaric skills "locatable" (in space-time) and the extra-samsaric, or nirvanic skill, "unlocatable," i.e., outside of space-time or "non-referential" (which is a synonym of Transparency).

Since the first five skills are intra-samsaric, there is nothing specifically Buddhist about them. It is said that they can be attained by anyone, Buddhist or not, who undertakes the proper training. They become Buddhist only when they are used in the service of the Dharma. Without this, they are extraordinary, but not very helpful. Indeed, if one attains them without the Dharmic motivation of universal compassion, they may lead to pride and thus become an obstacle to liberation.

The skill that is listed first by Theravada and fifth by Mahayana is called *iddhi* (Sanskrit: *riddhi*). Literally it means wealth or prosperity, and it refers to the magical powers that are possessed by some advanced meditators. In the Theravada tradition it is described as follows:

> *Now, O Bhikkhus, the monk enjoys the various Magical Powers* (iddhi-vidha), *such as being one he becomes manifold, and having become manifold he again becomes one. Without being obstructed he passes through walls and mountains, just as if through the air. In the earth he dives and rises up again, just as if in the water. He walks on water without sinking, just as if on the earth. Cross-legged he floats through the air, just as a winged bird. With his hand he touches the sun and moon, these so mighty ones, so powerful ones. Even up to the Brahma world he has mastery over his body.*[2]

What has been attained here is mastery over, or perhaps better, flexibility within, the physical universe, regarded here as composed of the four elements, earth, air, fire, and water. We might call this psychokinesis.

The other four mundane supernormal skills are (in the order listed by Theravada, with the Mahayana order, where it differs, in parentheses):

> *1.* The divine ear: *While remaining a human, one gains an ear like that of a deity, being able to hear sounds from very far away. The mundane, or intra-samsaric, nature of this accomplishment is made clear by observing that such an ear, called bionic, was constructed, by fanciful but not altogether unreasonable technology, for the female companion of the American television character "The Six Million Dollar Man."*

2. Telepathy: *Without recourse to words, one knows the contents of other minds directly. We call this extra-sensory perception, because we count only five senses. Since Buddhism regards the mind* (mano-vijñana) *as a sense (a "sixth sense," as we ambiguously say), telepathy is not, for it, extra-sensory but acute mental sensing.*

3. The divine eye *(listed first by Mahayana): This is something like the six million dollar man's bionic eye, except that, in addition to being superhumanly sharp, it sees the fruiting of karma and the place of rebirth of other beings.*

4. Retrocognition *(listed fourth by Mahayana): One remembers a great many of one's own former existences, in clarity and detail.*

The sixth supernormal skill, being associated directly with enlightenment, will be dealt with in the next section.

Although these skills are listed in the texts of all Buddhist traditions, they are, in general, downplayed. In Theravada, indeed, it is an offense against the Vinaya not only to claim skills one does not have but even to demonstrate those one does have. For good and Dharmic reasons, however, they can be used.

I was once in the company of a certain Theravadin bhikkhu of superior attainment (I am sure he would want his anonymity preserved) when I was stung on the finger by a wasp. I shook the wasp off, and the bhikkhu held my finger for a few moments. I thought it was very kind of him to show such sympathy, but, after many minutes had gone by and there was no swelling, I voiced my surprise. "I held your finger for a special purpose," he said mysteriously.

THE SIDDHIS

Certain Mahayana lineages are not as reticent as Theravada, and incorporate the supernormal skills prominently in their traditions. The skills mentioned are not quite the same as the Theravadin *iddhi*, although there is some overlap, and are usually called *siddhi*, a Sanskrit word meaning success, achievement, or hitting the mark. In Tibetan they are called *nyö-dub (dngos grub)*, "concrete achievement," and in Chinese *ch'êng-chiu*, "complete accomplishment." The siddhis are the skillful achievements that may be manifested by accomplished practitioners.

In Tibet, certain unusual persons are identified as Mahasiddhas or Great Accomplished Ones, ones whose siddhi is great. They are noted for the eccentricity and apparent immorality with which they live and teach. Breaking all the rules, they show how, at the proper time, rules are to be transcended.

The best known collection of stories on the Mahasiddhas is the *Caturashiti-siddha-pravritti* or "Stories of the Eighty-four Siddhas," by Abhayadatta.[3] All the siddhas in this text are from the Indian subcontinent, but the text has become very popular in Tibet. Many of the Mahasiddhas come from lowly backgrounds, are married and have jobs, some are criminals, and four (a remarkable feature in the culture of the time) are women. None of them are monks of restrained mien and obvious virtue. Their lineage is sometimes called the Crazy Wisdom Lineage.

The best known of all of them is Saraha.[4] He was a brahmin, but not a very respectable one. Although he lived like a high-caste Hindu during the day, he practiced tantric Buddhist rituals at night, and he drank alcohol, a beverage that is so repugnant to orthodox Hindus that even today it is known as *apeyya*, or "non-drink." Accused of evil living and hypocrisy, Saraha justified himself by the common Indian method of "acts of truth" *(sat-karma)*. The act of truth is of the form "If such and such be true, then may so and so [here, some extraordinary event is named] come to pass." An act of truth is said to work because truth itself is the way things are (*sat* means both "truth" and "being"). It was this power that Mahatma Gandhi used to free India from the British. He called it satyagraha, which he translated as non-violence, but which literally means "holding on to truth."

The act of truth does not have to be connected with virtue, but it must not be a lie. For example, in one famous act of truth, a prostitute was able to make the Ganges flow backwards, after many Hindu holy men had tried by spells but had failed, by saying, "If it be true that I have dealt with all my customers fairly, giving them all a good time without discriminating whether they were rich or poor, high or low caste, handsome or ugly, then let this mighty river Ganges flow backward."

Saraha performed the act of truth by plunging his hand into

boiling oil and drinking molten copper without being harmed, then he floated in water while one of his accusers sank, and finally had himself weighed and came out lighter than three iron weights each as heavy as a man. In all of these cases he had said, "If it be true that I do not drink alcohol, let my hand not be burnt, my throat not be scorched, my accuser sink in water while I float, and my weight be less than that of three men."

Now, the shocking thing about Saraha's acts of truth is not that they were connected with immorality, but that they were lies. He *did* drink alcohol. So, the only explanation (supposing that we take the stories at face value) is that Saraha caused the events to occur through the power of his superior siddhi.

The acts of truth being concluded, Saraha sang his didactic songs, known as *doha* from the name of their meter.

The account of his life concludes with an incident in which, having gone into an enstatic meditative state for twelve years, he came out of it and at once demanded the radish curry that his wife had prepared for him twelve years before. Understandably, she told him that it was no longer waiting for him. Well, he said, then he would be off to the mountains to meditate in solitude.

> But the girl replied, "A solitary body does not mean solitude. The best solitude is the mind far away from names and conceptions. You have been meditating for twelve years, yet you have not cut off the idea of radishes. What good will it do you to go to the mountains?" Saraha thought, "This is true." And so he abandoned names and conceptions.[5]

From the story of Saraha we learn that neither social rules nor one's life situation have any inherent existence. Saraha broke the rule against drinking alcohol, and lied about it, but by his miracles showed that reality was larger than such rules. Then, rather than going off into the mountains as a hermit in order to obtain the highest realization, he "abandoned names and conceptions" as a householder.

It must be noted, however, that his achievement was extraordinary. An ordinary person who drinks and lies about it is probably an alcoholic, or on the way to becoming one, and is anything but clear headed, and it is very difficult for most of us to abandon names and conceptions without going into retreat from society, at least for a time. The stories of the Mahasiddhas are not given as models for emulation, but as demonstrations that "all things [are] as space."[6]

In China, a group of Buddhist adepts known as *Lohan* (from the Sanskrit [*A*]*rahan*, i.e., Arhat in its root form with the first syllable omitted) are revered for their strange and magical behavior. There are variously said to be sixteen, eighteen, or five hundred Lohan. They are depicted as having a bizarre physical appearance (e.g., Chia-li-chia, whose eyebrows are so long he has to hold them up), or as having fantastic powers (e.g., P'an-t'o-chia, who can make himself smaller and smaller, bit by bit, until he vanishes). They are first brought to the attention of the Chinese in the Sutra of Forty-two Sections (Ssŭ-shih-êrh Chang Ching), which says

> *The Arhat is able to fly through space and assume different forms; his life is eternal, and there are times when he causes heaven and earth to quake.*[7]

The Sutra is a collection of sayings that appear to have been assembled in China on the model of the Analects of Confucius, and this particular passage has a very Taoist feel to it, describing the Arhats as if they were Taoist Immortals *(hsien-jên)*. The popularity of the Lohan may be due to this appeal to both Taoist and Confucian elements in Chinese culture.

The tradition of the Lohan passed into Korea, and also into Japan, where it merged with the indigenous Japanese tradition of the *hijiri* or mountain holy man. Many tales are told, for example, of Kobo Daishi performing acts similar to those of a *hijiri*.[8]

The stories of the Mahasiddhas and the hijiri certainly, and of the Lohan perhaps,[9] have a strong Tantric element. The Mahasiddhas and the hijiri are Tantric practitioners. In Tantric practice, one functions as a liberated being at the center of a brilliantly sparkling mandala (see chapter 10), performing, as it were, extra-samsaric magic. From this perspective, the intra-samsaric magic of the supernormal skills naturally arises.

TALISMANS

A form of intra-samsaric magic which is found throughout the Buddhist world is the use of charms and amulets. Anyone who has contact with living Buddhism notices this, but the phenome-

non has been little studied,[10] perhaps because, although researchers cannot dismiss it as a fantasy, they can discount it as
superstition. But it is too central to be ignored.

In Theravada, one finds bazaars specializing in amulets near
certain temples. They do a brisk business. In Japan, "protec-
tions" *(omamori)* may be obtained at many temples, particularly
(as it seemed to me) temples dedicated to Fudo (see chapter 1).
The *omamori* is often in the form of a miniature reproduction
of the Heart Sutra (Makahannyashingyo, The Larger Sutra on
the Heart of the Perfection of Wisdom, which, despite its name,
is quite short) packaged in such a way that it hangs neatly on a
car's rear view mirror. Some paper charms *(mamori-fuda)* are
now produced in the form of small, reflective bumper stickers.[11]
In the Tibetan tradition, a protective red thread, to be worn
around the wrist or neck, is usually handed out in connection
with a Tantric initiation.

The most elaborate ceremony involving a protective thread,
called *Paritta,* is a prominent feature of Theravada Buddhism.[12]
It is used for all kinds of intra-samsaric blessings, and can hardly
be called a corruption or a gross superstition, since it is performed by bhikkhus, often of the highest rank, and its reintro-
duction was an important part of the reform movement of the
Sangharaja, ("Leader of the Sangha,") Saranankara (1698–
1778).[13] The fact that it began as "choral recitation by monks"
(ganasajjhayana)[14] before it evolved into its present form, gives
us the clue to what might be going on.

All Buddhist traditions ascribe meritorious efficacy to the
word of the Buddha. Just hearing his words brings great merit.
In the Visuddhimagga, for instance, Buddhaghosa recounts that
once, when the Buddha was teaching, a human member of the
audience accidentally crushed a frog.[15] The frog died and was
instantly reborn as a glorious deity in the Trayastrimsha heaven,
on the top of Mount Sumeru (see appendix to chapter 6). Won-
dering what had happened to him, he reflected with his new,
divine mind, and saw that he had been a frog who had gained
merit just by hearing the sound of the Buddha's words, even
though, being a frog, he had not understood them. Thereupon,
he descended from his heaven with his retinue, gave reverence
to the Buddha, told him what had happened, and requested instruction in the Dharma, which he then received.

It is important to note that, in this account, although the Buddha's words were meritorious of themselves, they only produced

intra-samsaric happiness. The frog who became a god needed to apply himself so as to build the practice of Dharma on this fortunate foundation in order to move towards nirvana.

The Triple Jewel—the Buddha, the Dharma, and the Samgha—is one jewel with three aspects. The Dharma is expressed by the Buddha in his actions of body, speech, and mind, and it is preserved and again manifested, by the Samgha. Thus, contacting any part of the Triple Jewel in any aspect is meritorious. However, unless the good fortune produced by this merit is appropriated for the practice of Dharma, no progress will be made and one will slip back into a less fortunate rebirth.

Buddhist talismans, then, being an aspect of the Triple Jewel, ward off intra-samsaric evil so as to provide the opportunity for practice that will lead beyond samsara.

Breaking the Cycle

The last of the six abhijñas is called *ashravakshaya-jñana* (in Sanskrit) or *asavakkhaya-ñana* (in Pali). The translation of this term has given scholars a lot of trouble. It is clear that it refers in general to the ending of samsara for the individual who experiences it, and is more of a know-*what* than a know-*how* (a supernormal knowledge rather than a supernormal skill) but what it means precisely is more difficult to understand. Jñana is knowledge or wisdom, and *kshaya* means destruction. That part of the compound does not present a problem: it is the certain knowledge (jñana) that something has been destroyed *(kshaya)* finally and for ever.

What has been destroyed is called *ashrava,* and this is the word which is not clear. *Ashrava* is a Buddhist Hybrid Sanskrit word that appears to have been incorrectly generated from a Prakrit word, which is perhaps more authentically preserved in the Pali as *asava.* This comes from *sru,* to flow, with the prefix *a,* which means towards. So, something is flowing "towards," either out or in. The standard *Pali-English Dictionary* suggests "outflow or influx."[16] The Tibetans translated the word with *zag pa,* "contamination," while the Chinese decided on the character *lou* meaning "to leak," literally, "what happens when there is an ill-fitting door which admits rain."

Both the Pali and the Sanskrit traditions mention a fourfold division of *asava* (ashrava):

1. Kamasava (kamashrava), *"sensual flux";*

2. Bhavasava (bhavashrava), *"life flux";*

3. Ditthasava (drishtyashrava), *"view flux";*

4. Avijjasava (avidyashrava), *"ignorance flux."*

When samsara ends for an individual, these fluxes are destroyed (kshaya) and one realizes this for certain (jñana): they are, therefore, written as *kamashravakshayajñana,* "the certainty that the sensual flux has been finally destroyed," and so forth. What happens, apparently, is that sense data, attachment to life, or death (the eros/thanatos drive) viewpoints about how reality truly is, and all-pervading ignorance, no longer "flow."

It may not be possible to understand what this condition is like when we try to examine it from the point of view of intra-samsaric ignorance. However, we may be able to understand by analogy what it is that has been destroyed.

The child psychologist Jean Piaget has described how human babies construct their reality.[17] The very young baby lives in a state of primitive self-absorption, which Piaget would call solipsism were it not for the fact that the child is not even aware of itself. Objects and subjects are all one big blur. Gradually the child learns the skills of accommodation to objects and assimilation to itself as subject, and increasingly differentiates between the operations of accommodation and assimilation. The activities are complementary and reinforce each other.

> *Intelligence[18] thus begins neither with knowledge of the self nor of things as such but with knowledge of their interaction, and it is by orienting itself simultaneously toward the two poles of that interaction that intelligence organizes the world by organizing itself.[19]*

The result of the process is that

> . . . the object is fully constructed in correlation with causality to the extent that this coordination of schemata results in the formation of an intelligible spatio-temporal world *endowed with permanence.*[20]

Reality is then constructed as one containing autonomously existing subjects and objects, with an interface between them across which something seems to flow.[21] It is this flow, perhaps, that is the *ashrava* of Buddhism.

Piaget tells us that when the child successfully understands the subject-object distinction it has correctly understood reality. Buddhism would prefer to put more weight on Piaget's word *construction* than Piaget does himself. Samsara is a construction, and samsara is suffering. A child's reality is constructed, and he or she openly suffers and makes no bones about it. So, the child has constructed samsara, with the assistance of its parents and teachers, and conditioned by the fruiting of its karma. Piaget has given us a very insightful account of this process. According to Buddhism, the child now feels locked into a circle of repetition that inherently exists.

Nirvana is release from this circle, and in some way or another it must involve the deconstruction of the circular delusion that we call reality. This deconstruction, however, is not the demolition of existence leaving only non-existence. As we shall see more clearly when we examine the Madhyamika system in the next chapter, nihilism is just as much a delusion as inherent existence. The deconstruction of samsaric reality involves the understanding of the relativity of *all* world-views, without coming to the conclusion that relativity is the true world-view.

If ashrava is indeed the subject-object flux as identified by Piaget, we can then understand its fourfold division, and the certain knowledge of its destruction, as follows:

1. "The certainty that the subject-object flux of sense data has been finally destroyed": neither objects nor subjects are now regarded as inherently existing.

2. "The certainty that the subject-object flux of living has been finally destroyed": we no longer see life as inherently good, so that we want to live forever (the eros drive), nor as inherently bad, so that we want to kill ourselves (the thanatos drive).

3. "The certainty that the subject-object flux of viewpoints has been finally destroyed": we see reality as spacelike, not imposing apparently autonomous patterns on it.

4. *"The certainty that the subject-object flux of* ignorance *has been finally destroyed": this is the root flux; it looks less like a separate flux than a comprehensive way of speaking of the other three. Perhaps for this reason it is omitted from the list in some traditions.*

The circle of repetition, which the Buddha saw at his enlightenment and then broke, is usually explained as a wheel of twelve members.[22] The members do not, strictly speaking, *cause* each other, they arise in dependence on each other, according to the formula "this being so, that appears." This is called interdependent arising (*pratitya–samutpada*, "coming up together next to each other"). The twelve members, in the order which they condition each other, are as follows:

1. Avidya: *beginningless ignorance, symbolized by an old, blind woman feeling her way uncertainly with a stick.*

2. Samskara: *conditioned or composite reality, symbolized by a potter who, from a lump of clay that could become anything, is making particular pots. So we find that although reality is in itself open, for us it is "fired" into one shape and not another.*

3. Vijñana: *consciousness, symbolized by a monkey leaping about from object to object just as our conditioned mind moves constantly from one idea to the next.*

4. Nama-rupa: *"name and form," the codependence of body and mind, symbolized by two men in a boat.*

5. Shadayatana: *the six senses (the five physical senses and the mental sense), symbolized by a house with six windows (or, sometimes, two houses with three windows each), representing by windows that we might prefer to call "the doors of perception."*

6. Sparsha: *touch (mentioned here as the typical sense, as it is in Abhidharma, since the data "touch" or contact the sense organ), represented by a man and woman embracing.*

7. Vedana: *sensory input, represented by a man being pierced through the eye by an arrow. The symbolism here is not the direct one of pain, but the indirect symbolism of the entry of sense data through the sense organ to the sense consciousness.*

8. Trishna: *craving or thirst, symbolized by a man drinking alcohol.*

9. Upadana: *grasping, symbolized by a monkey (or sometimes a human) picking fruit from a tree. Craving and grasping are closely related but distinguishable. Buddhaghosa says a person in the desert who thinks about water is a symbol of craving, whereas arriving at the oasis and actually drinking the water is a symbol of grasping. We may have a desire for something, that is to say, but not necessarily act on the desire.*

10. Bhava: *the craving to become (to become immortal or to continue living after one's death) or to be annihilated (to kill oneself or to cease living after one's death), i.e., the eros/thanatos drive, symbolized by a woman who is either in a seductive pose or pregnant.*

11. Jati: *birth, represented directly by a woman giving birth.*

12. Jara-marana: *aging and death, again represented directly by a corpse being carried to the cemetery.*

As it is a circle, member twelve becomes the condition for the arising of member one again, in another rebirth.

This circle can be cut at any point, but the most effective place to cut it is at avidya. We could, for instance, try to stop the circle between sparsha and vedana, saying to ourselves, "Sense data is out there, but I'm not going to feel it," but, apart from being very difficult, this has the danger of leading either to mental disorder or, at best, to the extreme enstasis of the state of neither notions nor non-notions, which the Buddha entered during his seventh act and found that it was not liberation. By dispelling avidya, however, the whole cycle falls apart. We come unstuck, samsara and rebirth is finished. If we are bodhisattvas, of course, we will choose to remain in samsara, although no longer trapped in it, to assist all other sentient beings.

NOTES
to Chapter Eight

1. Thomas S. Kuhn, *The Structure of Scientific Revolutions,* 2nd edition, enlarged (University of Chicago Press, 1970). For some of the controversy raised by Kuhn's book, see *Paradigms and Revolutions: Appraisals and Applications of Thomas Kuhn's Philosophy of Science,* ed. Gary Gutting (University of Notre Dame Press, 1980).

2. Quoted from the entry *ABHIÑÑA* in *Buddhist Dictionary: Manual of Buddhist Terms and Doctrines* by Nyanatiloka. Fourth, revised edition, edited by Nyānaponika (Kandy: Buddhist Publication Society, 1980). For an extended treatment, from an orthodox Theravadin standpoint, see Buddhaghosa's *Visuddhimagga,* chapter 12 (for English translations, see chapter 7, note 4).

3. There is a literal translation from the Tibetan version by James B. Robinson, *Buddha's Lions: The Lives of the Eighty-Four Siddhas* (Berkeley, CA: Dharma Publishing, 1979). A freer version, which mixes translation and commentary (unfortunately, without warning the reader as to which is which) is that of Keith Dowman, *Masters of Mahamudra: Songs and Histories of the Eighty-Four Buddhist Siddhas* (Albany, NY: SUNY Press, 1985). In his glossary, Dowman (p. 429) lists the "eight great siddhis" as: power to wield the sword of awareness, to pass through matter, to create, to destroy, to dispense the pill of third-eye vision, to dispense the eye-salve of omniscience, to speed–walk, alchemical powers. Speed–walking is a supernormal power of locomotion making special use of the element air. A spontaneous occurrence of speed–walking (which he calls trance walking) is reported by Lama Govinda in his autobiographical *The Way of the White Clouds* (1970 Shambhala reprint of the British edition of 1966), pp. 77–78, and discussed in chapter 5 (pp. 80–83).

4. See the study of him, with a translation of the King *Dohas,* by H. V. Guenther, *The Royal Song of Saraha* (Shambhala, with Routledge and Kegan Paul, 1973).

5. *Buddha's Lions,* p. 43.

6. *Masters of Mahamudra,* p. 69.

7. Quoted from the translation of the sutra in *Sermons of a Buddhist Abbot* by Rt. Rev. Soyen Shaku, translated by Daisetz Teitaro Suzuki (New York: Samuel Weiser, 1971 reprint of the 1906 edition), p. 5. For an English translation with commentary from the oral tradition of Chinese Buddhism, see Ven. Master Hsuan Hua, *The Sutra in Forty-Two Sections* (San Francisco: Buddhist Text Translation Society, 1976).

8. See, for example, "Saint Kobo's Well," "The Willow Well of Kobo," and "The Kobo Chestnut Trees" in Richard M. Dorson, *Folk Legends of Japan* (Rutland, VT: Tuttle, 1962).

9. A Chinese Buddhist gentleman once showed me his rosary, consisting of beads carved to represent the heads of the Lohan, on which he said a Tantric mantra consisting of OM MANI PADME HUM and something else ("You can't say," he explained, meaning, I suppose, that I did not have the initiation which authorized me to say whatever it was) before an image of Amitabha Buddha. This synthesis may have been unique to him, and I cannot generalize from it.

10. An important recent book on the subject is *The Other Side of Theravada Buddhism: The Buddhist Saints of the Forest and the Cult of Amulets,* by Stanley Jeyaraja Tambiah (Cambridge University Press, 1984). Dr. Tambiah's approach is sympathetic, but he interprets the data by means of the anthropological categories of "indexical symbol" and "shifter," and I cannot say that I follow him.

11. Such a reflective sticker is pictured in *Japanese Religion: Unity and Diversity,* 3rd edition (Belmont, CA: 1982), p. 196.

12. Lily De Silva, "PARITTA—A Historical and Religious Study of the Buddhist Ceremony for Peace and Prosperity in Sri Lanka," *Spolia Zeylanica* (Bulletin of the National Museums of Sri Lanka), vol. 36, part 1 (1981), pp. 1–175.

13. De Silva, p. 149.

14. De Silva, p. 148.

15. Translated by Henry Clarke Warren, *Buddhism in Translations* (New York: Atheneum, 1962—and subsequently—reprint of the 1896 Harvard University Press edition) pp. 301–302.

16. Pali Text Society Dictionary (1921–1925 and subsequently), columns 114b to 115a.

17. *The Construction of Reality in the Child,* translated by Margaret Cook (New York: Basic Books, 1954 and subsequently) from Jean Piaget, *La Construction du réel chez l'enfant* (1937).

18. By "intelligence" Piaget seems to mean something like *vikalpa* (judging or classifying mind). The difficulty of understanding western psychological texts from a Buddhist standpoint, and vice versa, arises from the disparity between the richness of the Buddhist psychological vocabulary and the (at present) poverty of the western psychological vocabulary.

19. Piaget, pp. 354–355.

20. Piaget, p. 88. The italics are mine.

21. Piaget, p. 355, figure 2.

22. *King Udrayana and the Wheel of Life* (cited above in chapter 6, note 7). See also figure 9.

Chapter 9

TEACHING

(Act 11 of the Buddha)

Having attained complete freedom of body, speech, and mind, Shakyamuni, who can now be called "Buddha" without qualification, remained for some time resting in his achievement. Then, one of the deities, variously called Shakra, Brahma, or Indra, requested that he speak of his enlightenment and explain how he obtained it, so that other beings could follow him out of the cycle of suffering.

Theravada regards this as a request that was really necessary. The Buddha did not know, they say, if there were any beings who would understand him, but after the deity had told him that there were, the Buddha looked at samsara with his divine eye and saw that there were "beings with little dust on their eyes." For Theravadins, the Buddha can know anything he wishes, but he must first apply his mind to it. Mahayanists, however, say that the Buddha is omniscient, so that he already knew about the beings with little dust on their eyes. However, he pretended he did not, so as to give the deity the chance to gain merit by requesting the teaching.

In any case, it has become standard practice that before any Buddhist teacher speaks of the Dharma, the audience makes a formal request for it. The Dharma is not imposed upon those who do not wish to hear it, but once it has been requested, the teacher is bound by compassion to teach as well as possible.

The First Sermon

All Buddhist traditions are unanimous in recording that the first teaching given by the Buddha was the Sutra Turning the Wheel of Dharma (Dharmachakrapravartana Sutra). The Dharma is compared to a wheel (chakra) that is set turning by these first public words of the Enlightened One. In Indian symbolism, the wheel has stood for power ever since the Aryans conquered the subcontinent around 1500 B.C.E. with their secret weapon of the war chariot. A war chariot is mostly wheel and very little chariot, so by synechdoche a turning wheel came to mean a conquering chariot. A wheel is therefore appropriately placed in the center of the flag of the Republic of India.

At his birth, it was prophesized that Shakyamuni could either become a world emperor (*chakravartin*, "wheel turner") or a Buddha. The wheel of conquest is taken over by Buddhism and used to refer to the conquest *of* samsara rather than conquest *within* it. Once again, it is relevant to point out that the Buddha was born into the kshatriya or warrior caste.

The first teaching, called by the Chinese the Wheel Sutra (Lun Ching) and often known in English as the First Sermon, is a summary of Buddhism. If one decides to follow the Buddhist path, it is the best place to start, but it is something one never leaves until final enlightenment. The Abhidharmakosha, for instance, structures its explanation of the path as a spiral of progressively greater understanding of the teaching proclaimed in the Wheel Sutra.

THE FOURFOLD TRUTH

The heart of the Wheel Sutra is the exposition of the Fourfold Truth. It is better to call this teaching the Fourfold Truth than the Four Truths, since they are not four separate truths, but one truth in four aspects. The Fourfold Truth is not a creed or set of concepts proposed as "the faith of Buddhists," but a diagnosis of the problem of existence and the prescription of an appropriate therapy.

The Fourfold Truth can be put simply in four Sanskrit words: *duhkha* (suffering), *samudaya* (arising), *nirodha* (stopping) and *marga* (path).

1. Duhkha

The first part of the Fourfold Truth contains the only word that is difficult to translate. It says that conditioned existence, or samsara, is duhkha (Pali: *dukkha*). English equivalents of duhkha that have been offered include pain, misery, suffering, and ill. The most satisfactory translation, ironically, is perhaps "unsatisfactory." For the moment, we will leave it in Sanskrit and Pali, so that we can come to understand it in the light of the standard explanations.

Theravadins usually teach dukkha directly out of the Wheel Sutra as it has been preserved in the Pali.[1] The Buddha gives there a list of things that are dukkha: birth, aging, sickness, death, sorrow, grief, weeping, despair, meeting things that are not liked, losing things that are liked, and not obtaining what is desired. In short, the body, the five clusters *(skandha;* Pali: *khandha),* is dukkha.

This means that the normal events of life, from birth to death, and associated difficulties, whether physical or mental, are dukkha, and indeed the very fact of having been born at all (i.e., of being embodied) is dukkha. When dukkha is stated thus baldly, a common reaction is to point to all the joys of life and accuse the Buddha of pessimism. But joy is not being denied, it is being pointed out that joy is impermanent, so that even if we do experience joy, we are going to lose it. This is the aspect of "losing things that are liked." In fact, it is impossible to explain why beings would be attached to samsara if there were no joy at all in it.

Tibetan Buddhism tries to convince us of the truth of duhkha by analyzing it on three levels.[2]

The first level is "the suffering of pain" (*duhkha-duhkhata,* literally "the duhkha of duhkha"). This is physical or mental pain, which all beings, even animals, experience and recognize as suffering. However, when we experience pain, we look forward to a time when it will end. "Sure, work is bad, but I have a vacation coming up." Change is imagined to be the end of suffering. But, even on vacation we experience suffering. Packing, traveling, overeating, guarding our possessions, and spending too much, are all suffering. Even if we really are "having a wonderful time," we have to leave and go back to work. So we say, "When I retire, I'll move to that place where I had a wonderful vacation and I'll never leave." Then we find that, once there, we get bored, we get sick, and, eventually, we die. So, the second level of duhkha is the suffering of change *(viparinama-duhkhata)* where change *(viparinama)* has the nuance of "decay," or "change for the worse." Until we look closely at it, we mistake change for happiness. When we look closely, we see that it is suffering.

The suffering of change is clearly evident during the practice of sitting meditation. When we first take our seat, we try for a comfortable position. After some time, however, it becomes uncomfortable, and we want to change our position. This indicates that our first position, although undeniably comfortable at the time, was not *thoroughly* comfortable. It was uncomfortable, but the discomfort was very small. Then, it grew until we became painfully aware of it. In other words, sitting is suffering.

The third level of duhkha is derived directly from the observations made at the second level. Since we have discovered that, whether we are at work or away on vacation, that is, wherever we are in samsara, we are still suffering, we conclude that samsara itself *is* suffering. And, since we have found, during sitting meditation, that no position of the body is intrinsically comfortable, we have to admit that the body *is* suffering. This is called *samskara-duhkhata,* the suffering of conditioned existence, and it is what the Buddha meant when he said, in the Wheel Sutra, that the five clusters are themselves suffering. It is not that there is suffering *in* samsara, along with no suffering, but that samsara *is* suffering, through and through. Samsara and duhkha are synonymous. This is something that is not readily apprehended. It is said to be like a very fine hair in one's eye. Because of the extreme fineness of the hair it is only noticed by someone whose pain threshold is very low. So, only when the mind has been sensitized to suffering by Dharma practice can it appreciate this aspect of misery.

2. The Arising of Duhkha

The first part of the Fourfold Truth identifies the disease that afflicts all samsaric beings. The second part of the Fourfold Truth gives the etiology of the disease. *Samudaya,* arising, refers to the origin or the source of suffering. The root of suffering is *upadana,* grasping. Reality is flowing, but we attempt to freeze it; it is spacelike, but we attempt to parcel it up. From this comes, at the very least, disappointment, since when look at what we have grasped, we find it is not what we thought it was.

Four types of grasping are traditionally identified: grasping at sense objects, at viewpoints, at ceremonies, and at the word "I."

Grasping at sense objects *(kamopadana)* leads to suffering because anything physical decays. A new car, for example, is magically enticing, and apparently permanently glistening, in the catalog. In the showroom, meticulously polished, it looks immune from decay. But when we have bought it and driven it for a time, the reality of its impermanence becomes very clear.

So, we may say, of course I know that sense objects are impermanent, but I am an intellectual, I go for the seemingly enduring world of ideas. This is the second type of grasping: grasping at ideas or viewpoints *(drishty-upadana).* However, ideas are not enduring: we cannot hold onto them any more than we can hold on to sense objects. Views about the world such as the existence of phlogiston or the value of blood-letting seem foolish today. We cannot imagine that sane, intelligent people took such things seriously. Yet they undoubtedly did. How do we know that our views on oxygen or vitamins will not look equally foolish to our descendants?

When grasping at viewpoints is very strong, we call it dogmatism. The dogmatic person (the person with overmuch trust [*saddha*] whom we met in chapter 7) is so attached to views that he or she forces them on others and may even kill for them. Most of us feel uncomfortable (that is, experience suffering) in the presence of such a person. Whether they are trying to sell us their brand of politics, religion, or vacuum cleaner, we wish they would leave us alone to make our own decision.

Grasping at viewpoints is often subdivided into four *viparyasa* or topsy-turvy viewpoints: what is impermanent is viewed as permanent, what is characterized by suffering is viewed as not characterized by suffering, what is without inherent existence is viewed as possessing inherent existence, and what is ugly is viewed as lovely. When we turn these views the right way up, we are entitled, like Joshu, to put our shoes on our head.

The third type of grasping is grasping at ceremonies (*shila-vratopadana*, "grasping at rules of conduct"). This is the belief that I can purify my mind simply by some ritual. It is what we might call superstition. When this aspect of grasping was formulated, Hindus and other non-Buddhists, who were thought to have empty rituals and meaningless ascetic practices, may have been chiefly in mind, but it is also a warning that if even Buddhist practices are done mindlessly rather than mindfully, liberation from samsara cannot be obtained.

Finally, and most perniciously, is the grasping at the word "I" (*atma-vadopadana*). Because we use the word, we think it must refer to something in an objective, autonomous sense. When we think like this, we know that we have to protect our "self" at all costs. This leads directly to the suffering of isolation, to the fear of others, and the wish to harm them in order to protect oneself.

Grasping at "I" is the root grasping, since if there is no grasping at the sense of self, the kind of self that needs to grasp onto sense objects, viewpoints, or ceremonies is not experienced. It needs to be carefully noted that the problem arises by grasping at the *sense* of self and at the *words* "I," "me," "mine," and so forth. Grasping at the real, inherently existing self does not create a problem, for it cannot be done: there is, according to Buddhism, no such self to grasp. Grasping at the "self" is like falling in love with a hologram of a man or woman.

We call a person selfish when they spend all their time amassing wealth, grasping onto sense objects. We could notice also, perhaps, a certain hardness of ego in dogmatic people, who grasp onto viewpoints. They often hold themselves stiffly, as if they were under attack, and indeed they may feel they are, for if their views are not accepted by others, doubt is thrown on the validity of their views, and, therefore, they feel, on themselves. Again, ceremonies for the sake of ceremonies can be a way of defending the supposed inherently existing self. In severe cases, this can become the imprisoning psychological disorder of obsessive-compulsive repetition.

3. The Stopping of the Arising of Duhkha

The third part of the Fourfold Truth is a message of hope. Our disease is not incurable. The Buddha, as the Master Physician

(Bhaishajya-guru), has identified the disease as duhkha and the cause as grasping *(upadana)*. Now, he analyzes the cause in more detail. Suffering does not come to us because of fate or the decree of a deity, it comes from our own past actions, and, therefore, we can do something about it. When the mechanism of the fruiting of action is understood, suffering can be stopped. This part of the Fourfold Truth is therefore called *nirodha*, stopping or extinction. The analysis is done according to the twelvefold circle of interdependent origination. (see chapter 8).

4. The Way to the Stopping of the Arising of Duhkha:

The last part of the Fourfold Truth is the remedy for the disease of suffering. It is called *marga* or the path. More precisely, it is the Holy Eightfold Path *(aryashtangika-marga)*. The practice is called a path because suffering is ended bit by bit, with many reversals, and it is something we have to tread. The remedy is not a pill that works all at once and without our cooperation.

The eight limbs of the path are as follows:

1. Right View (samyag-drishti): *understanding reality as it truly is, rather than as our deluded consciousness thinks it is. The basis of right view is the correct understanding of the Fourfold Truth.*

2. Right Attitude (samyak-samkalpa): *judging or classifying mind, the mind that we ordinarily use in going about our business, is to be free of attachment, hate, and confusion.*

3. Right Speech (samyag-vak): *helpful and compassionate speech, free from lying, backbiting, and so forth.*

4. Right Action (samyak-karmanta): *helpful and compassionate conduct, free from killing, stealing, and sexual misconduct.*

5. Right Livelihood (samyag-ajiva): *earning our living in a manner that helps, rather than harms, sentient beings. Careers that are traditionally contraindicated are selling weapons, selling animals for slaughter or people for slavery, and selling alcohol or poison (which would include dealing in drugs); working in a slaughterhouse or fishing; military service; and any employment necessarily involving deceit or treachery.* There is considerable variation in how Buddhists choose to follow these recommendations.

6. *Right Effort* (samyag-vyayama): *actively working to overcome our hindrances and negativities, and cultivating our wholesome qualities.*

7. *Right Mindfulness* (samyak-smriti): *maintaining awareness of reality as it truly is.*

8. *Right Concentration* (samyak-samadhi): *meditation according to proper Buddhist principles.*

These eight limbs can be condensed into the Triple Practice *(trishiksha):*

1. *Conduct* (shila): *limbs three through six, and the recommendations of the* Pañcha-shila *(see chapter 3).*

2. *Concentration* (samadhi): *limbs seven and eight. Concentration, or focusing the mind, is meditation in a formal session. Mindfulness is the maintenance of awareness, or a meditative attitude, in ordinary activities.*

3. *Study* (prajña): *limbs one and two.*

All three parts of the Triple Practice interact and support each other. By study of the Dharma, the true nature of reality is understood intellectually. This intellectual understanding is directly experienced in meditation, and by proper conduct action is brought into line with understanding. Then, proper conduct helps to calm and purify the mind, which in turn assists Dharma study.

Progress along the path is marked in various ways. A common set of signposts goes from hearing to thinking to practicing. At first, we listen to the teaching, memorize it, and try to make some basic sense of it. This is the path "composed of hearing" *(shruta-mayi).* Then, we investigate it critically. This is the path "composed of thinking or reflection" *(chinta-mayi).* We then incorporate the teaching into our lives by meditation and moral conduct. This is the path "composed of practice or cultivation" *(bhavana-mayi).*

This triple division can refer to the appropriation of any aspect of the path. When the entire path is looked at, it is sometimes taught as fivefold. The beginning is the path of preparation *(sambhara-marga),* also called the path of "putting on the armor." The second level is the path of application or putting forth effort *(prayoga-marga),* in which the Fourfold Truth is understood intellectually. At the next level, the path of seeing *(darshana-marga),* the Fourfold Truth is directly experienced, and this insight is applied in the path of practice *(bhavana-marga).* Finally, there is the path of completion or attainment *(nishtha-marga),* also called the path of no more learning or no practice *(ashaiksha-marga),* since at that level the virtues are performed automatically.

A path structure often taught in Theravada has four main divisions: the one who has "entered the stream" *(sotapanna),* i.e., definitely moving or streaming towards enlightenment; the one who will return only once *(sakadagami)* to the human world before attaining liberation; the one who will never return to the human world *(anagami),* being destined to attain liberation after rebirth in one of the heavens; and the one who is fully liberated *(arahat).*

At some point along each of these paths a condition of "non-lapsing" is identified, that is, of being definitely on course to final liberation with no possibility of slipping back or being reborn in the "defiled realms" of the animals, the pretas, or the hells. The identification of the non-lapsing point seems to vary with the lineage. In Theravada, the "stream-winner" *(sotapanna)* is said to be firmly established. In the Mahayana, non-lapsing is said to occur at the level of the Path of Seeing. In Far Eastern Mahayana, the seventh or eighth level of the Bodhisattva Path (see chapter 1) is identified as the non-lapsing stage, but this is only one of many traditions taught in Tibetan Mahayana. The relationship of the various paths to each other, across and even within lineages, is unclear.

Transmission of Teachings

Buddhism appears to have a Canon of Scripture. However, when such a supposed Canon is looked for, it proves troublesome to find.[3] The notion of Canon is Jewish, Christian, and Muslim, but it is not Buddhist. There has never been a Buddhist equivalent of the Rabbinate, the Episcopate, or the Caliphate charged with the establishment of a closed and authoritative list of writings, and indeed the very idea of the centrality of Book is foreign to Buddhism. The center of Buddhism is not the word of the Buddha, nor even the Buddha. It is bodhi, the enlightened mind. Buddhas are of supreme importance because they manifest bodhi completely, but exactly that same bodhi is also the goal, and in some sense the essence, of all sentient beings. The speech of a Buddha *(buddha-vachana)* is of great significance, for it is both liberated and liberating, but it does not come from on high, it points back to the bodhi that is incipiently in the unliberated being who hears the speech. The text is, in the final analysis, expendable in favor of the practitioner's own bodhi. Zen Buddhism says it is "not dependent upon words and letters." This does not mean that it can decide that anything at all is true Buddhism but that bodhi is the true teacher, and once it has been realized, the texts may be ignored.

Therefore, although it was, according to the traditional account, only three years after Shakyamuni's final nirvana that his words were assembled into a body of teaching, the transmission was oral for more than four hundred years. A collection of the teachings as preserved in Pali was committed to writing, apparently for the first time, between 43 and 29 B.C.E. in Sri Lanka, but even then this was not done to establish an authoritative canon but to gain merit in the hope of ending a disastrous famine.

This being said, there is a great amount of authoritative literature in Buddhism, and it is a highly revered source of teaching. Something must therefore be said about it.

The Buddha spoke when requested and as needed on whatever topic came up. After his final nirvana, these *ad hoc* teachings were seen to fall into two main groups: teaching especially about monastic regulations (Vinaya) and general teachings (Dharma). The tradition grew up that all the Vinaya texts had been remembered by Ven. Upali, and all the Dharma texts by Ven. Ananda. Each text was then introduced by the formula "Thus have I heard." The "I" was understood to be either Upali or Ananda, as appropriate, and the presence of this formula at the head of a text became a mark of its authenticity. It had been heard by a reliable witness.

The opening formula goes on ". . . at one time." This is said to indicate that the teaching was given on a definite occasion, but because the Dharma is timeless, the actual date is not specified. Then there follows an indication of the place of the teaching, e.g., ". . . the Blessed One was at the city of Shravasti," and any other information that is thought to be useful in setting the scene. The Buddha is then requested to teach on some matter, and the teaching accordingly follows.

The form of the teaching is oral in style even in its written form, full of the repetitions and stock phrases which assist memorization. This indicates that for many centuries the teachings were remembered by "reciters," and when one wanted to hear a teaching one had not memorized, the appropriate reciter had to be called in. It is still the custom to memorize as much as possible, although the written texts are now used as an *aide memoire*. In English translations, the repetitions are sometimes replaced by dots. Standard lists are indicated by the phrase "until you come to," which was originally a rubric (i.e., "recite the standard list from 'A' *until you come to* 'Z'") rather than part of the text.

At some point the corpus known as Dharma was split into two: elementary or general teachings (Sanskrit: Sutra; Pali: Sutta) and advanced or specialized teachings (Abhidharma or Abhidhamma). This tripartite division became standard and is called the Triple Basket (Sanskrit: Tripitaka; Pali: Tipitaka). The image is that of Indian street vendors who carry their wares of nuts, fruits, and so forth in baskets on their heads. The baskets are joined together to make a single utensil, but only one sort of food is in each basket. So, Vinaya, Sutra, and Abhidharma (usually mentioned in that order) are gathered in clearly distinguishable baskets, but order within an individual basket is not readily discernible. Sometimes the texts are arranged by length, sometimes by the feeling that they are linked in some way, sometimes they are merely lists of increasing length, and then again the system breaks down into "miscellaneous." There is some attempt at ordering by topic in the Vinaya, and indeed the Vinaya, because of its supreme practical importance, is the most organized and probably the oldest of the baskets.

The most succinct collection of texts is that preserved in Pali. Known as the Pali Tipitaka, it is indeed just that. Three baskets and no more. If the tripartite division is very early, as it seems to be, then the claim of Theravadins to have the oldest surviving (if not the original) collection of texts is worthy of respect. Its relative brevity, and the fact that it is closed, probably gave rise to the illusion, in the minds of Christian and quasi-Christian Buddhologists, that they were dealing with a canon. They unhesitatingly dubbed it "The Pali Canon," and so it remains in textbooks to this day. The fact that this "canon" is never presented by itself, as the Bible might be, but is always set forth by a specific living teacher in the context of a specific commentarial lineage, mostly escaped their notice. When they did suspect something of the kind, they invented the mystifying category "semi-canonical" for the texts that did not seem to them to be "canonical."

The other two major extant collections of writings, in Tibetan and Chinese, can only be called a canon in the loosest possible sense. A number of texts appear to be variants of those found in the Pali, but by far the greater number of them are known only to the Mahayana.

Theravadins sometimes accuse the Mahayanists of inventing texts, while Mahayanists reply that the Theravadins did not receive the fullness of the teaching. Western Buddhologists have often sided with the Theravadins, but on the un-Buddhist basis of "earlier is better." This standard appears to be an amalgam of Protestant prejudice and the claimed objectivity of the modern historical-critical method. Protestantism regards the words of Jesus, insofar as they can be recovered, as more reliable than the writings of the Church Fathers. This Protestant assumption is found in a secularized form in historical-critical method, which calculates authenticity as inversely proportional to the distance from the authoritative source, a founder who lived at a definite historical time.

But what is the authoritative source in Buddhism? It is bodhi as it continues to be manifested in the lineage of truly realized teachers. It is always fresh. The Large Sutra on Perfect Wisdom, a Mahayana sutra, says that any teaching by a realized disciple is a teaching of the Buddha because all bodhi is the same.[4] It is notable that when a teacher is asked about his authority to teach he does not point to a body of approved texts but traces his ordination lineage, all the way back, if possible, to Shakyamuni Buddha himself.

With this in mind, it seems that the arrangement of the Tibetan collection is the most logical. It divides the teachings into Kanjur (bka' 'gyur), "Translations of the Buddha Word," and Tenjur *(bstan 'gyur),* "Translations of Teachings," that is, broadly, what the Buddha said and what the authorized commentators said. Interestingly, the Abhidharma and the Vinaya, which are part of the supposed "canon" in Pali, are found in the Tenjur.

The Chinese collection is quite diffuse. It exists in many versions, and it is not closed. Generally, the words of the Buddha are collected in the earlier volumes and the commentaries of the teachers in the later volumes. There are, in addition, histories, biographies, and dictionaries, catalogues of other versions of the collection, and even a volume on Hindu, Manichean, and Nestorian writings. Despite the complete absence of any discernible tripartite division, it is still referred to as San Tsang, "The Threefold Treasury," an attempt to translate Tripitaka into Chinese. More accurately, it is also called Ta Tsang, "The Great Treasury."

Remarkably little has been translated into any European language. The situation in regard to the Pali texts is the most satisfactory. Most of the Pali Tipitaka is available in an at least serviceable English translation, due to the tireless efforts of the Pali Text Society,[5] but only relatively tiny portions of the Mahayana texts have been translated into any language other than Japanese. Even when translations are done, scholars, particularly of the Chinese texts, still manifest a quasi-Christian reverence for the sutras, which are almost *as a rule* published without commentary, and are therefore largely incomprehensible.[6]

By an auspicious conjunction of karmic fruits, however, Buddhism is now being taught in the west by living teachers of all the major lineages. The pioneers of European and American Buddhist studies had to rely almost entirely on texts, and, having learned the languages as best they could, they made intelligent guesses at the meaning. Sometimes these guesses were good, but all too often they were bad. Western Buddhology is currently undergoing rapid changes as it realizes, by contact with the living tradition, its mistakes, and seeks to correct them. But, there is still a long way to go.

In the face of the mountain of untranslated, and often unedited, material, it is perilous to make generalizations about Buddhism. This book is, of course, an attempt to do just that, but it can be no more than an attempt. When all of the texts have been translated and studied in the light of their authoritative commentaries, this book will need, at the least, a new edition.

Skillful Means

Language is inextricably intra-samsaric. Therefore, it cannot describe anything extra-samsaric. The Buddha's reluctance to teach his vision is indicative of this central difficulty. If unliberated beings misunderstand everything that is said, and reality is in any case spacelike so that it cannot be parceled up and analyzed, can the Buddhas say anything meaningful at all? And yet, if they say nothing, unliberated beings remain unliberated. So, *something* must be said.

The rule is, as I said when discussing Abhidharma: Buddhist teaching is transformation manifesting as information. This rule will now be explained.

Buddhist teaching is called, in Sanskrit, *upaya-kaushalya,* skillful means or skill in means. In Chinese it is called *fang-pien,* appropriate method. That is, the teaching is a tool, and it must be applied appropriately. Since beings are different, different things must be said or done to aid them. This technique is compared to that of a skilled physician who diagnoses different diseases and prescribes different remedies appropriate for each disease. Non-Buddhist teachers, on the other hand, are compared to quacks who prescribe the same remedy for every disease. The variety, and even the logical incompatibility, of Buddhist teachings is seen as a strength rather than a weakness.

Skillful means does not describe reality, since that is impossible, but seeks to transform the mind of the suffering being so that it may itself come to see reality as it truly is. In Chinese, a Buddha's teaching activity is called *chiao-hua.* The first character means "teach" and the second means "change" or "transform," so the compound means "teaching so as to transform," "transforming by teaching," or "teaching, that is, transformation." What appears to be philosophy in Buddhism is more like pedagogy. The unliberated being is regarded as a child or fool *(bala).* Because we cannot teach children all at once everything that adults know, we tell them stories, even white lies, until their minds are mature enough to understand more.

Although skillful means is practiced in all Buddhist traditions, it is of particular importance in Mahayana, which teaches apparently contradictory doctrines at different times to different people. The *locus classicus* of skillful means is the parable of the burning house in the Lotus Sutra. It is noteworthy that this is a Mahayana sutra.

In the parable,[7] an old and very rich man has three sons. He comes home one day to find that his house, which is sadly in need of repair, has caught fire. He thinks about going into the house to gather the children up, one by one, and carrying them out, but he realizes that this will be difficult, since the house is very large and there is only one small door. He calls in to them to leave the house at once, but the children are playing with their toys, and cannot understand what their father is worried about. So, since he "knows the children's preconceptions, whereby each child has his preferences, his feelings being specifically attached to his several precious toys and unusual playthings"[8] the father decides on a skillful means. He tells them that the specific toys that each of them has always wanted are waiting for them outside the house. One child will get a goat-cart, another a deer-cart, and the third an ox-cart. At once the children rush to the door, pushing and shoving each other in their race to be first. When they are outside, and safe, the father is happy, but the children are puzzled. The carts that their father had promised them are nowhere to be seen. There are, however, three huge and impressive carriages, bejewelled, tasseled, carpeted, and cushioned, surrounded by attendants and drawn by magnificent, fleet-footed white oxen. "These are for you," the father tells them, "one each." The children happily mount them and forget about the little carts that they had imagined they would get.

"Has the father tricked his children?" the Buddha asks his disciple Shariputra. "No," says Shariputra, "for the children have not only been rescued from death by the promise of the imaginary little carts, they have also received a much larger vehicle than they ever could have hoped for." It is as if, we might say, the children had asked for a scooter, a motorbike, and a small automobile, and each has been given a starship.

The Buddha then explains the meaning of the parable. The children are unliberated beings. They are suffering in the burning, decrepit house of samsara, but they don't realize it because they are absorbed in their playthings. "He who dies with the most toys, wins." When the Buddha tells us directly about suffering, we do not understand him. He seems like a foolish old man who is worrying over nothing. So, the Buddha tells us that there are even better toys somewhere outside of samsara. As the poet Rupert Brooke put it, concerning heaven as imagined by fish,

> Somewhere, beyond both space and
> time,
> Is wetter water, slimier slime . . .
> And in that heaven of all their wish
> There shall be no more land, say
> fish.

When we imagine liberation, we think of it as containing something like the nice things we have now, only more so. But the things we have now are not nice, they are suffering, as we learned in the first part of the Fourfold Truth. Liberation from suffering is truly unimaginable. But if it is unimaginable, we will imagine it as full of nothing, the absence of all our nice things. This is because of the limitations of our present thought processes. (On this, see also the parable of the frog in "Nirvana as Skillful Means" in chapter 10.) Our thoughts need to be transformed, enlarged, and purified before they can make any sense of extra-samsaric peace. We may, however, be lured away from our nice things if we think there really are nicer things "out there." So, I must be given what appears to be (and *really* appears to be, or it will not work as skillful means) information that, in fact, is transformation.

MAHAYANA AND HINAYANA

There is some precision in the symbolism of the three imaginary carts and one real chariot in the parable. The three imaginary carts are drawn by progressively stronger and more impressive animals. The real chariot is enormous and is drawn by the most powerful animal of all. This is an allegory of the Mahayana understanding of the Dharma as being divided into different "vehicles" (*yana,* literally "a means of going"; Chinese *ch'êng,* "chariot") that are said to be (to change the metaphor) different medicines for different beings, that is, different *upayas.*

All Mahayana traditions speak of more than one yana, but the number of them, their names, and how they relate to each other, differs according to the lineage. The most basic division, upon which all Mahayana traditions agree, is into two:

Hinayana or Lesser Vehicle (*hina* means inferior and carries the nuance of elementary or "to be abandoned"), and Mahayana or Greater Vehicle. Hinayana is taught as the vehicle of negative ascesis (e.g., refraining from harming beings) and self-benefit or work on one's own problems, while Mahayana is taught as the vehicle of positive ascesis (i.e., actively giving good things to beings) and compassion or other-benefit. The content of the Hinayana teaching is similar to Theravada, but it is petrified and reified, as we saw in the discussion of Hinayana Abhidharma in chapter 5.

The three imaginary carts of the parable are identified in the Lotus Sutra itself as the vehicles of the Shravakas, the Pratyekabuddhas, and the Bodhisattvas. Shravakas and Pratyekabuddhas, collectively regarded as Hinyana, are the stock fall guys of Mahayana Buddhism. Shravaka means "one who hears" and refers to a direct disciple of Shakyamuni Buddha who attains his own liberation by following the Buddha's advice, but does not remain in samsara to assist other beings. A Pratyekabuddha also attains his own liberation, but has no teacher, nor does he teach. Pratyekabuddhas are also featured in the Pali texts (where they are known as Paccekabuddhas[9]) as self-realized beings who cannot teach because they are deficient in skillful means. They might, for example, try to communicate their experience by levitating, and then saying, "See what I mean?" "No," the puzzled observers reply. It is not clear why Pratyekabuddhas are not only mentioned by Mahayanists, but mentioned repeatedly, only to be excoriated. Perhaps these noble but tongue-tied gentlemen are Buddhist parodies of non-Buddhist teachers, especially Hindu and Jain eremitical ascetics.[10]

The point of the story, in any case, is to focus on the Bodhisattvas, who are, for the Mahayana, the true Buddhists. Shravakas and Pratyekabuddhas then become a catechectical device, psychologized into Mahayana Buddhists who work only for their own benefit and liberation, with or without a teacher.

The real chariot is something of a mystery. It is called the One Vehicle (*eka–yana*), and it is somehow the only vehicle there is. The Buddha says, in the Lotus Sutra, that he divides the One Vehicle into three as a skillful means. The problem is that nobody calls themselves an Ekayana Buddhist. The Ekayana is much discussed, but it remains an abstraction. Actual Mahayana Buddhists identify themselves simply as Mahayanists.

GRADED PATH AND DIVISION OF TEACHINGS

Two of the most prominent Mahayana methods of classifying Buddhist teachings in an "upayic," or skillful means hierarchy, are the Graded Path *(lam rim)* of Tibetan Gelugpa and the Division of Teachings *(p'an-chiao)* of Chinese T'ien-t'ai.

The Graded Path

The Graded Path tradition is the simpler of the two. Tibet received the Dharma more or less directly from the great Buddhist universities of the Indian Subcontinent, just before they went into decline and finally disappeared. In consequence, Tibetan Buddhism has a markedly academic appearance. A professor feels very much at home in it. Courses have been designed, and they are offered in a specific order, some being the prerequisites for others, and theory and practice (as it were lectures and lab sessions) are directed to be taken together.

The text that has been most influential in the development of this tradition is the Lamp for the Path to Enlightenment *(Bodhi-patha-pradipa)* of Atisha,[11] who (see chapter 7) is also the root teacher of the thought transformation *(lojong)* practices. Atisha makes a tripartite distinction, but it is not quite the same as that of the three imaginary carts in the Lotus Sutra. He says:

> *One who by every means he finds,*
> *Seeks but the pleasure of samsara,*
> *And cares but for himself alone, that*
>   *one*
> *Is known as the Inferior Person.*

> *One who puts life's pleasures behind*
> *And turns himself from deeds of sin,*
> *Yet cares only about his own peace,*
> *That person should be called*
>   *Mediocre.*

> *One who wholly seeks a complete*
>   *end*
> *To the entire suffering of others*
>   *because*
> *Their suffering is his own,*
> *That person is a Superior.*[12]

Atisha sees three sorts of people of differing abilities. The first is the unreflective hedonist who looks for happiness either in this life or by rebirth in one of the realms of the deities. Such a person is hardly a serious Buddhist at all. The second person understands about the limitations of samsara and seeks liberation from it ("peace" here means nirvana) but does not work compassionately for the liberation of other beings. This is the Hinayanist. The last person, who sees all suffering, whether his own or others, as one, makes the Bodhisattva Resolve and seeks to liberate all beings from samsara. This is the Mahayanist, the truly insightful and earnest practitioner.

Towards the end of his text, Atisha makes some ambiguous references to the Tantras. These come to be regarded as a third vehicle, the Vajrayana or Supreme Vehicle. Tantra is a way of looking at reality from the point of view of its goal rather than its path. It does not introduce any teachings that are not found in the Mahayana, but the way it puts them into practice is distinctive. Its special vision will be discussed in the next chapter.

Based thus on Atisha, most Tibetan lineages arrange their teachings along a spectrum of increasing profundity called Teg-sum *(theg gsum)*, the Triple Vehicle.[13] The standard brief explanation of their distinctive characteristics is that the Hinayana is the practice of self-benefit, the Mahayana is the practice of other-benefit, and the Vajrayana cuts off ordinary perception, that is, allows us actually to see samsara as nirvana.

It it also customary in Tibetan Buddhism to relate the Triple Body (Trikaya, see chapter 1, fig. 3) to the Triple Vehicle, by saying that the Hinayana was taught by the Buddha in his Nirmanakaya and was offered to everyone, the Mahayana was taught by him in his Sambhogakaya to a select group of disciples, and the Vajrayana was taught by the Dharmakaya in secret to a very highly select group of disciples.

Of the many Tibetan variations on the Triple Vehicle theme, that of Tsongkhapa (1357–1419 C.E.), to whom we owe the technical term *lam rim*, is the most comprehensive. Tsongkhapa was the inheritor of a number of different lineages, both academic and practical, and he unified them in a reform movement called Gelugpa *(dge lugs pa)* or Virtuous Ones (a reference to the restoration of the Vinaya), and composed The Great Book on the Stages of the Path (Lam Rim Chen Mo), the standard compendium of the Gelugpa teachings.[14]

Division of Teachings

China did not inherit the Dharma in the neat course packets that went to Tibet. Texts, teachers, and customs drifted in through Central Asia more or less haphazardly, without any coherent explanation of why some teachings seemed to contradict others. The Chinese Buddhists had to work out more or less on their own what to do with the astonishing amount of material that was coming in.

They decided upon, by and large, three principles of skillful means, and arranged the teachings in accordance with them: (1) the Buddha taught differently at different times to different people, in accordance with the occasion and the capacity of the audience; (2) the Buddha taught the same thing all the time, but people heard him differently according to their capacities; (3) depending on the capacity of the audience, the Buddha either taught the final truth all at once (Sudden Teaching or Subitism) or led up to it in stages (Gradualism).

These principles may appear logically inconsistent, but that depends on what we mean by logic. If our logic is linear, unidimensional, and conceptual, based upon Aristotelian assumptions of the real efficacy of language, the three principles contradict each other. But if our logic is spatial, as Chinese logic appears to be (when yin and yang have been shown to be balanced, a phenomenon has been satisfactorily explained) and multidimensional (as Buddhist reality certainly is), the three principles are seen to be mutually supportive, like descriptions of a three-dimensional object in terms of each of its coordinates.

The first of the three principles is common to all Buddhist traditions, while the second is peculiar to the Mahayana. The third is distinctive to Chinese Buddhism and its offshoots. The controversy between Subitists and Gradualists is, indeed, so distinctive a feature of Chinese Buddhism[15] that when the Tibetans staged a debate between an Indian and a Chinese Dharma Master, in order to decide which tradition to accept, they saw the issue in terms of Subitism and Gradualism.[16] Most Tibetan lineages opted for Gradualism. The Nyingma lineage has retained the Subitist position, but Subitist lineages (some forms of Zen and of Pure Land Buddhism) are found chiefly in Far Eastern Buddhism.

The tradition of *p'an-chiao* (division of, or judging between, teachings) began in China during the fifth century C.E.[17] and

various systems were devised. The T'ien-t'ai system, traditionally but probably incorrectly attributed to Chih-i (538–597 C.E.),
the lineage founder,[18] is a development of that proposed by
Hui-kuan (fl. 420–429 C.E.), who grouped the sutras into five
classes corresponding to five periods in the life of Shakyamuni
Buddha.

The T'ien-t'ai system is very complicated, since it attempts to
produce a balanced spread-sheet of all the texts in regard to their
profundity, their audience, their content, and their upayic
mode.[19] The result is known as the "Five Periods and Eight
Teachings." The five periods are periods in Shakyamuni Buddha's life. They differ from the Twelve Acts in that all five periods
are subsequent to the Enlightenment, and are an elaboration of
the ninth and tenth acts.

The first period is very short but contains extremely profound
teaching. The Avatamsaka Sutra, it is said (which was the subject
of Fa-tsang's Essay on the Golden Lion, see chapter 1), was
taught by the Buddha immediately after his enlightenment, in
the short space of three weeks. Because of its exalted nature, it
was taught almost entirely in the deity realms. Coming back to
the human realm, the Buddha modified his teaching, beginning
with the Hinayana, which he taught for twelve years, and moving through elementary and intermediate Mahayana (taught respectively for eight and twenty-two years) until, in the final period, lasting eight years, he gave his last and most exalted
teachings in the Lotus and Nirvana Sutras.

The Eight Teachings are composed of the Four Methods and
the Four Types. The Four Methods are: sudden, gradual, secret,
and variable. The Four Types are: the Pitaka or Hinayana type;
the Common or shared Hinayana and Mahayana type; the Special or Bodhisattva type; and the Round or Perfect type, which
is the final teaching.

All of this makes a magnificent chart in the finest tradition of
Chinese spatial logic, and it brings order to what had been the
chaotic library of Chinese Buddhist texts, so that a practitioner
is able to find out what teachings are available, judge which
might be more suitable than others, and know in what order they
might best be studied. When the Division of Teachings was combined, in the T'ien-t'ai lineage, with a parallel gradation of meditations, a coherent and comprehensive approach to Chinese
Buddhism had been established.

Teaching by Silence

THE SILENCE OF THE BUDDHA

When the Buddha was asked his opinion on certain topics, he purposely made no intelligible reply. These came to be known as the undecided topics (Pali: *avyakata-vatthuni*). They are:[20]

1. The universe is eternal.

2. The universe is not eternal.

3. The universe is spatially finite.

4. The universe is spatially infinite.

5. Mind and body are identical.

6. Mind and body are different.

7. After final nirvana, one continues to exist.

8. After final nirvana, one is annihilated.

9. After final nirvana, part of one continues to exist and part of one is annihilated.

10. After final nirvana, one neither continues to exist nor is one annihilated.

When asked these questions by, one imagines, genuine enquirers who had come to have their philosophical doubts laid to rest by an Omniscient One, the Buddha would either remain completely silent or would answer, "The question is incoherent" (*Nopeti*, "It can't come up like that. It's not really a question"). When the enquirer would then observe that it appeared that the Buddha did not know the answer, and it would be better for him to be honest and say so, the Buddha would again respond with silence or with "Nopeti."

The questioner having gone away thoroughly frustrated, the disciples asked for an explanation. He told them that he would not elucidate metaphysical questions. He would only speak of suffering, its origin, its stopping, and the path to its stopping, because this was helpful, whereas metaphysics was not. He illustrated this by telling a parable of a man shot by a poisoned arrow. The wounded man says he will not accept medical assistance until he has found out for certain who it was who shot the arrow, what was his name and family background, how tall or short he was, what was the color of his skin, what materials were used in making the bow and the bowstring, and what materials were used to make the shaft and flight of the arrow. What do you think, asks the Buddha, will the man die before he gets all that information? Just so, one who insists on asking metaphysical questions before attending to the real problem, the suffering of birth, sickness, aging, and death, will die before he can attend to his suffering.

It is noteworthy that these ten questions are still live issues today for philosophers and scientists, and we do not seem to be much nearer a solution, two and a half millennia after the time of the Buddha. But even supposing I did know for certain, for instance, whether or not the universe was eternal, how would it help my suffering? If, however, I work to end my suffering, which comes from ignorance, the intrinsic clarity of my mind will manifest, and such questions will answer themselves.

THE SILENCE OF THE PHILOSOPHERS: MADHYAMIKA

Ordinary, defiled mind asks questions that it thinks are real questions, and seeks for answers. The Buddha's silence frustrates defiled mind by throwing the questioning back on itself. A corpus of Mahayana sutras that began to appear around the beginning of the Common Era picks up on this frustration and pushes it to its limit.

The corpus is known collectively as the Perfection of Wisdom (Prajñaparamita) literature, that is, the wisdom (prajña) that has gone to (ita) the further (param) shore, to nirvana or enlightenment. It is extensive, and it comes into being over a fairly long period of time.[21] In this literature we meet the word "shunyata," used in a definitely philosophical sense, for the first time. The viewpoint of the Perfection of Wisdom sutras is encapsulated in this extract from one of the shorter texts in the corpus, the Diamond Sutra (Vajracchedika Prajñaparamita Sutra, "The Sutra on the Perfection of Wisdom that cuts ignorance like a Diamond or Thunderbolt"):

> *Subhuti asked: What then, O Lord, is this discourse on dharma, and how should I bear it in mind? The Lord replied: This discourse on dharma, Subhuti, is called "Wisdom which has gone beyond," and as such should you bear it in mind! And why? Just that which the Tathagata has taught as the wisdom that has gone beyond, just that He has taught as not gone beyond. Therefore it is called "Wisdom which has gone beyond." What do you think, Subhuti, is there any dharma which the Tathagata has taught? Subhuti replied: No indeed, O Lord, there is not. The Lord said: When, Subhuti, you consider the number of particles of dust in this world system of 1,000 million worlds, would they be many? Subhuti replied: Yes, O Lord. Because what was taught as particles of dust by the Tathagata, as no-particles that was taught by the Tathagata. Therefore are they called "particles of dust." And this world-system the Tathagata has taught as no-system. Therefore is it called a "world system."*[22]

This sounds like a conversation between two schizophrenics. "A" is "not-A" and therefore it is called "A." Ordinary, judging mind *(vikalpa)* finds no foothold here.

It is pressed and frustrated still further in an even shorter text of the Perfection of Wisdom corpus, the Heart Sutra (Prajñaparamita Hridaya Sutra, "The Sutra on the Heart of the Perfection of Wisdom"):

> *Here, O Shariputra, all dharmas are marked with emptiness; they are not produced or stopped, not defiled or immaculate, not deficient or complete.*[23]

That is, everything (*dharma* here means "thing" or "event") never came to be and will never cease to be, all the opposites that ordinary mind sees are not reality.

Maximum frustration is put upon dualistic, judging mind in

the shortest text in the corpus, the Sutra on the Perfection of Wisdom in One Letter (Ekakshara Prajñaparamita Sutra). The Buddha says:

> *Ananda, do receive, for the sake of the weal and*
> *happiness of all beings, this perfection of wisdom in one*
> *letter, i.e., A.* [24]

The Sutras do not explain what is going on. In order to understand these strange statements, we need to go to the treatises of the Madhyamika system, which traces its origin to Nagarjuna (second/third century C.E.).

Madhyamika is one of the two great Mahayana explanatory systems. The other is Yogachara, which was discussed in Chapter 7. The name means "Middleist." "The Middle Way" is another name for Buddhism. In regard to conduct, Buddhism teaches the middle way between surfeit and abstinence. In the Madhyamika system, it takes the middle way between affirmation and denial, without collapsing into agnosticism. Madhyamika dialectic can thus be seen as a direct descendant of the conversations on the undecided topics.

Nagarjuna opens his principal text, The Root Verses on the Middle (Mulamadhyamaka Karika), with eight negations. Reality, he says, is not characterized by coming into being, passing away, termination, non-termination, unity, difference, movement into the future, or movement away from the past.[25]

The eight negations do not negate reality, rather they affirm it, by negating *concepts or ideas about* reality. Nagarjuna calls the faculty of the mind that classifies reality into "this" and "that," *prapañcha,* false imagining. When we look at reality directly, prapañcha does not operate, reality is found to be "quiescent" *(shiva)* of prapañcha.

As an example of what he means, he analyzes the concept "going." Suppose something is moving. Let us call it the Goer. There must be something that makes the Goer go. Let us call that the Going. Now, let us look for the Going so that we can see how it is that the Goer goes. If the Going exists, it must exist in the past, the present, or the future. But if it is in the past, the Going has already stopped before the Goer has gone, and if it is in the future, the Goer has gone before the Going has come. Either proposition is absurd. So, perhaps it is in the present. If so, the

Going must be either the same as the Goer or different from it. But if it is the same, it is just a synonym, as a woman may be called both wife and mother. So, the Goer must be different from the Going. But if so, it has no connection with the Goer and it cannot make the Goer go. There must, then, be an intermediary, let us call it "Going$_1$," which makes the Goer go and is made to go by the Going. But "Going$_1$" must also be either the same as or different from both the (original) Going and the Goer. So we would have an infinite series of "Going$_n$," asymptotically approaching the Goer but never actually making the Goer go.

We are forced to conclude that there is no Going and that, therefore, the Goer does not go. Yet, it observably goes. So, what we have shown is not that nothing goes, but that *how* it goes is not discoverable by linguistic or conceptual analysis. By applying prapañcha to reality, we have watched prapañcha put itself out of business.

It is now possible to make some sense out of the schizophreniform dialogues in the Perfection of Wisdom sutras. The statement "the universe exists" is clearly true, if anything is true at all. The Buddha in the Diamond Sutra puts this colorfully as "the particles of dust in all the world-systems exist and are very many." But then, when we try to find these particles by pointing to the inherent existence of their concepts, we are unsuccessful, just as, in the Abhidharma system, we were unable to discover inherent existence by minutely observing our awareness of things and their components. We find, then, that "the universe does not exist." Nevertheless, the universe exists, and we must agree that it does. "What was taught as particles of dust, as no-particles that was taught by the Tathagata, therefore are they called 'particles of dust.'"

Nagarjuna explains this double aspect of reality by means of a model called the Twofold Truth *(satya-dvaya)*. There is, first, the ordinary truth of judging mind, which asserts that things exist, that is, that some things exist and others do not, but that, in general, there *is* a universe. This is the Conventional Truth *(samvriti-satya)*. Then there is the discovery that, taken as it is, before it is muddied by conceptualization, nothing is found. This is the Higher Truth *(paramartha-satya)*. Both Truths are true. If only one Truth were true, it could be established, and the other Truth would be shown to be a falsity. But both Truths can be equally established. No error can be found. That it seems that there *must* be an error somewhere, that all this is just playing with words, is nothing more than the screams of protest of deluded mind that is so accustomed to having ground under its feet, to having a viewpoint and a position, that it trembles in fear[26] when it finds itself in free fall in open space, "unsupported by anything" as the Diamond Sutra puts it.[27]

This complete openness is the Middle Truth *(madhyama-satya)* and is the Madhyamika demonstration of Emptiness or Transparency.

When "all the dharmas are marked with emptiness," then reality is seen as "not produced and not stopped," as conforming to the Eight Negations. The letter "A" is a symbol of this, since it is both the first letter of the alphabet and a negative prefix.[28] As the beginning of the alphabet, it can be seen as the origin of all language, as the root affirmation that the universe exists. And as a negative prefix, it can reverse itself and deny everything it has just created. Because the letter "A" is *simultaneously* an affirmation and a denial, without either affirmation or denial being dominant, without affirmation or denial being mixed or compounded together, but having both affirmation and denial (the two opposite operations of whole mind), equally and entirely present, it *is* the Middle Truth, or the Perfection of Wisdom.[29]

BACK TO BODHI: THE ZEN KOAN

The silence, or the baffling "Nopeti," of the Buddha in the Pali Suttas turns back the questioning of ordinary mind. The schizophreniform dialogues between the Buddha and Subhuti in the Diamond Sutra question what questioning is. Nagarjuna's eight negations leave dualistic mind with no questions to ask. The Zen koan employs this questioning of questioning, the turning back of questioning on itself, as a skillful means.

Both Madhyamika and Zen began as reform movements. The Abhidharma, which Nagarjuna knew, was in the petrified form taught by the Sarvastivadins. Abhidharma had begun as reports of the freshness of every moment, open in its evanescence, and had catalogued itself into a metaphysical, samsaric prison. Nagarjuna unlocked this prison by showing that the dharmas of the Sarvastivadins could not possibly exist. The essences that they taught were fantasies, evading all attempts at finding them. Nagarjuna demonstrated that the only logical conclusion was, as the Perfection of Wisdom Sutras had said, that the true mark of all the dharmas is Emptiness. The freshness of every moment had been recovered.

As Buddhism became established in China, it organized itself in magnificent and ponderous systems such as the T'ien-t'ai. The value of this was obvious, but the danger was that it provided something to cling to. Practitioners became involved in doctrinal minutiae and controversies over meditational techniques. They were absorbed into large monastic institutions and fell victim to "grasping at ceremonies." An outrageous teacher from the southern part of the Indian subcontinent, Bodhidharma (*circa* early 6th century C.E.), "the blue-eyed, red-bearded barbarian from the west," burst rudely through all of this and initiated a "back to bodhi" reform. The only value of the Dharma, Bodhidharma shouted at monks and emperors, is that it leads to Enlightenment. If some form of the Dharma is not leading beings to Enlightenment, then, no matter how sacred it may seem, it must be discarded. "Gold dust is valuable, but in the eyes it causes blindness."

Bodhidharma's lineage is called Ch'an, an abbreviated transliteration of the Sanskrit dhyana, meditation, to emphasize that meditation or mind transformation is the heart of Buddhism, and where it is obscured or lost there cannot be said to be true Buddhism. The word was passed, with the lineage, to the rest of East Asia, being pronounced *Sŏn* in Korea, Thien in Vietnam, and Zen in Japan, from where it has come into English.

The most distinctive practice of Zen, zazen or sitting meditation, has been mentioned above, in chapter 6. The most bizarre practice, and the one that has attracted a lot of attention in the west, especially from those who have no intention of seriously following the Dharma, is the koan.

It was noticed that those who came to Zen practice wrestling with an existential problem made faster progress than those who did not. In zazen, there are no distractions. So, if one has a problem, it will keep showing up. Try as we might to sit in the freshness of the moment, this nagging question about the meaning of life, or whatever, will keep coming back, troubling our minds and clouding our vision. If we can dispel the problem, clear mind may manifest.

Occasionally, a practitioner would see through a problem, and the freshness of reality would open before him. The moment of breakthrough from the dualistic mind, which asks about the undecided topics, into the non-dualism of reality as it truly is, was recognized as an "awakening" (Chinese: *wu;* Japanese: *satori*) or a glimpse of final enlightenment. The incident of breakthrough was put on record and so came to be called a koan (Chinese: *kung-an*), literally "public notice-board." Since a koan had worked once, it was "publically posted" so that it could be taken up by others in the hopes that it would work for them also.

Koans began to be collected. There are now said to be 1,700, of which only a few have been translated into English, mostly in versions of the Gateless Gate (Mumonkan)[30] and the Blue Cliff Record (Hekigan Roku).[31] The usefulness of these collections is that they raise genuine problems, and recount how they were solved. The danger is that, knowing the "correct" answer, one can imitate it and pretend to a satori one does not have.[32] Once again, there is a handhold for "grasping at ceremonies."

The true "answer" to a koan, however, is not like an answer to a riddle. A riddle is a question put by and to dualistic mind, albeit in a confusing way, and it is solved when the confusion is straightened out and the mind has moved to the right answer. A koan is not a question, it is a problem, and in order to solve it the questioning, the feeling of problemness, has to be turned back on itself. A riddle is solved when the answer is found. A koan is solved when the question disappears.

A koan is not, however, completely unintelligible. One can pull it apart and suggest why it worked for whomever it worked. Take, for example, the famous koan of One Hand. The question, or problem, is: two hands brought together make the sound of clapping; what is the sound of one hand? If I answer "No sound" I have stated the obvious, based on dualistic mind. If I answer that it has a sound, I am factually incorrect.

The sound of two hands clapping can be regarded as a symbol of the statement "the universe exists." The absence of sound when there is only one hand is then a symbol of the statement "the universe does not exist." The "sound" of the one hand is the coexistence of sound and no-sound. It is Transparency, or the Middle Truth.

This is what the koan "means," or at least, can be thought to mean. But an explanation of it is not an answer to it (or what Zen calls a "penetration" of it): it is a more precise understanding of what the problem is.[33] When dualistic mind has been turned back upon itself repeatedly, frustrated in all its attempts to answer, non-dualistic bodhi mind will respond by seeing the incoherence of the question. What response I will then give, I cannot predict. I might just make a loud noise, the Zen Shout, *"KA!"* It should, however, be clear to the teacher that the student has penetrated the koan, for the teacher's bodhi mind will recognize the student's bodhi mind.

Ch'an, Sŏn, and Thien balance koan with sitting practice, and add other practices as well. Zen tends to be more exclusivistic. Of the two largest branches of Zen, Rinzai and Soto, Rinzai uses koan practice directly while Soto emphasizes sitting and uses koans indirectly. The Rinzai technique, based on the teachings of Hakuin (1686–1769 C.E.), is designed to raise what he called the Great Doubt. By sitting with the koan that one's teacher has assigned, living with it day in and day out, not trying to solve it but *living* with it "like a red-hot iron ball in one's mouth that can neither be swallowed nor spat out," a point of crisis is reached. This is called "descending into the cave of the green dragon." The mind no longer doubts some things and not other things, it is all one big Doubt. There is no escape. Every attempt at explanation, or answering, is blocked. Then, if all goes well, "suddenly, it will be as though a sheet of ice were broken or a jade tower had fallen. He will experience great joy, one that never in forty years has he seen or heard. . . . The ten directions melt before your eyes, the three periods are penetrated in an instant of thought. . . ."[34]

The technique can be dangerous, for there must be a real and complete blockage, and something like a mental breakdown. When the breakdown is fruitful, it leads to enlightenment. When it goes wrong, it brings on mental disorder. For this reason, Rinzai koan practice should only be done under the supervision of a competent teacher.

Soto Zen uses koan technique more diffusely. Anything can be a koan. Life itself is a koan. Zazen is a koan.

Koans can also be used as the focus of a rapid fire question and answer session, reminiscent of Tibetan debate (see chapter 5), called "Dharma Combat" *(shuso hosen).*

Whatever method is used, the aim of Zen is to turn the mind back from questioning and let it come to rest in the present moment, awakening to what is.

> *I was once asked to give a talk at the local Roman Catholic Church. They asked me, "What is the whole of the essence of Zen Buddhism?" I said, "The whole of the essence of Zen Buddhism is toilet paper. How much do you use? Do you just pull, or do you reflect?" And they said, "Is that the whole of the essence of Zen Buddhism?" And I said, "Yes. That is all."*[35]

Whether the question is the infinity of the universe or the finitude of toilet paper, the Zen response is that of the Buddha in the Pali texts: either silence or "Nopeti."

NOTES
to Chapter 9

1. This has been translated into English from the Pali many times. A convenient place to find it is *The Buddhist Tradition in India, China and Japan*, ed. Wm. Th. de Bary (New York: Modern Library, 1969), pp. 16–17. The Chinese version, which has some special features, such as the refrain "this is a Dharma never previously heard," and the account of the joyful news being passed up the various levels of the sensuous realm, does not seem to have been translated into English.

2. These three levels are found in the Pali tradition, but are taught there as three *aspects* of *dukkha,* and they are mentioned in a different order: the suffering of suffering, the suffering of conditioned existence, and the suffering of change.

3. The standard survey in English is Maurice Winternitz (translated by V. Srinivasa Sarma), *A History of Indian Literature* (Delhi: Banarsidass, revised edition, 1983), vol. 2, section 3. Although Winternitz's treatment is extensive, it needs to be supplemented by the equally extensive study of Hajime Nakamura, *Indian Buddhism: A Survey with Bibliographical Notes* (Delhi: Banarsidass, 1987). A readable but somewhat idiosyncratic account is *The Eternal Legacy* by Sangharakshita (London: Tharpa, 1985). The author's problems with the notion of canon are evident. Kogen Mizuno, *Buddhist Sutras: Origin, Development, Transmission,* is concerned only with the transmission to the Far East, but is useful within that limitation. A table of the main contents of the Pali, Chinese, and Tibetan collections is given by Richard H. Robinson and Willard L. Johnson, *The Buddhist Religion* (Belmont, CA: 1982), pp. 270–272.

4. Edward Conze (translator), *The Large Sutra on Perfect Wisdom* (University of California Press, 1975), p. 89.

5. These were prepared in the days when anything that the English viewed as a sacred text was required to be translated into "Anglican Hieratic," so as to resemble the King James version of the Bible. The language is consequently stilted, and it is not error free. The collection is, however, under active revision.

6. There are two notable exceptions to this rule. Almost no Tibetan text appears in English without material derived from the oral commentary of a living teacher, and all the translations from the Chinese published by the Buddhist Text Translation Society of San Francisco contain extensive commentaries by their teacher, Master Hsüan Hua.

7. For an accessible English translation, see Leon Hurvitz (translator), *Scripture of the Lotus Blossom of the Fine Dharma* (New York: Columbia University Press, 1976), pp. 58–64.

8. Hurvitz, p. 59.

9. Ria Kloppenborg, *The Paccekabuddha* (Leiden: Brill, 1974). She also presents a brief discussion of the *savaka,* the Pali equivalent of the shravaka.

10. I have argued that the Mahayana polemic against the so called Hinayana is remarkably similar to the Christian polemic against Judaism. That it misses its mark (to put it mildly) is clear, and I have suggested that it is an emic catechetical device masquerading as an etic polemic. "The Hermeneutics of Polemic: The Creation of 'Hinayana' and 'Old Testament,' " paper delivered at the conference on Buddhism and Christianity, Berkeley, California, August 1987.

11. Translated and annotated by Richard Sherburne, S.J., as *A Lamp for the Path and Commentary* (London: Allen and Unwin, 1983).

12. Sherburne, p. 5. (Translation of next to last line modified.)

13. The Nyingma (Old Transmission) lineage is distinctive in teaching nine vehicles. The first three are those of the Lotus Sutra (Shravaka, Pratyekabuddha, and Bodhisattva Vehicles), and the remaining six are subdivisions of the Vajrayana (three Outer Tantra Vehicles and three Inner Tantra Vehicles). This is still, however, closely related to the Tegsum of the three Sarma (New Transmission) lineages.

14. No complete translation into English is as yet available. Alex Wayman has translated the sections on meditation, and given a brief overview of the full text, in *Calming the Mind and Discerning the Real* (New York: Columbia University Press, 1978). The "seed verses," which Tsongkhapa wrote immediately after receiving a revelation from the Bodhisattva Mañjushri on how to write the book, and two of his own preliminary outlines, have been translated by Sherpa Tulku, *et al.,* under the editorship of Robert Thurman, in *The Life and Teachings of Tsong Khapa* (Dharamsala, India: Library of Tibetan Works and Archives, 1982), pp. 57–89. *Tibetan Tradition of Mental Development* (Dharamsala: Library of Tibetan Works and Archives, 1978) contains the oral teachings of Geshey Ngawang Dhargyey based on his expertise in the *Lam rim chen mo.*

15. Peter N. Gregory (ed.), *Sudden and Gradual: Approaches to Enlightenment in Chinese Thought* (University of Hawaii Press, 1987). Also see Sung Bae Park, *Buddhist Faith and Sudden Enlightenment* (Albany: SUNY Press, 1983).

16. The debate is supposed to have occurred about 792 C.E. at the monastery of Samyay *(bsam yas)* but believing in its historicity has gone in and out of academic fashion. I think it is in again. For an account in English, see Giuseppe Tucci, *Minor Buddhist Texts, Part II* (Rome: Istituto per il Medio ed Estremo Oriente, 1958) (Serie Orientale Roma IX,2), pp. 5–154. Also see G. W. Houston, *Sources for a History of the bSam yas Debate* (Sankt Augustin: VGH Wissenschaftsverlag,, 1980) (Monumenta Tibetica Historica, Abt. 1, Bd. 2).

17. Mizuno, *Buddhist Sutras,* chapter 8.

18. The basic traditional handbook on *T'ien-t'ai p'an-chiao*, written in Chinese by the Korean monk Chegwan, has been edited and published with an English translation by the Buddhist Translation Seminar of Hawaii, with David W. Chappell and Masao Ichishima, as *T'ien-t'ai Buddhism: An Outline of the Fourfold Teachings* (Tokyo: Daiichi-Shobo, 1983; distributed by the University Press of Hawaii).

19. See the charts on pp. 31–35 of the work cited in the preceding note.

20. The same or a similar conversation is given at a number of points in the Pali texts. Two of them are printed in Warren, *Buddhism in Translations*, pp. 117–128.

21. The standard scholarly survey is *The Prajñaparamita Literature* by Edward Conze ('s-Gravenhage, 1960; revised edition, Tokyo, 1978).

22. Edward Conze (translator), *Buddhist Wisdom Books: The Diamond Sutra and the Heart Sutra* (London: Allen and Unwin, 1958), pp. 51–52. (Text only quoted.)

23. *Buddhist Wisdom Books*, p. 85.

24. Edward Conze (translator), *The Short Prajñaparamita Texts* (London: Luzac, 1973), p. 201.

25. My interpretative translation of part of the opening *vandana* (invocation). For the Sanskrit text and another English translation, see Kenneth K. Inada, *Nagarjuna: Mulamadhyamakakarika* (Tokyo: Hokuseido Press, 1970), pp. 38–39. Also see the commentary on the *vandana* by Chandrakirti, translated by Mervyn Sprung as *Lucid Exposition of the Middle Way* (Boulder: Prajña Press, 1979), pp. 32–33.

26. For this reason, Emptiness is not to be taught to persons whose Dharma practice is insufficiently advanced (*The Large Sutra on Perfect Wisdom*, p. 271). It is a peculiarity of the modern educational system that any kind of information is supposed to be freely available to all enquirers, regardless of their moral or spiritual condition. This bodes ill for the future rebirths of many of us academics, and indeed here I am, teaching Emptiness to anyone who can read English.

27. Conze, *Buddhist Wisdom Books*, p. 26.

28. Through an auspicious karmic conjunction, the letter "A" works in this respect just as well in English as in the Sanskrit of the original sutra.

29. Because of the importance of "A," there is a specific practice devoted to its visualization. It is briefly referred to in *Open Secrets: A Western Guide to Tibetan Buddhism* by Walt Anderson (Penguin, 1980), pp. 73–74.

30. For example, Koun Yamada, *The Gateless Gate* (Los Angeles: Center Publications, 1979).

31. For example, Thomas and J. C. Cleary, *The Blue Cliff Record* (Boulder: Prajña Press, 1978).

32. A great deal of fluttering amongst the priestly dovecotes was created by the publication in 1916, in Japan, of *Gendai Sojizen Hyoron* ("A Critique of Present-day Pseudo-Zen"), a koan "crib book," which had previously been circulating amongst grateful students in surreptitious manuscript form, listing the standard koans and the different "correct" responses expected by the various sub-lineages in order to be awarded one's certificate of "roshification" and, thus, a temple and an income. It quickly disappeared from bookstores under mysterious circumstances. An English translation by Yoel Hoffmann, *The Sound of the One Hand: 281 Zen Koans with Answers,* was published by Basic Books, New York, in 1975, and has likewise become difficult to find.

33. Gyomay M. Kubose, *Zen Koans* (Chicago: Henry Regnery, 1973), p. x.

34. Philip B. Yampolsky (trans.), *The Zen Master Hakuin: Selected Writings* (New York: Columbia University Press, 1971), p. 145.

35. This is my imperfect memory of a talk given by Katagiri Dainin Roshi in Chapel Hill, North Carolina, on October 3, 1985. I hope Roshi will forgive any inaccuracies in my reporting.

Chapter 10

COMPLETE OPENNESS

(Act 12 of the Buddha)

The end of Buddha Shakyamuni's life in the human realm is
called final nirvana *(pari-nirvana).* It resembles death, but
it cannot strictly be called death, since death, in Buddhism, is
merely disappearance from one part of samsara followed by
reappearance, or birth, in another part of samsara. Final nirvana
is disappearance from samsara itself. Samsara is a closed circle.
Final nirvana is complete openness.

In this chapter we will look at what the word nirvana means,
how many kinds of nirvana there are, and what "disappearance"
might mean, for Buddhas, for the Dharma, and for the universe
in general. We will ask the question "What is the goal of Buddhist
practice? What can I expect from it, and where (and what) will
I be when I finish it?"

The answers to these questions can only be a skillful means.
Extra-samsarically, nothing can be said. But if nothing is said,
we cannot move out of samsara.

Nirvana

The word nirvana has entered the English language, but perhaps the worst approach to understanding what it means is to consult an English dictionary. Most English dictionaries do not distinguish between Hindu, Jain, and Buddhist uses of the word, and they leave us with the confusing impression that it is, at one and the same time, eternal bliss and complete extinction.

Textbooks on Buddhism commonly note that the word comes from the root *va*, "blow," with the negative prefix *nir*, so that it means "blown out" or, possibly, "cooled." This is philologically correct, but it is not especially helpful. What is blown out or cooled, and what happens then?

Theravada distinguishes two sorts of nirvana (or nibbana as it is called in Pali): nirvana with the graspable *(sopadisesa-nibbana)* and nirvana without the graspable *(anupadisesa-nibbana)*. The graspable *(upadi)* means the five clusters (Sanskrit: *skandha;* Pali: *khandha*). The two sorts of nirvana are therefore distinguished as to whether or not the clusters are present, which means, in effect, whether one is living or not. When the clusters disperse, we say that death has occurred. If what we have observed is in fact death, the fruiting of karma will condition the subsequent appearance of a new set of five clusters, and we will say that we have observed a birth. If, however, what has occurred is anupadisesa-nibbana, the clusters are dispersed but karma is not operative and no new set of five clusters comes into existence, that is, there is no rebirth.

It is the lack of the operation of karma, in some way or another, that is the distinctive characteristic of nirvana. At the moment of enlightenment, when, according to Theravada, a sentient being attains sopadisesa-nibbana and becomes a Buddha, the *fruiting* of karma is operative but its *production* ceases. It is the production of karma which is "blown out" or "cooled." An Enlightened One does not act in such a way as to sow seeds of karma that must eventually fruit. He is compared to a bird that, when it flies through the air, does not leave a track. A sentient being, still sowing karmic seeds, is like a land animal that leaves footprints.

The acts of body, speech, and mind of a Buddha, between preliminary and final nirvana, go cleanly into the moment without splattering into the past or the future. They are observed in time, and they are observed as wise and good, but they do not occur in time nor within the dualities of ignorance and wisdom, good and bad. Liberated mind is always in the present, always in step. It does not appear to move. In Japanese it is called Unmoving Mind *(fudo-shin)*. Unliberated mind moves rapidly between past and future in order to reach a decision in the present by comparing what is going on with what has gone on before and what might go on later. It splatters across the moment and produces karmic effects.

There is a Taoist story of a master butcher whose knife remained sharp no matter how much meat he cut up. Asked how this was, he replied, "I only cut where there are spaces." Since his knife met no resistance, its edge never dulled. This is an analogy of a Buddha's actions. They go sharply into the dimensionless NOW, making no wound or mark in the space-time continuum so that, in the absolute sense, nothing has happened.

The fruiting of karma continues, however, after the attainment of preliminary nirvana (sopadisesa-nibbana), since there is still a body and a mind within samsara. When all the karma of all previous lives has fruited, final nirvana (anupadisesa-nibbana, also called *pari-nibbana*) occurs, and a Buddha disappears from samsara or, as it superficially appears, dies. Preliminary nirvana is like removing one's foot from the gas pedal while driving: the car does not stop at once but keeps going until the energy that started it has been used up. The stopping of the car is like final nirvana.

Mahayana teaches the same two sorts of nirvana as Theravada (pari-nibbana is called *pari-nirvana* in Sanskrit), but it finds problems in them and calls final nirvana the Hinayana or incomplete nirvana. It explains the Hinayana nirvana as a true nirvana, in as much as there is liberation from samsara, but a flawed one, in as much as the being who enters final nirvana has left the rest of us behind and so has failed in compassion. This is due, says Mahayana, to not having made the Bodhisattva resolve. Mahayana then posits another nirvana, unsupported nirvana *(apratishthita–nirvana)*, which is neither in nirvana (i.e., in Hinayana nirvana) nor samsara. It is only, says Mahayana, in unsupported nirvana that karma ceases to operate and that action goes cleanly into the moment. Such action is said to be effortless or spontaneous *(anabhoga)*. It is the basis of some distinctively Mahayana teachings, which we will examine later in this chapter.

It needs to be said at once that it is not at all clear that the final nirvana taught by Theravada has the deficiencies which Mahayana sees in Hinayana nirvana. As with the distinction between Theravada Abhidhamma and Hinayana Abhidharma, it seems that Mahayanists are here fighting a corruption of Buddhism as a whole rather than of a living Buddhist lineage. Both Theravadins and Mahayanists agree that complete nirvana is complete nirvana. The controversy seems to be over how this is understood.

An important consequence of the controversy is that it highlights the teaching that true nirvana is not annihilation into cosmic nothingness. Non-being *(abhava)* is the opposite of being, and it appears to be just this sort of non-being that the Mahayana identifies as the Hinayana nirvana. The Hinayanist is out of samsara, but just by being out he is not in. A dualism is thus set up between samsara and nirvana, but since nirvana is non-dual, any nirvana which is dualistically distinguishable from samsara cannot really be nirvana. Theravada has preserved a similar rejection of a dualistic understanding of nirvana, as either eternal life or annihilation, in the Pali account of the Buddha's silence on the post-nirvana state (see the discussion of the undecided topics in chapter 9).

When non-Buddhists define Buddhist nirvana as annihilation, and then object to it, they should note that they are taking a Buddhist position.

What could happen to a being in such a supposed nihilistic nirvana is not clear. Generally, Mahayana teaches that those who attain the Hinayana nirvana, whom it calls Arhats, stay in lesser nirvana for some "time" (even though it is, presumably, a timeless state), and then experience a fortunate fruiting of karma, due to which they hear about the Mahayana path, and so resume their practice until they reach unsupported nirvana. A minority of Mahayana texts have the Arhats bemoaning that they are stuck in lesser nirvana and now cannot come back to assist other beings because their "roots" are destroyed, but this is not usually taught.

Disappearance

DISAPPEARANCE OF THE BUDDHA
After the breakup of the clusters that had constituted the last life of Shakyamuni as a human, his physical body remained to

be disposed of like that of any other being. It was cremated,
following the most usual custom of the Indian subcontinent.
After the cremation, some remains were found that had resisted
the flames. These are known as *sharira* (literally "body") and are
worshipped as relics.

There followed an unedifying fight over the relics: the kings of
the surrounding region went to war for sole possession of them.
Tradition says that the war was ended by the arbitration of a
brahmin called Drona, who divided up the relics equally between eight claimants. Or, not quite equally. He is said to have
kept one for himself, concealing it in his sacred topknot. A deity,
however, spotted the deception, swooped down, and took the
relic back to his heaven where it was suitably enshrined.

The relics that remained on earth were enclosed in large burial
mounds called *stupa* (Pali: *thupa*). By tradition, eight stupas
were built over the eight original relics. There are now many
thousands of stupas throughout the Buddhist world: it has
become the most distinctive architectural feature of Buddhism
and has undergone a complex development.[1] The major forms
are sketched in figure 11.

In its earliest form, the stupa is a large hemispherical mound
of earth with the relic at its center. The mound is covered with
masonry facing and pierced by a central pillar topped with ceremonial umbrellas (the symbol of royalty). The whole structure
is surrounded by a walkway and bounded by ornamental gateways.

A typical stupa of this early type, which is still in a good state
of repair, is that at Sañchi near Bhopal, India. The gateways are
elaborately carved with secular, and indeed erotic, subjects, serving as a transition from the realm of the passions to the realm
of the Dharma. Reverence is paid to the relics by walking around
the stupa in a clockwise direction, according to the ancient Indian practice of *pradakshina* (literally "keeping it on the right")
that is found in some form or another in all parts of the Buddhist
world. As one keeps close to the plain bulk of the stupa on one's
right, and the world of ordinary experience goes by on one's left,
the feeling may arise that one has found a center, an island of
refuge, amidst the confusion of samsara.

As the architectural form developed, its symbolism more and
more overwhelmed its utilitarian purpose. The mound was first
raised on a base, then the base became larger than the mound,

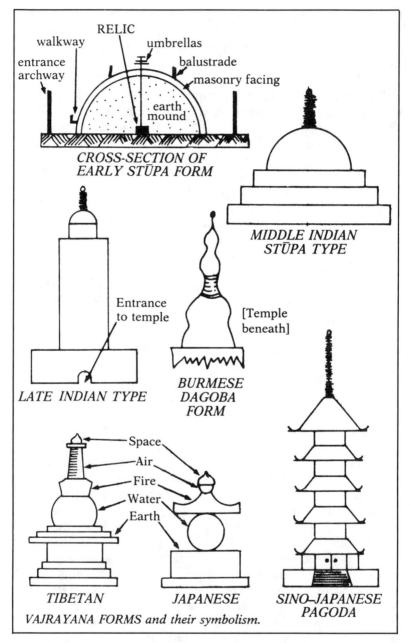

Figure 12: STŪPA DEVELOPMENT.

eventually opening up into a temple with the mound becoming reduced to a dome or elongated into a spire. In the Far East, the central pillar expanded to produce the distinctive multistoried structure, modeled after pre-Buddhist Chinese watchtowers, and generally known in English as a pagoda. A small dome or ball surmounting the spire is all that remains of the original hemispherical stupa form.

When the stupa is in the form of a temple, the relic will not be invisible, as it is at places like Sañchi, but exposed for veneration. The most famous of these relics is what is purported to be a tooth of the Buddha, housed in the Temple of the Tooth in Kandy, Sri Lanka, and carried about in procession once a year. Other relics are, like many Christian relics, quite small. Typical of these is the relic in the stupa-shaped temple on the roof of the headquarters of the Buddhist Churches of America (a Pure Land lineage—on which see later in this chapter) in San Francisco.

When there is no relic inside a stupa (whether it is in the form of a temple or a mound) an image or a sacred text may function as a substitute, on the basis of the unity of the Triple Jewel: a properly consecrated image, or a true word of the Buddha, is non-dual with the Buddha himself. Nevertheless, a true relic, when available, is held in greater esteem.

Sometimes the stupa is regarded as a symbol of the entire Buddhist worldview, a microcosm of the Dharma. This is most obviously the case with the Tibetan form, called *chörten,* and a stupa of similar shape found in Japanese Tantric (Shingon) Buddhism, both of which are used as funerary monuments. Even the Theravadin *dagoba,* however, can be seen in this way, according to the elaborate explanations given by Lama Govinda.[2]

The stupa can also be an offering. Miniature stupas are placed on Mahayana altars, and bamboo slips, with the name of the deceased and an appropriate prayer or mantra written on them, are tied onto Japanese funerary stupas as a part of the yearly festival of the dead called *Obon matsuri.* That these bamboo slips are regarded as supplementary stupas seems clear from the fact that they have curved tops reminiscent of stupa domes.

Stupas are now being erected in the United States. For example, a Tibetan chorten near Bloomington, Indiana, was dedicated in October 1987 by the Dalai Lama as a memorial to those who died resisting the takeover of Tibet by the Peoples' Republic of China, and a small but influential Japanese lineage, Nichihonzan Myohoji, which conducts vigorous campaigns for nuclear disarmanent, has erected a Peace Pagoda in Kitsap County, Washington, near a Trident nuclear submarine base.

PILGRIMAGE

Although a Buddha, after final nirvana, is not locatable within space and time, it is helpful to have something within the space-time continuum as a focus for practice. Stupas are one such focus. Pilgrimage sites are another, related, focus. Any pilgrimage site that is in a good state of repair can be expected to have a stupa, but it will be subsidiary in importance to the site itself.

A pilgrimage differs from a journey in that a journey is merely an outward movement from one place to another, whereas a pilgrimage is both an outward and an inward movement. It is what is called enantiodromic, that is, it goes in opposite directions at the same time, like going "into" a mirror by walking away from it.

A pilgrimage is, also, a journey towards a place of great significance. It is a journey to a place which is "close to one's heart." The baseball enthusiast, for example, makes a pilgrimage to the Baseball Hall of Fame because it is, for him at that moment, the center of his external and internal universe. And so we say that players are "enshrined" there.

If a pilgrimage is explicitly religious, the pilgrim says that the goal is not just *a* center but *the* center, the most important place in the world. For a Buddhist, this is Bodh Gaya, the place of the Buddha's enlightenment. When one has arrived at the center outwardly, one has also reached, or striven to reach, the center inwardly. Standing before the Bodhi Tree the Buddhist tries to be aware of the bodhi mind within.

There are important pilgrimage sites all over the Buddhist world, but the four most important are those associated with the birth, enlightenment, first teaching, and final nirvana of Shakyamuni Buddha. The custom of going on the "Buddhist pilgrimage" *(dharma-yatra)* is probably quite old, but the first record we have of it is given by Emperor Ashoka (see chapter 2). He set up memorial inscriptions at each of the sites, and, since he gives us the dates of his visits, calculated as so many years after the final nirvana, he unwittingly provides us with the only reliable way of arriving at a historically credible date for the Buddha's life.

The four great pilgrimage sites, three of which are in the Republic of India while the fourth is in the Kingdom of Nepal, are as follows:

1. Lumbini: *This is in Nepal and is locally known as Rupadei, Rupandehi, and Rummindei as well as Lumbini.³ All Buddhist traditions identify it as the place of the Buddha's birth. It no longer has its* sal *trees and is at present quite isolated. Although it is near the Indian border, it is normally reached by air and then bus from Kathmandu, the capital of Nepal. A multinational project, endorsed by the United Nations and actively supported by the Nepali royal family, is slowly moving ahead with plans to develop it as a world Buddhist center.*

2. Bodh Gaya: *The place of the enlightenment. The most fully developed of the four sites, it is dominated by the magnificent Mahabodhi Mandir (Temple of the Great Enlightenment), next to which is the Bodhi Tree and the space that is the symbol of this book. Temples and/or monasteries have been built by the Burmese, Thais, Tibetans, Chinese, and Japanese, and bhikkhus from Sri Lanka run a bookstore. It is thus possible to spend a day experiencing in quick succession the different cultural flavors of the Dharma. Bodh Gaya is otherwise a sleepy little village near the important Hindu pilgrimage town of Gaya, sometimes distinguished as Hindu Gaya, in the Indian state of Bihar.*

3. Rishipatana: *The place of the first teaching or Wheel Sutra. Locally it is called Sarnath and is today a suburb of Benares, the most important of all Hindu pilgrimage towns. The site contains a large, ancient stupa, modern temples from many parts of the Buddhist world, and a small but excellent museum. Known in the Buddhist texts as Mrigadava, the Deer Park, a fenced-in copse has been stocked with deer to give an authentic appearance.*

4. Kushinagar: *Locally known as Kasia, west of Gorakhpur, India, this is the place of the final nirvana. There is a large mound, which may have been a stupa, on the spot where the Buddha's body is said to have been cremated, with a temple nearby containing a statue of the Buddha in the so-called "lion pose," i.e., lying on his right side as he passes into final nirvana.*

The Buddha is reported to have been very ambiguous about the setting up of pilgrimage sites after his final nirvana. He was afraid that people would become attached to them, in a form of "spiritual materialism," and was at first in favor of not having any sites at all. He was, however, prevailed upon to approve these four. We misuse them, then, the Buddha seems to say, if we go to them simply as tourists. That would be merely a journey. By making a pilgrimage to them, we are assisting our progress to our own enlightenment.

THE DECAY OF THE DHARMA

Everything which comes into being, said the Buddha, will be destroyed. Although the Dharma is eternal in its essence, when it comes into being as a phenomenon, that is, as a teaching proclaimed by a Buddha, it is subject to decay along with the universe in general.

The decay of the universe is followed by the birth of another universe. It is not the end of samsara, it is like the death and rebirth of a being within samsara, but on a very much grander scale. The cyclic death and rebirth of the universe as it is taught in Buddhism is similar to that which is taught in many forms of Hinduism: the universe goes through a sequence of "ages" *(yuga),* and, for both Hinduism and Buddhism, we are now on the down side of one of the final ages.

The standard Theravada teaching on the death and rebirth of the universe is given by Buddhaghosa in his Visuddhimagga.[4] He says that the universe will be destroyed, at one time or another, by fire, by water, and by wind. There are to be, he says, seven destructions by fire followed by one by water. This cycle of eight will be repeated seven times, until there have been fifty-six such cycles. Next, there will be seven destructions by water, giving a total of sixty-three cycles of creation and destruction. After that, the destructions will be by wind. The process goes on, but Buddhaghosa does not give us any more details. We have already looked so far into the future (he accepts astronomical time scales quite matter-of-factly) that any further information would scarcely be meaningful. The point is that whatever has come to be, whether apparently stable civilizations or even the world itself, will disappear and so cannot, in the final analysis, give anything but suffering.

Buddhaghosa describes the process of destruction in detail in the case of a destruction by fire. First, there will be refreshing rains, bringing joy and the promise of a good harvest, but then they fail, and the terrible heat begins. Deities known as Loka-bhyuhas descend from their heaven and, with their hair dishevelled and screaming in distress, go through the world urging beings to practice compassion and the other virtues, since the end of a world system is near. Many earth beings die and, through the fruiting of their virtue from lives in the distant past, are reborn in the higher heavens. The heat increases, and spreads upwards to the lower heavens. One after another, supplementary suns appear, until there are seven suns and the world dies in a universal conflagration. Then, after a very long time, a cloud appears and begins to refertilize a reborn earth. Beings appear once more on earth, but in subtle bodies of light, moving around without pressure. They taste the earth, find that it is (at that time) edible and appetizing, and begin to take on the nature of earth, becoming fully physical and producing the openings necessary for bodily functions. As a consequence they develop the physical passions, including sex, of which they are ashamed (because "the wise" criticize them for it) so they invent clothing and shelter. Next they establish boundary lines, and, as Karl Marx wrote centuries after Buddhaghosa, begin to fight over the possession of private property. Civilization and all its ills comes into being, and continues until the destruction of the world system, after which the whole sequence starts again.

In general, the cycle of destruction begins in the human realm and spreads upwards, while the cycle of regeneration begins in the deity realms and spreads downwards.[5] Buddhaghosa says that there is a connection between the three poisons (attachment, aversion, and confusion) and the three modes of destruction. When confusion dominates a world system, it is destroyed by wind. When attachment or aversion dominate, the destruction is either by fire or by water. He gives us two conflicting traditions on this, and does not decide between them.

The Dharma, being manifest, decays along with the world. In one Pali text, the Buddha states that the Dharma would normally remain in its pure form for a thousand years, but he cuts this period in half after admitting women to the Samgha as nuns.[6] Another Pali text accepts one thousand years as the period of the pure, or true Dharma, during which time complete enlightenment is possible, and then catalogs its degeneration through a further five thousand or more years, as monastic conduct, the scriptural texts, the ritual paraphernalia, and the relics successively and gradually disappear, until nothing whatsoever of Buddhism remains. The destruction of the world itself then follows.

Mahayana commonly teaches the decay of a world cycle under five aspects:

1. Kalpa-kashaya: *the decay of the age (the yuga, here, however, called a kalpa) in general.*

2. Drishti-kashaya: *the decay of right viewpoint, or true understanding of the Dharma.*

3. Klesha-kashaya: *the decay of conduct, with the rise to greater prominence of the Three Poisons.*

4. Sattva-kashaya: *the decay affecting sentient beings, in which their suffering increases.*

5. Ayuh-kashaya: *the decay of lifespan, in which the life expectation and the stature of humans will progressively decrease until we are an average of (at the most pessimistic estimate) one foot tall and live for only one year.*

The decay of the Dharma is normally divided by the Mahayana into three periods, called successively True Dharma (*sad-dharma*), Shadow Dharma (*pratirupa-dharma*), and Withered or Final Dharma (*vipralopa* or *paschima-dharma*). The length of these periods is variously set at either five hundred or a thousand years for each of the first two, and ten thousand years for the last, giving four possible combinations, all of which have been, at different times, taught as the correct one by some lineage or another. This triple periodization is found in various sutras, but most clearly in a large, apocalyptic Chinese text called Ta-chi Ching, The Great Collection Sutra.

The first lineage to make extensive use of this periodization was the Teaching of the Three Stages (San-chieh Chiao) of Hsin–hsing (540–594 C.E.).[7] He accepted the values of 500 and 1,000, respectively, for the ages of the True and Shadow Dharma, and, since it was widely believed in China at the time that the Buddha had passed into final nirvana in 949 B.C.E., he calculated that the Age of Final Dharma had begun in 551 C.E. He preached that the One Vehicle had been taught during the Age of True Dharma and the Triple Vehicle during the Age of Shadow Dharma, when only the form but not the substance of Buddhism was generally accessible, and that in his day, during the Age of Final Dharma, only his own doctrine was appropriate. Everything, he said, was Buddha, just as it is. Therefore, one should prostrate even to animals as if to exalted teachers. Unfortunately for his popularity, he taught that not only no other Buddhist lineage, but also no government, was efficacious during the Age of Final Dharma. He thus managed to offend everybody who was anybody, and his lineage was suppressed.

In Japan, the periods of the True and Shadow Dharma are commonly understood as lasting one thousand years each. With the final nirvana of Shakyamuni Buddha set at the Chinese date of 949 B.C.E., 1051 C.E. was obtained for the beginning of the Age of Final Dharma. This happened to coincide, as did the date of 551 in China, with a period of political and social unrest, and gave an opportunity for some Buddhist reformers to proclaim that the time had come for the overthrow of governments and other Buddhist lineages. The most vocal such reformer was Nichiren, whose vigorous teaching has been discussed in chapter 2. Less strident, but just as convinced, were the reformers of the Pure Land Lineage, to be discussed later in this chapter.

Japanese Buddhists explain the decay of the Dharma as a threefold process. During the Age of the True Dharma *(Shobo-jidai)*, the true teaching *(kyo)*, practice *(gyo)* and attainment *(sho)* are manifest. When attainment decays, the Age of the Shadow Dharma *(Zoho-jidai)* has begun. On the surface, Buddhism seems healthy, the texts are extant and their meaning is understood, and the temples with their rituals still survive, but upon investigation it is found that no one is attaining enlightenment. The form (or shadow) remains, but the living spirit has gone. In the next phase, practice disappears, and only the teaching, which no one any longer really understands, remains. This marks the beginning of the Age of the Final Dharma *(Mappo-*

jidai), which is sometimes said to last until the end of the world-cycle, "ten thousand years" being regarded as a symbol for "unto the end of time as we know it." Certain texts are sometimes identified as being more likely to remain than others, with the Pure Land texts (see below) surviving the longest, until, at last, even the name "Buddha" is forgotten.

Hsin-hsing and Nichiren are just two examples of teachers who have proclaimed the Age of the Final Dharma, and they have been chosen from the East Asian Mahayana traditions. Theravadin and Tibetan Final Dharma traditions, which are more closely associated with notions of reform and restoration, will be discussed in the next section. The general trend is that whenever there is social or political unrest, or a series of natural catastrophes, it is open to some Buddhists to announce that, according to their calculations, the Age of the Final Dharma has appeared, and a major religious and social revolution is due to occur. They then provide us with what they regard as the only form of the Dharma which it is feasible to practice in such degenerate times. The continuation of other forms of Buddhism, and of the world in general, is as much a perplexity and embarrassment to these Buddhist millenarian movements as it is to similar movements in other religions.

A prominent opponent of Final Dharma teaching, especially in Japan, is the Zen lineage. Zen masters typically bypass the proclamation of difficulties and say: Just sit, and you will find that you can do it.

It is not easy to square Final Dharma teachings with what we think we know about reality through modern science. On the one hand it might seem that the world is headed for disaster, through overpopulation, pollution and the threat of global nuclear warfare, that materialism is increasing and religion is declining, so that it is clear that the end of the age is near. On the other hand, people seem to be living longer and to be growing taller (witness, for example, second generation Japanese Americans [Nisei], who are almost always taller than their Japanese-born parents) and the Dharma, though struggling in the east, is flourishing in the west. Again, the teaching of progressive degeneration seems to be flat contrary to the scientific teaching of evolution, unless we take the larger view that evolution is occurring in the context of universal entropy, in which case we might see any improvement as merely the refreshing rains which bring false hopes of a good harvest.

Reappearance

FINAL NIRVANA AS SKILLFUL MEANS

It has already been noted that nirvana is not a negative condition, a state of cosmic annihilation. However, it is often expressed in negative terms, and so the impression may still remain that there is something nihilistic about it.

There is a famous passage in the Pali texts, which uses positive and quasi-positive terms for describing nirvana. It is Udana 80, and runs as follows:

> *There is, monks, that state wherein is neither earth nor water nor fire nor air; wherein is neither the state of the infinity of space nor of the infinity of consciousness nor of nothing whatsoever nor of neither-notions-nor-non-notions; where there is neither this world, nor a world beyond, nor both, neither moon nor sun; this, monks, I say is free from coming and going, from duration and decay; there is no beginning and no establishment, no result and no cause; this indeed is the end of suffering . . . There is, monks, a not-born, not-become, not-made, and not-compounded. Monks, if that not-born, not-become, not-made, and not-compounded were not, no escape from the born, become, made, and compounded had been known here. But, monks, since there is a not-born, not-become, not-made, and not-compounded, therefore an escape from the born, become, made, and compounded is known.*[8]

This passage is a positive assertion of nirvana, even though it is still couched in negative terms. Nirvana exists, it seems to say, but not in terms of "existing" as we know it, therefore we can only say what it is not.

The story is told of a tadpole who evolved into a frog. He left his fellow tadpoles behind, and went out of the pond to examine the strange new realities of air and dry land. Excitedly he re-

turned to his tadpole friends and tried to explain to them what
he had experienced.

"There is air," he said.

"What is it like?," they asked.

"It is everywhere, like water, only it is not wet."

"How can water not be wet?"

"Because it is not water."

"But there cannot not be water!"

"Well, then, there is dry land."

"What is that like?"

"It is like mud, only it is not wet."

"Not-wet, not-wet, that's all we hear from you. But *everything*
is wet. Wet is how things are. You are babbling. Your 'air' and
'dry land' are just nothing at all!"

"No, no! They are something, but they are not wet."

When a liberated being tries to describe nirvana to an unliberated being, similar difficulties arise. It is beyond existence,
yet it is not another world. It is not nothing, yet it is not anything
like something. It is not life, death, both or neither.

When the other tadpoles become frogs, they see for themselves
what their apparently insane companion meant. At liberation,
our consciousness is transformed (in Yogachara terms, our consciousness or *vijñana* becomes wisdom or *jñana*) and we no
longer need to define reality in terms of existence or non-existence.

Mahayana takes this denial of nihilism one step further and
actually teaches nirvana as if it were a positive condition. The
classic statement of this is chapter 11 of the Lotus Sutra, in which
an enormous, richly ornamented stupa suddenly erupts from the
earth. Shakyamuni Buddha opens a door in the front of it and
reveals another Buddha, Prabhutaratna, sitting inside. Prabhutaratna Buddha had passed into final nirvana many ages ago,
and on opening his stupa one would have expected to see only
his relics, but Prabhutaratna is still alive and healthy. He invites
Shakyamuni to sit next to him, indicating by this that the two
Buddhas are equals, and Shakyamuni climbs up.[9]

The point of this incident is that Mahayana views the "final
nirvana" of the Hinayanists as a skillful means which the Buddhas display for those of inferior capacity. If we think that our
practice really has no goal, we may lose heart. So, the Buddhas

tell us that a definite end is attainable, and we feel encouraged enough to practice diligently. It is like teaching a child to walk: "Just one more step dear; good! now another one . . ." and so forth. However, if nirvana really were a condition of final rest, it could be distinguished from samsara, and so could not really be nirvana. The Lotus Sutra is giving us a simile of the Mahayana "unsupported" nirvana, which is inconceivable in terms of the duality of goal and no-goal.

Nirvana as a skillful means is related to the Bodhisattva resolve to return to samsara even though one might have acquired enough merit to leave it. It is a commonplace of Mahayana Buddhist liturgies to beseech the Buddhas, Bodhisattvas, and teachers not to depart into final nirvana until all beings have been liberated. In Tibet, this has become institutionalized, in some lineages, in what is known as the Hubilganic Succession. Certain teachers have the ability to employ a death yoga (the details of which vary according to lineage) in order to "bring death into the path," that is, to use the perfect openness and freedom of the Clear Light, which comes at a certain point in the death process, as a door to liberation from bondage to samsara, so that, Great Compassion arising spontaneously, they take an appropriate rebirth.[10] Such beings are known as tulku *(sprul sku)* in Tibetan (or *hubilgan* in Mongolian, hence the term "hubilganic"), a translation of the Sanskrit word Nirmanakaya (see the discussion of the Trikaya in chapter 1). His Holiness the Dalai Lama is a prominent tulku. The present Dalai Lama is the fourteenth in the line of rebirth.

Even within the Mahayana, final nirvana is, it will be noted, still mentioned. It therefore seems that there will come a time when it will be appropriate to enter it. Indeed, it is common to resolve that one's bodhisattva activity will continue "until samsara is emptied." The question then arises, what happens then? A Tibetan teacher of whom I asked this gave a very practical reply: "Don't worry about it, it won't be any time soon."

REFRESHING THE DHARMA

Many Buddhist traditions, while accepting that the Dharma, once manifested, will decay, speak of ways in which it will be restored or refreshed. Prominent among these is the belief in the appearance of the Bodhisattva Maitreya, known in Theravada countries as Metteyya.[11] Maitreya, it will be remembered, was appointed by Shakyamuni to be the next Buddha, and he is said to be living now in the Tushita heaven awaiting the time when it will be right for him to descend. It is therefore possible for some Buddhists to assume that, whenever the teachings of Shakyamuni are endangered, Maitreya's appearance is imminent.

This "messianic" expectation (as it has sometimes been called) has been an important part of the political history of Southeast Asia from time to time. For instance, the Burmese revolution against colonial domination was fueled in part by the identification of one or another revolutionary hero with Metteyya in the form of the righteous Buddhist king Satkya-Min (a Burmanization of the Pali *Chakkavatti*, "Wheel Turning Emperor").[12]

In the Tibetan tradition, the restoration of the Dharma is expected to be accomplished not only by Maitreya but also by Rudra Chakrin, a future king of a region known as Shambhala. Rudra Chakrin is regarded as a form of Mañjushri, the Bodhisattva of Wisdom, and is associated with the Kalachakra Tantra.[13] Shambhala is said to be a fertile valley hidden somewhere in the otherwise hostile snowy wastes of the Himalayas, where all is peaceful and the Dharma flourishes. The legend has entered western literature through the story of Shangri-la.[14] There will come a time, according to the legend, when evil, materialistic rulers will take over the earth, exerting control by means of the most destructive weapons ever known. Just as the supreme ruler has assured himself that no opponents remain, he hears of the tiny kingdom of Shambhala. Enraged, he throws all his fearsome weapons at it, and a terrible battle ensues. Victory for the dictator, who has superior physical forces, seems certain at first, but Rudra Chakrin and all his subjects are great Bodhisattvas who have been reborn in Shambhala at this time expressly for the purpose of defeating the evil ruler.[15] Their spiritual power overcomes the physical power of the attacker, and a golden age of the Dharma begins, at the end of which the Dharma will decline until it is restored by Maitreya.[16]

A tradition of renewal which is specific to the Nyingmapa, the most ancient lineage of Tibetan Buddhism, is that of the *terma* (*gter ma)* or hidden treasures.[17] The great Indian teacher Padmasambhava, who is credited with the conversion of Tibet to the Dharma in the eighth century c.e., is said to have used his supernormal skills to plant seeds of Dharmic renewal. These seeds take the form of, amongst other things, relics, ritual objects, natural phenomena (such as rocks, trees and lakes), precious metals, jewels, and, most importantly, texts. The texts are written in a special language, either a non-human language or a form of Tibetan incomprehensible to ordinary speakers. In addition, they are under a kind of "time lock" that preserves them from unauthorized interference until the proper time. When that time arrives, a certain person, usually identified as a *gongter* or emanation *(dgongs gter)* of Padmasambhava, discovers the treasure, uses the key or formula *(gtsug las khan)* to unlock it, decodes it, and proclaims its liberating message. Such a person is known as a *terton (gter ston)* or discoverer of a hidden treasure. A terma is like a piece of the True Dharma that has, as it were, been frozen in its pure state, so that when it is released at the time of the degenerate Dharma it has lost none of its purity and it can restore the true teaching, even if, at the time of its release, the entire body of teaching and practice has disappeared. The Nyingma canon contains a section devoted to textual terma that have already been discovered (many more are said to be still awaiting discovery), and some of these are now available in English.[18]

The Chinese cultus of Maitreya, which has a respectable history, produced a strange offspring in the figure of Pu-tai (Japanese: Hotei).[19] Pu-tai is the so-called "laughing Buddha," the fat, dishevelled monk whose image, either standing up with arms raised, or sitting down grinning inanely, can be found in practically every curio shop in Chinatown.

Pu-tai, a nickname meaning Hemp Bag (his real name being unknown) may have been a Taoist folk hero, or, more likely perhaps, a Buddhist monk from Chekiang province in China who lived sometime in the first half of the tenth century C.E. If he was a Buddhist monk, he was the sort that did not have a permanent monastic home, but traveled from place to place as a "cloud and water" *(yün-shui)* monk. He never seemed to mind the weather, and was often seen talking and laughing to himself. Over his shoulder he carried the hemp bag which gave him his nickname, in which he put anything he found or was given. This bag of junk was an object of derision and fascination to onlookers. To children, it was the bag of wonderful things. After Pu-tai died, the tradition developed that he had been a form of Maitreya, since Maitreya means the Kindly One (Sanskrit: *mitra,* friend) and Pu-tai had been nothing if not kind and jolly. In the course of time he came to be identified with a Chinese god of luck, so that the only thing some people know about Buddhism is that "You rub the Buddha's tummy and he brings you luck."

More importantly, he was chosen by the Zen lineage as a type of "anti-monk." An important aspect of Zen is the fun it makes of other, more staid forms of Buddhism, as a way of cutting through the hypocrisy or "spiritual materialism" (as Chögyam Trungpa called it) that, in any religion, keeps coming in the back door after it has been thrown out of the front. Pu-tai is a monk, as his shaved head and robe make clear, but he does not take the trappings of monasticism very seriously: his robe is improperly arranged, so that his stomach is showing (an offense against both the Vinaya and Confucian etiquette); he seems to have forgotten his sandals (showing that he is not very good at the practice of mindfulness); and he is overweight (apparently having ignored the precept about moderation in eating). Zen never suggests, however, that the Buddha is a fraud or that enlightenment is an impossible fantasy. The fun is poked at the inessential shell of the Dharma, never at the Dharma itself.[20] So, Pu-tai's image is properly enshrined, and offerings are made to it just as to a more solemn image. I noted, however, that in Japanese Zen temples, the shrine to Hotei was often near the entrance, as if the monks were saying to visitors "We do serious *work* here, but we try not to take *ourselves* too seriously."

Spontaneous Joy

VAJRAYANA

The Tantric Perspective

The experience of Buddhism, I have said, is the experience of joy. This joy is, as we have seen, generally expressed negatively, as the absence of duhkha. There is a reluctance to express liberation positively, calling it joy, bliss, or eternal happiness, since there is the danger that this will be misunderstood in samsaric terms, and samsaric joy is not the absence of suffering, but the experience of very subtle suffering.

There is an old joke about a man banging his head against a wall. "Why are you doing that?" someone asks. "Oh," he replies, "it's so lovely when I stop." The relief the man feels at the reduction of his suffering is samsaric joy. Extra-samsaric joy is not capable of being expressed, understood, or even felt, intra-samsarically, that is, it is neither joy nor suffering as we unliberated beings know it.

But, so long as the term "joy" is hedged around with these caveats, it is possible to speak of liberation in positive terms. In Tantric Buddhism it is called "Great Bliss" *(Mahasukha). Sukha* is the antonym of duhkha, the opposite of the first part of the Fourfold Truth. Wherever there is the absence of duhkha, there is sukha. We can think of this the way we think of a minus quantity. If I have two apples and take away four, I have −2 apples. I cannot *picture* this, but I can work with it. I can grasp it intellectually, though not experientially. So with sukha. I can understand what it is, but I cannot experience it until I am enlightened, or at least until I have a momentary flash of enlightened mind.

Tantric Buddhism is so called because it preserves special texts called Tantras, which we will examine later. It is also called Vajrayana, the vehicle or method (yana) of the vajra. Vajra is a Sanskrit word with a rich history in the culture of the Indian subcontinent.[21] In Buddhism it stands for the perfection of wisdom, pure mind, reality-as-it-is, which, like space, is unconquerable. It is symbolized by the indestructible clarity of the diamond. Vajrayana, then, means the Supreme Vehicle.

In the Tibetan Buddhist "Three Vehicle" classification (see "The Graded Path" in chapter 9), Vajrayana is the third vehicle. It is not, however, an entirely separate vehicle, since it leads to the same goal as the Mahayana. It is, more precisely, a sub-vehicle of Mahayana, distinguished as a separate vehicle only because of its different, and, it claims, more efficacious, practices.[22]

The Tantric perspective is called "pure perspective" because it sees reality as unconditioned, totally blissful, forever liberated from duhkha. Although duhkha is not a fantasy, it is dreamlike, it is not the way reality "really" is. Duhkha has been brought about by causes and conditions. When reality is seen without the defilements of causes and conditions, duhkha disappears.

This is like seeing space. Seeing purely is seeing spaciously, seeing Transparency. It is Complete Openness.

When reality is seen thus, it is called *Vajradhatu,* "Diamond

Realm." This is the Tantric equivalent of the Realm of Indra's Net. We see everything as pure, sparkling, and free from sorrow, and as it were full of magic. Our vision is filled with Buddhas, Bodhisattvas, and Dharma Teachers in their glorious rainbow bodies, seated on lotus thrones in the midst of huge, awe-inspiring, glittering mandala palaces. The dirt, disappointment, pain, and limitations of our ordinarily perceived universe disappears. Beauty can be appreciated without attachment and the negative attitude of Hinayana is no longer needed, since the addictive mind has been transformed into Buddha Mind. Every moment is experienced as fresh, as it is when reality is seen as the openness of the scintillation of the dharmas (see chapter 5), and as it is known to be (but perhaps not experienced as such) through the study of Madhyamika and Yogachara.

Perfect wisdom and perfect compassion become inseparable and are experienced as perfect energy. Tantric activity is *anabhoga* (Tibetan: *lhun grub*), goalless,[23] playful, spontaneous.

I complained once to a lama that taking the Bodhisattva vow to remain in samsara as long as there were beings to be liberated was very discouraging. So many beings, and so much time! I felt exhausted at the very thought of it. "Yes," he said, "now it may seem that way. But when we are Buddhas, we have infinite energy."

Tantric Practice

Not only does Tantra speak of liberation in positive terms, it also speaks of Transparency, or reality itself, in positive terms. In Mahayana, the Dharmakaya (see chapter 1) is referred to only by negatives. In Tantra, the Dharmakaya is visualized as the activity of the Buddha.

Although all Buddhas are equal, since all are equally enlightened, one Buddha is given, by Tantra, a kind of pre-eminence as the hypostasization of Pure Mind itself. This Buddha is sometimes called the Primal Buddha (Adi-Buddha) or Cosmic Buddha and is identified as, according to the various sub-lineages of Tantra, the Buddha Vairochana (The Greatly Shining One), the Buddha Vajradhara (The Vajra Bearer), or the Buddha Samantabhadra (The Universally Auspicious One), and he acts.

The acts of sentient beings are said to be threefold: acts of body, acts of speech, and acts of mind. The Cosmic Buddha also manifests the actions of body, speech, and mind, but does so according to the energy mode of *anabhoga,* spontaneity or play-fulness. Whereas an unliberated being *(sattva)* acts out of a sense of inherently existing self and other, within a universe bound and defined by time and space, and having goals, a Buddha simply acts. His actions are non-referential. They occur (since they are observed within samsara), yet they do not occur (since their perspective and motivation is extra-samsaric). They express the non-duality of samsara and nirvana. Transparency, as it is understood by the skillful means of negation according to Madhyamika, is viewed positively.

Madhyamika can be mistaken for dualism or nihilism. It might seem as if liberation means going from an embodied state in samsara to a disembodied state in nirvana. Yogachara, with its predominantly positive terminology, partly removes this misunderstanding. Tantra goes further. Reality itself, shunyata, is taught as the universality of the body, speech, and mind of the Cosmic Buddha. However, since this, in its turn, can be misunderstood as monism (i.e., that samsara *just as it is* is nirvana) this universality of Buddha-embodiment has to be viewed in the light of the Madhyamika negations, as empty of inherent existence.

The theory of Tantra is not different from the non-duality taught in Madhyamika and Yogachara. The distinctive practice of Tantra is that this non-duality is lived, or embodied. The body, speech, and mind of the Tantric practitioner are seen as non-dual with the body, speech, and mind of the Cosmic Buddha, by means of *mudra, mantra,* and *smriti.*

Mudra is gesture. The hands of the practitioner are brought together in certain strictly prescribed ways in order to actualize the non-duality of the bodies of sattvas and of Buddhas. These gestures are sometimes very complicated, but they can be quite simple. One gesture, which is also found in other forms of Buddhism, is to bring the right and left palms together in a manner similar to the gesture of prayer in Christianity. In non-Tantric Buddhism, this is merely a gesture of respect. In Tantra, it means, in addition, the actualization of the non-duality of the realms of samsara (the left hand) and nirvana (the right hand).

This dual symbolism is present in much of Tantra. The non-Tantric meaning (e.g., the joining of hands as a mark of respect) is called the *exoteric meaning* because its significance is obvious, and the Tantric meaning is called the *esoteric meaning* because its meaning is not immediately evident. It is either a normal action with an unusual meaning or it is an apparently meaning-less action. In either case it needs a special, or esoteric, line of teaching transmission.

Mantra means an action of the voice or speech. The word has passed into modern English, but it is often misunderstood. In Sanskrit it has many meanings, always having something to do with sacred or special speech. Buddhism emphasizes its etymol-ogy as that which protects *(tra)* the mind *(man)* from ordinary or defiled perception.

A very popular mantra is OM MANI PADME HUM, pro-nounced by Tibetans "Ohm manny paymay hoom." Western text-books sometimes say that this means "Hail to the Jewel in the Lotus." It is not too much to say that this "meaning" is mischie-vous nonsense. A mantra is a sound, it is not language, and therefore it is not a sentence. Like music, a mantra may occa-sionally have a meaning separate from itself, but usually it does not. If a piece of music is supposed to conjure up pictures in our heads, such as the songs of various identifiable birds, we call it Program Music. This is like language, in which a word like "cat" refers to a furry animal that can purr and scratch. What we might call pure music, like a Beethoven symphony, is its own meaning. Any pictures we might see while listening to it are incidental and unimportant. We cannot meaningfully ask "What is the *meaning* of "Ta-ta-ta TUM" at the beginning of the Fifth Symphony?" Similarly, we cannot ask for the dictionary mean-ing of OM MANI PADME HUM. Certain elements of it, indeed, are linguistically identifiable—*mani* is "jewel" and *padme* is the vocative of "lotus"—but if we say "OM Jewel, Oh Lotus! HUM," we have not been very communicative.

The Chinese teacher T'an-luan (c. 488–c. 554 C.E.) clears this up for us. He says that there are two sorts of words (Chinese: *ming,* possibly "two sorts of *nouns*"). First, there are what he calls "words that are other than things." These are ordinary words, like "cat," and they are quite arbitrary. They *refer* to things, "like," says T'an-luan, "a finger pointing at the moon." We can call them "thing-words." If we wanted to use the word "dog" to refer to a furry animal that purrs and scratches, we could do so without ambiguity so long as everyone else agreed to this use (and that in fact is what we do, when we use a language other than English to refer to that animal).

Then, says T'an-luan, there are "words which are the same as things." These are mantras. A mantra is a *word-thing*, that is, it is a word that itself a thing, rather than a word that refers to a thing. It is as if a finger, rather than pointing at the moon, would itself emit moonlight.

A mantra, then, does not signify but it is what it signifies. That is, its meaning is not a dictionary meaning, its meaning is its sound or (as they might say in California) its "vibes." OM MANI PADME HUM is the mantra of Avalokiteshvara, the Bodhisattva of Compassion, and it therefore "means" Avalokiteshvara; it is Avalokiteshvara manifest as audible energy. It is compassionate mind actualized as speech.

Smriti means remembering or recollection. It refers to the mental activity of learning the mudras and the mantras, understanding their meaning (in the way I have just described "meaning"), and performing them with conscious awareness. A mudra or mantra will have some effect of itself, but it has much more effect when it is performed mindfully.

The primary meaning of the word tantra is similar to that of sutra. Both mean a thread or connection, that is, a link with the true teaching of the Buddhas. A sutra is an exoteric thread and is, in form, generally something like a sermon. It is an explanation or exposition of a doctrine. A tantra is a liturgy (sadhana). One listens to a sutra in order to understand it. One learns a tantra in order to perform it. The tantra will contain visualizations (see chapter 6), mudras, and mantras. When it is performed correctly by the properly prepared practitioner, a phenomenon that the Japanese Tantric teacher Kobo Daishi calls *sammitsu-kaji* takes place: the syngery *(kaji)*, or linking of energy between sentient beings and Buddhas, of the triple mystery *(sammitsu)* of mudra, mantra, and smriti. The actions of the Tantric practitioner *(sadhaka)* become non-dual with the actions of the Cosmic Buddha.

A distinctive feature of Tantric visualization liturgies is the mandala. This word has also passed into modern English, but, once again, not altogether accurately. We have already met two meanings of the word. In chapter 6 we saw that it could mean the physical world viewed as an ordered cosmos and offered to the Buddhas in gratitude for their teachings. We have also seen that in the Eighth Act, the Buddha searched for and found the bodhi–mandala or enlightenment space. Mandala can therefore mean either a sacred space or space as sacred or ordered.

A third meaning of mandala, which is related to the other two meanings but significantly different from them, is "palace of a deity." It is this meaning that has passed into English with some misunderstandings. Early western researchers found plans of palace-mandalas and noted that they were symmetrical, usually composed of a circle inside a square enclosed in another circle, with the diagonals of the square dividing the inner circle into a quaternity. This structure excited the psychologist Carl Jung, some of whose patients drew quaternities that reminded him of mandalas as he had seen them described by the Buddhologists. It subsequently became usual to speak of any quaternity, or even any circular diagram, as a mandala.

What the early Buddhologists, and therefore Jung, failed to notice, was that they were looking, not at mandalas themselves, but at *plans* for mandalas. It is therefore irrelevant that the mandala reproduced in figure 1 of Jung's *Mandala Symbolism*[24] is apparently similar to the wheel of existence in his figure 3. The circles in the wheel of existence are *abstract,* symbolic representations of the meaningless repetition of samsara. The outer circle in the mandala is a two-dimensional representation of an *actual* sphere of interlocking vajras that protects the cubic palace of the deity. Nothing samsaric, that is, nothing connected with the wheel of existence, can penetrate this sphere and enter into a mandala.

When a Tantric liturgy calls for the visualization of a mandala, the teacher communicates detailed descriptions about its form. This may include a plan of the mandala, which is hung on the wall of the shrine room. The student will be directed to inspect the plan minutely and commit it to memory, so that it can be used as an aid to seing the three-dimensional reality. When the visualization has been done successfully, the mandala appears of itself (for, from pure perspective, it is really there, it is not a [necessarily defiled] construct of the imagination) non-referentially, without regard to ordinary perceptions of space. It is neither in front of nor inside the practitioner, and has nothing to do with the size of the room in which the practice is being performed. The mandala is reality. The room is samsara.

A consequence of the mandala being reality is that the practitioner is him or herself the deity[25] in the mandala. This phenomenon is called Deity Yoga, and is one of the most distinctive features of Tantra. Once again, it is an actualization in the body of the practitioner of the teaching of the non-duality of samsara and nirvana. If it is true, as Mahayana teaches, that my defiled being is non-dual with the undefiled being of the Buddhas, then, from pure perspective, I see that I *am* a Buddha. I actually see myself as fully enlightened, having no suffering and acting in the energy mode of spontaneity. If, for example, I am performing a *sadhana* of Avalokiteshvara, I see and know myself as Avalokiteshvara himself, adorned with all his glorious marks, signs, and ornaments. This is called "pride of being a deity."

Deity Yoga works by my "acting as if" from the standpoint of the *goal*, rather than striving for attainment by moving along the *path*. Tantra is therefore called the Effect Vehicle, and it refers to other forms of Buddhism as the Cause Vehicle.

The danger in this practice should be clear. I can only generate pride of being a deity if I am securely grounded both in the wisdom of emptiness, so that I do not see myself as inherently a deity and other beings as inherently not deities, and in the practice of compassion, so that I automatically use the enormous power of a deity for compassionate rather than selfish ends. If either my wisdom or my compassion is deficient, the practice of deity yoga is actually harmful, since I will generate, not pride of deity, but pride of ego-grasping, binding me more closely to delusive samsaric reality.

Since it is not possible for me not to have deficiencies of wisdom and compassion until I am fully enlightened, it might therefore seem that there is no way that I could practice Tantra until I actually am enlightened. But this would defeat the purpose, since Tantra is a means of attaining enlightenment.

The way around this difficulty is to receive an initiation or *wong (dbang)* as it is known in Tibetan. *Wong* is a translation of the Sanskrit *abhishekha*, "sprinkling" or "annointing," a general word meaning initiation. In English, *wong* is coming to be translated as "empowerment," since, by receiving it, one is empowered to enter into a particular practice and given powerful protection from the negative influences of one's own defilements. However, it should be noted that the empowerment is not a gift from without, but the awakening of a faculty of the bodhi mind, which I already have but cannot yet access. It is a liberation of my own purity.

A Tantric liturgy is only to be performed by those whom the teacher has recognized as properly prepared, and to whom he,

or another qualified person, has given the requisite empowerment. Along with the empowerment there will be a detailed oral
exposition of the liturgical text, including certain vital details
without which the liturgy cannot be effectively performed. These
details are purposely kept out of the written text in order to
protect the tantra from the dangers of use by unauthorized persons.

Because of the variety of empowerments, and the different
states of preparation of students, there are many levels of tantras. They are distinctive to whichever sub-lineage of Tantra one
is following. In the Gelugpa lineage of Tibetan Buddhism, for
example, there are four levels, called Action, Performance, Yoga,
and Highest Yoga Tantra. The ascent through these levels is
compared to the progress of courting a lover: looking, laughing
or smiling, holding hands or embracing, and uniting.[26] A similar
system, not quite so colorfully described, is preserved in Japan,
in the Shingon[27] lineage. The most complicated system is the
division into six levels, three "Outer Tantras" and three "Inner
Tantras," taught by the Tibetan Nyingma lineage.

Tantric Ethics

When Tantra first became known in the west it attracted attention because of stories of ritual sex. The westerners, accustomed
to a somewhat disembodied spiritual environment, the sort of
thing that we succinctly if unfairly characterize as Puritan or
Victorian, suddenly came upon a religion in which, it appeared,
sex and sanctity need not be divorced, but could go hand in hand,
and even marry. Literally.

Persons who were interested in restoring what they supposed
to be the ancient, pre-Christian religion of Britain and Europe
found allies in those who were going to "the east," especially
"mysterious Tibet," and bringing back lurid, liberating tales of
lusty monks and nuns copulating in the snowy peaks. A certain
Sir John Woodroffe produced pioneering works on Hindu Tantra (incompletely distinguished from Buddhist Tantra) that
could be read in the privacy of an English gentleman's study for
spiritual titillation and mystical profundity. Sir John styled himself Arthur Avalon, boldly clothing himself in the mantle of Britain's most famous myth. The ambiguous and lonely American
scholar W. Y. Evans-Wentz wrote first of *The Fairy-Faith in Celtic
Countries* (1911), then produced four important books on Tibe-

tan Buddhism,[28] before returning to the topic of early, traditional religion, leaving us a manuscript on Native American religion that had to be published posthumously.[29]

The combination of interest in early religion and Tantra was a condemnation of western spirituality as Avalon, Evans–Wentz, and others like them, saw it. In essence, their fight was against the dualism that appears to be an endemic disease of western spirituality and metaphysics. The feeling was that somewhere, before or apart from Christianity, things had been simpler, more human, more spiritual, and more whole. Over the years, this view has strengthened, being identifiable today as Neo-Paganism.[30] Insofar as this movement is anti-dualist it is, Buddhistically speaking, moving in the right direction, and insofar as it seeks an embodied spirituality it is consonant with Tantra. Insofar as it concentrates on sex, however, it is a serious impoverishment of the Tantric vision.

The actual situation is much more interesting than the amazing rumors of randy lamas that deliciously shocked the spiritual demimonde of our straightlaced ancestors. If samsara and nirvana are non-dual, it follows that the defilments (such as the Three Poisons) are non-dual with Pure Mind. Whereas Hinayana ethical conduct *(shila)* stresses the removal of the poisons, and Mahayana emphasizes the cultivation of the virtues, Vajrayana plunges right into the defilements and, using pure perspective, sees them as undefiled.

This is symbolized by three possible ways of dealing with a cup of poison. One can, first of all, refuse to drink the poison. This, from the Mahayana standpoint, is the Hinayana path of negative ascesis. If one has developed strong antidotes against the poison, one can sip a little of it now and then without being harmed by it. This is the Mahayana path of identifying oneself with the sufferings and defilements of other living beings while not becoming trapped in them. Finally, if one is quite sure that one has the ability, one can drink the poison down in a single gulp, and transform it into nectar, "like the peacock."[31] This is the Vajrayana path in which suffering itself is mutated into bliss.

Another simile is found in the iconography of Padmasambhava, the Indian teacher who is credited with converting Tibet to the Dharma. He holds a staff on which are three heads, one above the other. The lowest head is blissfully smiling and represents the Hinayana path. The Hinayana practitioner is, as we say, on a pink cloud, experiencing the bliss of release from his addictions.

The next head is sorrowful. This represents the Mahayana path, in which the Bodhisattva feels keenly the sufferings of other beings. Once there was a lama who wept all day long.

"Why," his disciples asked him, "are you so unhappy, seeing that we know you to be of high attainment?"

"How can I not be unhappy," he replied, "when I see constantly the misery of all sentient beings?"

If we really could feel the universality of suffering as our own, from the horror of Auschwitz to the numbing sadness of the lives of ordinary people, and the continual fear of animals killing each other, we could not be serenely detached in our private world of bliss.

The head on top of Padmasambhava's staff is a skull. This represents the Vajrayana, in which death, the suffering which brings a life of suffering to an end, is taken into the path and used as a means of liberation.

In chapter 7 we saw two methods of dealing with obstacles to enlightenment. Buddhaghosa prescribed antidotes to the defilements, linking them with six personality types, and Chekawa recommended using obstacles as stepping stones to realization. In Vajrayana, obstacles are seen as non-dual with liberation. Five personality types are described and identified as impure modes of five aspects of Buddha Mind. These are called the Five Buddha Families (Sanskrit: *buddha-kula,* home, nest, or cell of Buddha).

Five Buddhas are arranged in a mandala. The central Buddha is Vairochana (or another of the Cosmic Buddhas) who is pure mind, pure light, or pure space. His color is white, or rather, a kind of translucent luminosity, impossible to achieve on the physical plane, that is both crystalline clear, as if it had no solidity, and radiating like flawless alabaster lit from within. He is the hypostasis of basic, spacelike Buddha Wisdom. The other four Buddhas encircle the Cosmic Buddha: Amoghasiddhi to the north, who is green and whose symbol is the sword; Akshobhya to the east, who is blue and whose symbol is the vajra; Ratnasambhava to the south, who is yellow and whose symbol is the brilliant, fiery *chintamani* (wishing-jewel); and Amitabha to the west, who is red and whose symbol is the lotus.

Each Buddha is associated with a certain quality of mind, and manifests it in its pure mode. The Buddhas at the four cardinal points are hypostases of the four wisdoms, which, according to the Yogachara system, are produced by the transformation of the defiled consciousnesses (see figure 10 in chapter 7). The Cosmic Buddha is the hypostasis of the foundation or source of the four wisdoms. Unliberated beings manifest the same five qualities, but impurely, and are therefore assigned to one or the other Buddha as their Buddha Family, as follows:[32]

1. Vairochana or "Buddha" Family: *The basic quality is spaciousness. In impure mode, it manifests as sloth, isolation, a spaced-out indifference to events. In pure mode, it is the complete openness of the Wisdom of All-Encompassing Space.*

2. Amoghasiddhi or "Karma" (action) Family: *The basic quality is activity. In impure mode, it manifests as busyness, perfectionism, and irritation at messiness. In pure mode, it becomes the Wisdom of Perfect Activity, always meeting events appropriately, neither doing too much nor too little.*

3. Akshobhya or "Vajra" (method) Family: *The basic quality is brilliance. In impure mode it manifests as criticism, self-justification and fixed ideas. In pure mode it becomes the clarity and openness of non-judgmental Mirror Wisdom.*

4. Ratnasambhava or "Ratna" (jewel) Family: *The basic quality is expansive richness. In impure mode it manifests as greediness and self-indulgence. In pure mode it becomes the Wisdom of Non-Duality, which gives universally and impartially of its own richness.*

5. Amitabha or "Padma" (lotus) Family: *Its basic quality is attraction. In impure mode it manifests as seduction and possessiveness, especially sexual possessiveness. In pure mode it becomes the Wisdom of Proper Comprehension, which clearly distinguishes the variety of delightful things and becomes itself attractive rather than seeking to attract.*

Tantric *shila,* ethical conduct, must first of all have a firm basis in detachment from the vices and the idea of an inherently existing self, according to the Hinayana path, and the cultivation of wisdom and compassion according to the Mahayana path. If this basis has been properly laid, it is possible to proceed safely to the Vajrayana practice of contacting our fundamental quality of mind as linked with one of the five Buddha Families. Then, seeing our defilements from pure perspective, we transform the vices into virtues as if we were drinking poison and transforming it into nectar. It is only in this context that our teacher might recommend some practice of sexual yoga, and even then, it will probably not be physical sex but some work with male and female energies.

Because Tantra is the *embodiment* of non-duality, and human bodies are sexual, Tantra cannot omit sexuality. The distinction which is made in Mahayana between wisdom and compassion becomes, in Tantra, embodied as female and male energy. Female energy is embodied wisdom (prajña). It is spacious, accepting, tranquil, and content to be rather than to do. In liturgical practice, it is symbolized by a bell (Sanskrit: *ghanta;* Tibetan: *dilbu* [*dril bu*]) held in the left, or "female" hand. Male energy is embodied skillful means *(upaya),* which is compassion *(karuna)* in action. Male energy is probing, questing, active, always wanting to do rather than to be. In liturgical practice, it is symbolized by a vajra (Tibetan: *dorje* [*rdo rje*]) held in the right or "male" hand.

Both men and women contain male and female energy, with the left side of the body associated with female energy and the right side with male energy. The energy that is predominant in any one person is usually the same as the sex of the genitalia. The use of sexual energy in the Tantric path, then, is a matter of realizing the non-duality of our male and female energies. The commonest way that this is done is by holding the dorje and dilbu and moving them in prescribed patterns. Sometimes, either in conjunction with the manipulation of dorje and dilbu or separate from it, the practitioner may be instructed to visualize him or herself as joined to an enlightened being of the opposite sex so as to facilitate the exchange, or uniting, of the energies. Very occasionally, and only in the practice of certain lineages and only with special instruction and proper preparation, actual coitus between two practitioners may occur.

It is this practice that attracted the attention of the early western researchers. It must be carefully noted, however, that if any such practice is performed improperly, or without due authorization, it is not a Tantric practice. It is samsaric, common or garden copulation, and nothing more. It can, indeed, since "the corruption of the best is worst," set back one's progress severely, particularly if one practitioner has seduced another with deceitful promises of spiritual benefits. Such a deception is explicitly prohibited in the Vinaya.

Another aspect of Tantra which has been commonly misunderstood is the presence of so-called "terrifying deities." Sometimes these entities are represented as copulating with each other, thus increasing the scandalized fascination of the uninitiated observer.

This is, once again, an expression of the embodiment of the non-duality of samsara and nirvana. The Tantric entities in sexual union embody the non-duality of attachment or lust *(raga)* and compassion *(karuna)*. The horrific entities embody the non-duality of aversion or hate *(dvesha)* and skillful means.

Skillful means, or compassion in action, is energy directed towards the liberation of all sentient beings. Hate, in Vajrayana perspective, is the same energy perverted to selfish and harmful ends. But hate, we may have noticed, is often the stronger form of the energy. If we are trying to be helpful to someone (i.e., to use our skillful means), we may become discouraged and give up when our efforts seem to be unavailing. Hate, however, can carry us, our families, and whole countries along in vendettas, blood feuds, and wars. We do not really have to work at being hateful. Hate more or less presents itself. It has the same self-generating quality as Tantric spontaneity.

Therefore, many entities who are known as calm, loving, and helpful Bodhisattvas at the Mahayana level appear as wrathful beings, regarded as more powerful forms, at the Vajrayana level. The peaceful Avalokiteshvara, for example, manifests as the bloodthirsty Mahakala. The blood that Mahakala drinks, however, is the blood of demons. Expressed psychologically, Avalokiteshvara encourages our positive emotions while Mahakala destroys our negativities.

A certain lama who had come to the west and discovered American television very much enjoyed watching *The Incredible Hulk*. It is, indeed, very Tantric. David (known as Bruce in the comic strip version) is an open-faced, gentle, and helpful young man who, when angry, changes into a terrifying green monster, always opposed to evil, never allied with it. David wants to be kind and generous, but his normal strength is no more than human and is inadequate against numerous or very powerful foes. When his real energy is aroused, however, he can tear concrete blocks apart and do whatever is necessary to obliterate harmful forces. His job finished, he changes back into a mild-mannered human (always finding, through the fortunate fruiting of karma, a new set of clothes which fits him perfectly).

The non-duality of David and the Hulk is quite close to the non-duality of Avalokiteshvara and Mahakala. Avalokiteshvara is white, smiling, and fully clothed, as David is human, good-looking, and conventionally dressed. Mahakala is black, growling, and practically naked, as the Hulk is green, growling, and wearing only shorts (the trouser legs having split off during the transformation, although the waist has held). Just as ordinary people are helped by David, Avalokiteshvara helps ordinary practitioners slowly and gently cultivate compassion. For a frontal attack on the forces of evil, the Hulk must manifest, and for a direct attack on negativities as non-dual with virtues, Mahakala must be invoked.

A final difficulty is the Tantric Secret. Tantric initiates are told not to discuss their practice with non-initiates. They are sometimes allowed to say in general what it is, but they cannot give detailed instruction, sufficient for actually contacting and manipulating the energies, to someone who is unprepared. This is another aspect of Tantra that has been held up to ridicule. The assumption of modern society in general, and of academia in particular, is that all information should be freely available to everyone. The American Constitution guarantees freedom of information, and, as a protection against dictatorship and official "disinformation" it is a very valuable right. But, it has problems. If I want to know how to make a nuclear bomb so as to blow up a country or two in my spare time then, in theory, I have the right to that information. We realize that this will never do, so we introduce exceptions such as "the national interest" or the insanity of the enquirer. These are ways of saying that if obtaining certain information could lead to my harming myself or others, I do not have an automatic right to that information.

And there's the rub. From the standpoint of the Buddhas, all unliberated beings are more or less insane and, while they seek happiness, in their confusion they obtain, and produce, suffering. Therefore, information on the real nature of mind, which is a power greater than any nuclear bomb, must be withheld until a being has attained a fair degree of sanity, clarity, and compassion. If we do not have David's virtues we will not transform into the Hulk, we shall be like Dr. Jekyll uncontrollably converting into Mr. Hyde, destroying ourselves and others.

PURE LAND BUDDHISM

The Path of Trust

If, as Buddhism says, my ignorance is complete and beginningless, how can I possibly remove it? If ignorance tries to remove ignorance, it is like trying to wash in dirt. Buddhism answers that my own ignorance is not the only thing that has existed from without beginning. Enlightenment, and enlightened beings, have also existed beginninglessly. Samsaric existence is shot through with suffering and ignorance, but it is intrinsically pure, like water. When we speak of "dirty water" we mean that dirt is found throughout the water, mixed wholly with it. Yet the water is still water and, in itself, is pure.

Therefore, there is some help for me when I wish to move towards enlightenment. Purity is already here, I just have to find the way to access it.

By Taking Refuge in the Triple Jewel of Buddha, Dharma, and Samgha, all Buddhists are accessing the purity of, or trusting in, the pure aspect of samsara. Mahayana forms teach that Buddha Nature is found everywhere, and that the Buddhas and Bodhisattvas are still available, actively aiding us. There is, then, in all lineages, an important component of trust (sometimes misleadingly called faith) in a higher, or at least a purer, power. The Buddhism which puts the greatest emphasis on this is called Pure Land, the most popular form of Buddhism in East Asia.

The name Pure Land (Chinese: *Ching-t'u;* Japanese: *Jodo*) refers to the realm in which the practitioner hopes to be reborn after dying from the human realm. The Pure Land is mentioned in a large number of Mahayana sutras as the abode of the Buddha Amitabha. In one form of Vajrayana, as we have seen, Amitabha is the Buddha in the western quadrant of the mandala, and is subsidiary to the Cosmic Buddha. In Pure Land Buddhism, he is the principal Buddha, and presides over the best of all possible realms.

Amitabha's realm is called the Pure Land because it is free of any imperfections. It is also called *Sukhavati* or the Land of *Sukha,* i.e., although it has the outward appearance of a deity realm or heaven *(deva-loka)* it is actually extra-samsaric and not characterized by duhkha. It is said to be located far away to the west, beyond all world-systems, (another way of saying it is outside of samsara) but also to reside in the heart of the practitioner. It is, in other words, non-referential. Its essence is Transparency.

Descriptions of the Pure Land and how it came to be are contained especially in three sutras, which have come to be identified as "the" Pure Land sutras: two texts, one long and one short, both called Sukhavativyuha, "The Array of the Land of Sukha" and one, extant only in Chinese, called Kuan Wu-liang-shou Fo Ching, "The Amitayus [i.e., Amitabha] Visualization Sutra."

In the Larger Sukhavativyuha, Shakyamuni Buddha tells the story of a brahmin named Dharmakara who became a monk under the former Buddha Dipamkara. Wishing to develop his own distinctive skillful means, he asked Buddha Dipamkara about "Buddha Fields" *(buddha-kshetra).* Buddha Fields are described in Mahayana as the realms within which Buddhas function. Each Buddha has his own "field" of influence. He does not rule over it like a God, but is its principal teacher, or its source of the Dharma. Wherever the Dharma is known, therefore, there is a Buddha Field. The world in which we humans live is a Buddha Field, and its Buddha is Shakyamuni.

Because realms differ in regard to their purity (their relative level of suffering) Buddha Fields also differ in purity. The hells are "defiled" Buddha Fields, our world is a "mixed" Buddha Field, and the heavens of the deities are "pure" Buddha Fields. The non-referential realms of the mandalas are the purest of Buddha Fields, and it was these Buddha Fields in which, the Larger Sukhavativyuha tells us, Dharmakara took an interest.

Buddha Dipamkara gave Dharmakara teachings, lasting very many years, on the precise characteristics of all of the purest Buddha Fields, after which Dharmakara went into an extended retreat in order to form a visualization of a single Buddha Field containing the best qualities of all the purest Buddha Fields. He then made his Bodhisattva Resolve with respect to this Field, saying, "When I become a full Buddha, may I have such a Buddha Field as this." One of the most distinctive qualities that the Bodhisattva Dharmakara resolved to have in his Buddha Field was the assurance that anyone, no matter how evil or deficient in practice, would be able to be reborn there merely by calling upon his name. Over many lifetimes, he moved towards the fulfillment of his Resolve, and Shakyamuni Buddha tells us that the Bodhisattva Dharmakara has now become the Buddha Amitabha, and has obtained the Pure Land in accordance with his resolve.

Whatever we are to make of this story as "history" or "myth," the point of it is that the Pure Land now exists, and that it is the realm in which conditions for attaining enlightenment are ideal. It is not just that the practice of Dharma is easier in the Pure Land than in other realms, but that the Pure Land, having the nature of Transparency, actually *purifies* those who enter it. Just as rivers become salty when entering the sea, beings take on the purity of Amitabha's Land as soon as they are born there. The passions of beings and the purity of Sukhavati are compared to fire and ice. When fire and ice meet, the fire is extinguished and the ice disappears. So, on entering the Pure Land, the desire of beings to go there, and the Pure Land itself as a place to go to, alike disappear. Everything is purified of samsaric, space–time defilements.

The Pure Land of Amitabha is mentioned in sutras which are still extant in Sanskrit, so it must have been known to Indian Mahayana Buddhism, and there are both Mahayana and Vajrayana practices based on it in Tibetan Buddhism, but it did not become the focus of a special lineage until T'an-luan, in fifth century C.E. China, wrote a commentary on a Sanskrit hymn in praise of the Pure Land.[33]

T'an-luan points out that the main reason why Amitabha brought the Pure land into being was to make it easier for beings to get to enlightenment. So, instead of having to rely on our own weak, imperfect, and defiled power, we can now rely on the infinite and pure power of Amitabha Buddha. T'an-luan calls this the Easy Path, and likens it to proceeding to one's destination by boat, assisted by the wind, whereas the traditional path, which he calls the Difficult or Holy Path, is like trudging to the same destination over land. The advantage of choosing the Easy Path is clear.

The heart of the Pure Land teaching, then, is other-directed trust in the power of Amitabha and his Land. The power of beings to effect their own liberation is downgraded or even, as we shall shortly see, denied altogether. T'an-luan teaches five ways (Chinese: *mên*, literally "gates") of focusing one's body, speech, and mind on Amitabha and the Pure Land. These five gates are quite traditional in form:

1. The Gate of Worship: *with the body, prostrations to Amitabha Buddha are performed.*

2. The Gate of Praise: *with the speech, the praises of Amitabha are chanted.*

3. The Gate of Resolution: *with the mind, the resolve is made to be reborn in the Pure Land.*

4. The Gate of Visualization: *again with the mind, the Pure Land is visualized in great detail, like a palace mandala.*

5. The Gate of "Turning Towards": *while one is in the human realm, one "turns" over the merits gained by one's practice "towards" (i.e., for the good of) all beings, and after one has attained birth in the Pure Land, one "turns" back and goes "towards" beings by reentering samsara as a Great Bodhisattva.*

T'an-luan devotes most of his text to the fourth gate. He was himself a monk, and had the time to practice the elaborate visualizations, but they had little appeal for busy laypeople. It was the second gate that became popular.

T'an-luan reminds us that Amitabha promised that all those who invoke his name will activate his compassion and be taken to the Pure Land. The invocation is known in Chinese as *Nien Fo* (Japanese: *Nembutsu*), meaning remembering, recollecting, or "recalling" the Buddha, and it has become so characteristic of Pure Land Buddhism that it is sometimes called the Nien Fo (or Nembutsu) lineage. Although T'an-luan probably practiced extended liturgies of invocation, one of which at least has come down to us, the popular form of the Nien Fo is extremely simple: just say *"Nan-mo A-mi-t'o Fo* (Japanese: *Namu Amida Butsu*), that is "Hail! Amitabha Buddha!," as many times as possible, and because Amitabha's name is, or at least functions like, a mantra, the practitioner will be actualizing the enlightened mind of Amitabha within his or her own unenlightened mind. This is something anyone can do, even while working in the home or the rice paddy.

In China, Korea, and Vietnam the practice of Nien Fo has continued to exist side by side with the more traditional practices of the Difficult or Holy Path. Generally, those who have the time, such as monks or nuns, will concentrate on the traditional practices, while laypeople will content themselves with invoking Amitabha's Name. Even within the monasteries, however, the Nien Fo has become a recognized and revered custom, often described as parallel with, rather than superior to, the traditional practices.

In Japan, the practice of Nembutsu, advocated at first as one practice amongst others, became more and more associated with its own lineage until, under Honen (1133–1212 C.E.) we see the emergence of the Jodo Shu ("Pure Land Lineage") in which the Nembustu was "selected" (Japanese: *senchaku*) as Honen put it, as the sole practice. Honen's chief disciple, Shinran (1173–1262 C.E.), had a major new insight into the significance of the Path of Trust, teaching that the Nembutsu was done, not by beings, but by Amitabha Buddha himself for the sake of beings. Although Shinran thought of himself as continuing his Master's teachings, he is credited with the founding of his own lineage, the Jodo Shinshu ("True Pure Land Lineage"), which has become the most popular of all forms of Buddhism in Japan.

The Path of Surrender

Shinran's insight cannot be understood apart from his life. He tried to solve in his own person the problem of how he, as an ignorant being, could remove his ignorance. He became a monk and practiced diligently, but he found that after twenty years he was no nearer to enlightenment. In despair he gave up, and in that moment of surrender he found his answer. His anguish and joy is recorded in a brief, almost off-hand, note:

So, I, Gutoku Shaku Shinran, in the first year of Kennin (i.e., 1201 C.E.) abandoned the miscellaneous practices and allied myself with the Primal Vow.[34]

The "miscellaneous practices" that he abandoned were all practices other than the Nembutsu, and he understood the Nembutsu in a new way. The Nembutsu that we practice is identical, said Shinran, with Dharmakara's "Primal Vow" (Japanese: *Hongan*) or Bodhisattva Resolve such that all practice is actually done not by beings but by Amitabha Buddha. This piercing and compressed insight needs a bit of unwrapping.

Various distinctions, which have been hinted at in the earlier Pure Land tradition, become, with Shinran, clear and sharp. First of all, the difference of emphasis between self-power (Japanese: *jiriki*) and other-power (Japanese: *tariki*) widens into a dichotomy between which we are forced to choose. However, there is no real choice, for only *tariki*, he said, has any efficacy. In *jiriki*, the defiled self blocks its own path to enlightenment. Furthermore, Shinran believed that he was living in the Age of Final Dharma (see above, "The Decay of the Dharma") so that it was no longer possible, he thought, for anyone to practice the Holy Path of *jiriki*.

As a consequence, the question, which had been hotly debated, of how many times one needed to say the Nembutsu in order to get the full effect, became irrelevant. The Nembutsu is not, said Shinran, a matter of quantity or calculation (Japanese: *hakarai*), it is the power of Amitabha Buddha overtaking us. The Nembutsu is not a mantra that beings recite to the Buddha, it is the Buddha's invitation to beings to accept the liberation that he has already obtained for them. It is, in short, the non-duality of beings' desire for liberation and Amitabha's power to liberate our defiled mind and his pure mind. There is no mixing of the two, with a gradual purification through repetetive invocation, as T'an-luan taught: the non-duality is simply the case.

When this realization is experienced, it comes as a moment of ecstatic, bodily, dancing joy. Nothing needs to be done! Everything is right as it is! *"Namu Amida Butsu!"* we shout in gratitude. This moment is called "the arising of the mind of true entrusting" (Japanese: *shinjin*) and is structurally comparable to a moment of satori, or awakening to non-duality, in the Zen tradition. It cannot be earned, it can only be awaited. Therefore, one need not be a monk or nun, or learned, or even virtuous. The realized individuals of the Jodo Shinshu tradition, called *myokonin*, "marvellously happy people", are often unlettered peasants who cannot even say the Nembutsu properly. They garble the strange foreign words and say something like *"Namandabu,"* but it does not matter, their liberation is due to Amitabha, not to their punctilious pronunciation.

When the shinjin has arisen, and the Nembutsu says itself, it occurs *jinen,* spontaneously, naturally, or automatically. *Jinen* is the Japanese pronunciation of the Chinese *tzŭ-jan,* "selfly," which is a popular term in Taoism. It came to be used by Buddhists for the manner in which Buddhas do without doing. It is a more or less exact equivalent of the Tibetan *hlundup (lhun drup),* the spontaneous activity of the Vajra Realm. The difference between *jinen* and *hlundup* is not in the spontaneity, but in how one obtains it. In Vajrayana, one must progress through the stages before spontaneous action takes over. Shinran found that, in his experience, Amitabha Buddha picked him up and placed him directly in the spontaneous energy mode. He called this action *ocho,* "the sideways leap," to indicate that he was accepted just as he was, without having to go through the traditional purificatory stages. All of a sudden, he found himself on the heights of the Bodhisattva Path.

However, he was still Shinran, and still, as Shinran, limited, defiled, and suffering. He could not, for example, commit murder and then excuse himself on the grounds of being an exalted being who was beyond any laws of right conduct. In his heart of hearts, he knew he was "firmly settled" in Amitabha's eyes, but he still had to allow this realization to express itself. The distinctiveness of Shinran's teaching is this *allowing* of the Buddha Nature rather than the *cultivating* of it.

Shinran has sometimes been compared to Luther, for it has seemed to some scholars that, as Luther found faith in Christ more efficacious than works, so had Shinran discovered faith in Amitabha to be better than the "miscellaneous practices." Another, and, I think, better way of understanding Shinran's original contribution, is to say that he had discovered how to *play* his practice rather than *work* it.[35]

Before Shinran, it was thought necessary to calculate how many Nembutsus one had done, using a rosary and keeping careful count, so that there was a feeling of progress, of having done so many invocations and having so many yet to do, like washing dishes. It was work. Play differs from work in that it is done just for the fun of it, it "flows,"[36] and it doesn't have a goal outside of itself. There may be something called a goal *within* a game, such as football, but play itself does not have a goal. We play only in order to continue playing,[37] and if it is truly play, it seems to play itself. So, Shinran found the Nembutsu was spontaneous, it just happened to him, but that did not mean that he did not do the Nembutsu. The Shin Buddhist still worships, and acts virtuously, but does not do so *in order to be liberated* but *in gratitude for having been liberated.* Ends and expectations are given up, and means play themselves.

This is the most radical answer to the question of how I can remove my ignorance, if all I am is ignorant. Of course I am ignorant! But Amitabha is wise, compassionate, and powerful, and he is already non-dual with my confusion. All I have to do is give up, and nirvana happens of itself.

The Nature of Liberation

So then, after all this, what is the goal of Buddhism? What is the payoff? Is it all worth the trouble?

Nirvana is the end of samsara. Samsara is reality as we know it. We experience ourselves as space-time beings with definite, demonstrable limits on our actions of body, speech, and mind. Nirvana, or liberation, is the disappearance of our reality. Theravada teaches this disappearance in terms of the individual. A general nirvana (in Pali, Nibbana) for all sentient beings is not denied or ignored, but it is hardly ever mentioned. In the Mahayana tradition, a universal nirvana is made explicit in the Bodhisattva's resolve to assist all beings "until samsara is emptied." This is the disappearance of time and space, or, to use an expression more familiar in the west, the end of the world.

If everything we know disappears, it is impossible to imagine what might take its place, for, as samsaric beings, we can only imagine the new thing as something like the old things. Yet the end of the space-time universe is *without analogy* and even to call it a "new thing" is to miss the mark.

We can, however, as we have already seen, characterize our reality, that is, samsara, and then indicate (rather than describe) nirvana as the unimaginable or incomprehensible (*achintya,* "not thinkable") negation of our reality. Then, as we did when describing the Vajrayana perspective, we can introduce positive analogies of the nirvanic state, but, as the modern linguistic theorists say, "write them under erasure." For instance, we can say that nirvana is joy, but we do not mean samsaric joy, for it is not a joy that is the opposite face of sadness and so it does not pall, that is, it does not decay into sadness. We still call it joy, not having a more appropriate word, but since it is the wrong word, we cross it out. So we write ~~joy~~.

Samsara is repetition. We get out of bed, go to work, come home, sleep, get up, go to work again. We eat, get hungry, and eat again. We wash, get dirty, and wash again. Samsara literally means "constantly moving." Like laundry, it can be more of a problem or less of a problem, but it is always a problem, and it is never finished. In samsara we think ahead and try to meet new circumstances with tools derived from old, apparently similar, circumstances. Nirvana, on the other hand, is ~~continual fresh-ness~~. Zen calls it *shoshin,* "beginner's mind," the innocent heart constantly awakening to the shock of wonder, like a child on Christmas morning. In nirvanic mode, the mind does not plan or work. It marries each moment flawlessly. It is spontaneous, it plays, it does not have an end in view nor a sense of time passing or space being passed through so as to get from here to there.

Samsara is limitation. Nirvana is ~~complete freedom~~ of body, speech, and mind in the ~~perfection~~ of ~~wisdom~~, of ~~love~~, and of ~~energy~~.

Samsara is winning and losing, one-upmanship and one-downsmanship, living and dying, good and evil, choosing between physical and philosophical opposites. "Does the world have meaning?" "Is it all meaningless?" Nirvana is the non-duality (i.e. the ~~oneness~~) of all opposites in Complete Openness.

We see an image on the television screen. We turn the television off and the image disappears. The image was real, but it had no inherent existence, it was brought about by causes and conditions, and those causes and conditions have now been removed. If the causes and conditions for all of samsara were to be removed, the television would disappear, we would disappear, everything would disappear. Yet there would not be a Nothing, for Nothing is a concept based upon the idea of Something, and only intelligible in samsaric terms. We can say that there is nothing on the television screen because there is a screen on which there could be something, but there is nothing.

When the framework that supports everything and nothing disappears, what is there?

Whatever it is, it won't be a disappointment.

NOTES
to Chapter 10

1. The classic study is "L'évolution du Stupa en Asie: Étude d'architecture bouddhique" by Gisbert Combaz, *Mélanges chinois et bouddhiques*, 2d vol. (1932–1933), pp. 163–305. An accessible summary in English is given by Dietrich Seckel, *The Art of Buddhism*, translated by Ann E. Keep (New York: Crown, 1964), pp. 103–132. *Psycho-cosmic Symbolism of the Buddhist Stupa* by Lama Anagarika Govinda (Emeryville, CA: Dharma Paublishing, 1976) is fascinating, but idiosyncratic and obscure.

2. *Psycho-cosmic Symbolism of the Buddhist Stupa*, pp. 20–32.

3. When I asked a group of Nepali university students which name was the correct one, they argued heatedly amongst themselves without coming to any conclusion.

4. Henry Clarke Warren, *Buddhism in Translations*, pp. 320–330.

5. Similar accounts of creation are found in non-Buddhist religions, which, from a Buddhist viewpoint, read like single episodes rather than the whole story.

6. Henry Clarke Warren, *Buddhism in Translations*, p. 447. What appears today as sexism in this passage is in fact astonishingly liberal for its time. Allowing a woman to choose her own life-style by, for instance, becoming a nun, rather than being married according to her parents' arrangements, is still a shocking idea to many Indians.

7. See the summary account in Kenneth K. S. Ch'en, *Buddhism in China* (Princeton University Press, 1964), pp. 297–300.

8. Translation adapted from Rune E. A. Johannson, *The Psychology of Nirvana* (Garden City, NY: Anchor Books, 1970), p. 47.

9. Leon Hurvitz, *Scripture of the Lotus Blossom of the Fine Dharma* (New York: Columbia University Press, 1976), pp. 183–188.

10. The Nyingma version of this yoga became known in the west through W. Y. Evans-Wentz's version of what he called *The Tibetan Book of the Dead* (1927). A more intelligible account, from the Gelugpa lineage, is that of by Lati Rinbochay and Jeffrey Hopkins, *Death, Intermediate State and Rebirth in Tibetan Buddhism* (Valois, NY: Snow Lion, 1979). See also Glenn H. Mullin, *Death and Dying: The Tibetan Tradition* (Boston: Arkana, 1986).

11. *Maitreya, the Future Buddha*, edited by Alan Sponberg and Helen Hardacre (Cambridge University Press, 1988).

12. E. Sarkisyanz, *Buddhist Backgrounds of the Burmese Revolution* (The Hague: Nijhoff, 1965), chap. 21.

13. A short teaching on the Kalachakra is given by the first Dalai Lama in *Selected Works of the Dalai Lama I,* translated by Glenn H. Mullin (Ithaca, NY: Snow Lion, 2nd ed., 1985), chapter 6. Another text, with an extended commentary by the fourteenth Dalai Lama, has been translated by Jeffrey Hopkins as *The Kalachakra Tantra: Rite of Initiation* (Ithaca, NY: Snow Lion, 1985).

14. Edwin Bernbaum, *The Way to Shambhala* (Garden City, NY: Anchor Books, 1980).

15. That this tradition is taken quite seriously is shown by the frequent Kalachakra initiations which have been given by the fourteenth Dalai Lama in response to the present global crisis. They are a contingency plan to provide a counterforce in case an evil empire takes over the world.

16. Tibetan opinion on this is divided. See Bernbaum, *The Way to Shambhala,* pp. 243–245. Myths similar to that of Shambhala occur in Hindu and Christian eschatology, perhaps by diffusion or borrowing. Interest in hidden valleys has now shifted to the Andes, popularized by the books and films of Shirley MacLaine. See also the strange report of Michael Brown, *The Weaver and the Abbey: The Quest for a Secret Monastery in the Andes* (London: Corgi Books, 1983), whose hidden valley is, like Shambhala, ambiguously physical and mental, prompting us to consider whether the place of regeneration is external or internal. Buddhism answers that external and internal reality are mutually dependent.

17. Tulku Thondup Rinpoche, *Hidden Teachings of Tibet: An Explanation of the Terma Tradition of the Nyingma School of Buddhism,* edited by Harold Talbott (London: Wisdom Publications, 1986). The review of this book by Matthew Kapstein in *The Vajradhatu Sun* 9:1 (Oct./Nov. 1987) includes reflections on the tradition and is a good place for the beginner to start. There is also a brief discussion in *Crystal Mirror V* (Emeryville, CA: Dharma Publishing, 1977), pp. 261–273.

18. For example, *The Legend of the Great Stupa and the Life Story of the Lotus Born Guru* (Emeryville, CA: Dharma Publishing, 1973).

19. Laurence G. Thompson, *The Chinese Way in Religion* (Belmont, CA: Wadsworth, 1973), chapter 13, "The Laughing Buddha."

20. Similarly, the Monty Python film *The Life of Brian* is a "Zen" view of Christianity since it pokes fun at the trappings of Christianity but never attacks the central doctrines.

21. The Aryans who invaded the Indian Subcontinent in c.1500 B.C.E. had throwing weapons which they called vajras. Their war god, Indra,

was also the god of storms, and his vajra was the thunderbolt. This was drawn as two crooked, intersecting lines and called the *svastika* or "lucky thing" because it brought the life-giving monsoon. Adolf Hitler apparently took the vajra or swastika as his symbol because he believed himself to be, like Indra, the divine general of the Aryans.

22. Tsong-ka-pa, *Tantra in Tibet,* trans. Jeffrey Hopkins (London: Allen and Unwin, 1977), p. 69.

23. Thus the title of Chögyam Trungpa's book *Journey without Goal: The Tantric Wisdom of the Buddha* (Boston: Shambhala, 1985). This is the best introductory book on Tantra.

24. C. G. Jung, *Mandala Symbolism,* translated by R. F. C. Hull (Princeton University Press, 1972).

25. "Deity" is a literal translation of the Tibetan *hla (lha;* Sanskrit: *deva),* but it has here a special meaning, referring to a pure or extra-samsaric entity, not to a being reborn in a heaven of the Triple World.

26. Tsong-ka-pa, *Tantra in Tibet,* pp. 201–209.

27. *Shingon* is a translation of *mantra* and literally means "truth word" (i.e., "a word which is itself Truth," not "true word" as some have misunderstood it).

28. *The Tibetan Book of the Dead* (1927), *Tibet's Great Yogi Milarepa* (1928), *Tibetan Yoga and Secret Doctrines* (1935), and *The Tibetan Book of the Great Liberation* (1954), all published by Oxford University Press.

29. *Cuchama and Sacred Mountains* (Chicago: Swallow Press, 1981).

30. Margot Adler, *Drawing down the Moon: Witches, Druids Goddess-Worshippers and Other Pagans in America Today* (Boston: Beacon Press, revised edition, 1986).

31. The peacock's blue neck is said to indicate that, although it can drink poison and transmute it, it does not escape entirely unscathed.

32. Chögyam Trungpa, *Journey without Goal,* chapter 9.

33. Roger Corless, *T'an-luan's Commentary on the Pure Land Discourse,* Ph.D. dissertation, University of Wisconsin, Madison, 1973. Available on demand from University Microfilms, Ann Arbor.

34. *Kyogyoshinsho,* chapter 6. My translation.

35. Roger Corless, "The Playfulness of *Tariki,*" *The Pure Land,* new series, no. 4 (December 1987), pp. 34–52. The vision of Shinran is well captured by Alfred Bloom in *Tannisho: Resource for Modern Living* (Honolulu: Buddhist Study Center, 1981).

36. Mihaly Csikszentmihalyi, *Beyond Boredom and Anxiety: The Experience of Play in Work and Games* (San Francisco: Jossey–Bass, 1975).

37. James P. Carse, *Finite and Infinite Games: A Vision of Life as Play and Possibility* (New York: Ballantine Books, 1986).

Appendix

The Story of the Dharma

Unity and Diversity

The Buddhas have only one message: liberation. "As the sea," said Shakyamuni, "though wide and deep, has only one taste, the taste of salt, so my teaching, though extensive and profound, has only one message, the message of liberation." In order to be heard, this message must be adapted to different times, places, and living beings, and as a result, the one flavor of liberation permeates and is permeated by many different cultures. The variety of forms of Buddhism is not an embarrassment, but rather a mark of its success. Every sentient being is trapped in samsara, but each is trapped in its own way. There must be as many remedies as there are sicknesses, as many ways out as there are traps.

The *divisions* of Buddhism have sometimes been called sects or schools, but in this book I have used the word *lineage*, as it seems to fit better with Buddhist experience. A Buddhist is one who has taken refuge, and he or she has taken refuge in a specific tradition whose teachers stretch back, or are claimed to stretch back, in an unbroken line or lineage to Shakyamuni Buddha.

Buddhism and Culture

There is one over-arching principle in the effective spread of Buddhism: *skillful means.* As Buddhism asks the individual, so it asks a culture: "What is it, do you think, that will bring you the most happiness?" When it has heard the response, Buddhism says, under its breath, "But that will only bring you samsaric happiness," and continues, out loud, "That is good, the Dharma can help you." Then, starting from that samsaric desire, it seeks a way of assisting the individual or culture to break out into extra-samsaric joy.

Most countries into which Buddhism spread were what we might call "low cultures," that is, they had rich local traditions but little sense of nationhood or broad cultural identity, and did not have a national religion or philosophy. Buddhism was able to supply this lack. It provided a "Great Tradition" perspective, encouraging local customs to coalesce into national polities and incorporating them in a supra-national worldview. The price was the downgrading of the local customs. Indigenous deities were said either to have converted to Buddhism, becoming Dharma Protectors *(dharma-pala),* or foolishly to have rejected it, thus being demoted to demons.

The only country in which this did not happen smoothly was China. It had already developed, in Confucianism and Taoism, sophisticated national systems, and so was not the "pushover" that, for example, Tibet was. Buddhism had to be more humble as it approached the Chinese, and it has often smelled, to good upstanding Confucians, of foreigners and their nefarious plots. Even so, the cultural blending was such that Buddhism came to be counted as the third religion of China, and the eirenic phrase "The three religions are a harmonious unity" *(San chiao ho i)* was coined. No other foreign system, other than Communism, has been able to penetrate Chinese culture so completely.

The corollary of nation building is that Buddhism also fueled wars over the new boundaries that it had helped to create. This is particularly evident in Southeast Asia where, on the one hand, there is a feeling of commonality in that all the Buddhist countries belong to the same lineage, and yet a climate of suspicion since the sub-lineages have developed along cultural and national lines.

Theravada and Mahayana

There are two major varieties of Buddhism: Theravada and Mahayana. Theravada is a single lineage with many sub–lineages, and is dominant in Southeast Asia (Sri Lanka, Burma, Thailand, Cambodia, and Laos). Mahayana is a family of lineages divided into two cultural branches: Central Asian (Tibet, Nepal, Sikkim, Bhutan, Kashmir, Mongolia) and East Asian (China, Korea, Japan, the Ryukyu Islands, Vietnam). Vajrayana is dependent on, and arises out of, Mahayana. It is popular in Central Asian Mahayana, where it is integrated with the Graded Path (see chapter 9). In East Asian Mahayana, it is sometimes blended with other traditions but most typically exists as the distinct Japanese lineage known as Shingon.

THERAVADA

Early Buddhism is supposed to have been divided into eighteen lineages, none of which has survived as such. Their most probable teachings have been catalogued by André Bareau in *Les Sectes Bouddhiques du Petit Véhicule* (Saigon: École Française d'Extrême Orient, 1955), who has recovered the outlines of thirty-four lineages. Theravada emerges from these as the oldest continuously existing lineage.

The first country to accept Theravada was Sri Lanka, in the third century B.C.E., and it has exercised considerable influence over other forms of Theravada. The great systematizer Buddhaghosa (see chapter 7) worked in Sri Lanka. The sense of easy superiority that Sri Lankan Theravada often assumes, because of its antiquity, can be a source of irritation to other Theravadins.

Burma, Thailand, and Kampuchea first heard of Buddhism in its East Asian Mahayana and Central Asian Vajrayana forms. The vigorous ornamentation of, for example, Thai temples, which contrasts so sharply with the simplicity of Sri Lankan custom, has been attributed to Vajrayana influence. All three countries became Theravadin in, respectively, the eleventh, thirteenth, and fourteenth century C.E., and from Kampuchea in the fourteenth century, Theravada went to Laos.

The flavor of Theravada is heavily monastic, with a prominent symbiosis between monastics and laypeople, as described above in chapter 4. Abhidhamma (see chapter 5), largely as explained

by Buddhaghosa, is the single theoretical system. Most controversies in Theravada have been over the correct interpretation
and practice of the Monastic Rule (Vinaya), and the relative
importance of doctrinal study and meditation.

MAHAYANA

Mahayana begins to be noticed around the first century C.E. on
the Indian subcontinent. Where it came from is still something
of a mystery. By its own self-understanding, it goes back to the
time of the Buddha, yet historical research cannot support this
claim. Mahayana, and especially Vajrayana, explains the lack of
historical evidence by saying that its teaching was given by the
Buddha as a skillful means for a later time, and that it was passed
down secretly until that time. An intelligent guess to assist in
resolving this issue from the standpoint of modern historical
criticism would be that the Dharma had become frozen in doctrinal formulae, and that the Mahayana restored the spirit of the
original teaching. But there are too many differences between
Theravada, which also understands itself to be the original teaching, and Mahayana, for this guess to be entirely correct.

There are two theoretical systems in Mahayana: Madhyamika
(see chapter 9) and Yogachara (see chapter 7). Central Asian
Mahayana preserves these as distinct systems, and prefers Madhyamika over Yogachara, although it arose later. East Asian
Mahayana blended them to produce the indigenous systems of
T'ien-t'ai (see chapter 9) and Hua-yen (see chapter 1). Central
Asian Mahayana teaches Vasubandhu's Abhidharma, superficially similar to Abhidhamma, as a preliminary or "Hinayana"
system. A form of it is found in East Asian Mahayana, but it is
rarely taught.

East Asian Mahayana

Mahayana passed first into China, being known at the imperial
court very soon after the beginning of the Common Era, but it
took until the sixth century before the native lineages of T'ien-t'ai
and Hua-yen developed. These awesome systems collapsed,
partly through persecution and partly under their own weight,
and have largely been replaced by the more folk-based lineages
of Ch'an and Ching-t'u (Pure Land), which then merged to form
the typically Chinese balance of Ch'an sitting and Pure Land
Nien-fo chanting.

The interaction of Buddhism with the indigenous systems of Taoism and Confucianism has been extensive and complex. In general, the Chinese saw Buddhism at first as a form of Taoism which promised health, longevity, and immortality without the dangers of the various Taoist elixirs, many of which were quite poisonous. Buddhism responded by proffering the Pure Land as a place superficially resembling a Taoist heaven but actually outside of samsara. Techniques of Taoist breathing to nourish the *ch'i*, "vital energy," were observed to be similar to the Buddhist use of the breath in Insight Meditation, and both systems borrowed from the other. The Taoist and Buddhist pantheons grew by mutual enrichment, and Ch'an picked up on and transformed Taoist ideals of spontaneity. Confucianism stood rather aloof from all this interaction, yet, as the established way of running things, it permeated everywhere. Especially, it contributed much to the etiquette of Buddhist monasteries (see chapter 4) and its formality became the focus of Ch'an iconoclasm (see the discussion of Pu-tai in chapter 10).

Korea received the Dharma from China, giving most importance to the Hua-yen (Korean: *Hwaŏm*) lineage. Wonhyo (617–686 C.E.) founded the native lineage of Popsong, "Dharma Nature," attempting a unification of all Mahayana teachings. Controversy between Ch'an (Korean: *Sŏn*) and scholastic lineages have been frequent, but repeated efforts have been made to resolve the differences. In 1935, all lineages were unified as Chogye.

Korea has used Buddhism as a way of establishing a national identity, particularly in its fight against Japanese domination.

The first transmission of the Dharma to Japan was in the sixth century C.E., from Korea. The importance of this fact has been underestimated, due perhaps to the long history of strife between Korea and Japan. Later, Japanese monks traveled to China (e.g., Zen Master Dogen) and some Chinese monks settled in Japan. Whereas Korea attempted to unify lineages, Japan has delighted in producing as many lineages as possible, so that nearly two hundred are currently listed. T'ien-t'ai (Japanese: *Tendai*) and Hua-yen (Japanese: *Kegon*) were prominent for some centuries, but have given way to Zen and Pure Land forms, which are not usually blended, and have produced many sub-lineages. A variety of Vajrayana called Shingon powerfully interacted with the local holy man *(hijiri)* tradition, and with the indigenous Shinto (teaching the identification of Japanese deities [*kami*] and Buddhist figures in the *honji-suijaku*, "soil and footprint," system—see chapter 3, note 19), and, though it has declined from its golden age, still maintains an impressive presence. Nichiren Buddhism (see chapter 2) is a distinctively Japanese lineage.

Practicality has been a keynote of the Japanese Dharma. Any form of Buddhism that was found to be irrelevant to daily life, either of the individual or the country, was allowed to die off. As a consequence, most of the theoretical structure of Japanese Buddhism is a modification of that developed in China, and its real genius is seen in the non-duality of thought and action in such intensely Japanese creations as Teaism (see chapter 2).

Vietnam received Theravada about the first century C.E. and Chinese Mahayana, in various forms, between the sixth and the seventeenth centuries. Theravada was used to make a foundation of Hinayana monastic asceticism on which was built an edifice of monastic and lay Mahayana, chiefly a combination of Zen (Vietnamese: *Thien*) and Pure Land, especially in the distinctively Vietnamese lineage of *Thao-Duong* (eleventh century) In 1963, all lineages were merged to create the Unified Buddhist Church of Vietnam *(Viet-Nam Phat-Giao Thong-Nhat Giao-Hoi)*. Vietnamese Buddhism has been a strong ally in revolts against foreign domination, first of all by China, and most recently by the United States. The fate of Buddhism in Vietnam since the withdrawal of the U.S. forces is difficult to ascertain.

Central Asian Mahayana

Tibet received Buddhism in the seventh century C.E. from the great monastic universities of the Indian Subcontinent. From the beginning, a distinction seems to have been made between Hinayana and Mahayana, and they were arranged in an academic style "sequence of courses." Vajrayana seems to have entered separately (the origin of Vajrayana, from the historical–critical point of view, is still very obscure), perhaps from the valleys in the far north or northeast of the Subcontinent. It was incorporated very early into the scholastic system, producing the ordered progression of the Triple Vehicle, which is the hallmark of Central Asian Mahayana.

Tibetan Buddhism was severely persecuted by King Lang-
darma *(glang dar ma,* 838–842 C.E.), who wished to restore the
pre-Buddhist religion of Bönpo, and it was not until about one
hundred years later that a new transmission of Buddhism was
received. The legacy of this hiatus is a split between the teachings
and practices of the "Old Transmission" *(Nyingma)* and the "New
Transmission" *(Sarma).* Nyingma *(rnying ma)* survives as a single lineage with a distinctive division of the Dharma into nine
yanas (see chapter 9, note 13). Sarma, based not only on a new
transmission but also on new translations of the texts, is divided
into three main lineages. The Kagyu *(bka rgyud)* and Sakya *(sa
skya),* both of which have many sub-lineages, were founded in
the eleventh century. In the fourteenth century, Tsongkhapa (see
chapter 9) founded the Gelug *(dge lugs)* as a reform and synthesis of the Sarma tradition. The Dalai Lamas belong to the Gelug
lineage.

Tibetan Buddhism incorporated the tribal society and sha-
manism of pre-Buddhist Tibet, and became the dominant ideological and social system of the region. Monks and high lamas
became the political leaders, accorded the wealth, prestige, and
influence of their secular forerunners, and the monastery buildings, set prominently on hilltops, took over the functions of the
"big house" of the chief. The figure of the lama has shamanistic
elements, for one who is called a lama *(bla ma)* (only some
monks are lamas and Tibetan Buddhism should not be called
Lamaism) is, for the practitioner who accepts that person as his
or her teacher, the embodied sacrament of the Dharma, the Triple Refuge in bodily form, and is expected, as a matter of course,
to be unusually accomplished both in the Dharma and in the
supernormal skills (see chapter 8).

In 1959, the symbiosis of Buddhism and Tibetan society was
ripped apart by the invasion by the People's Republic of China.
Despite the terrible suffering of the Tibetan people that this invasion produced, the event has had the fortunate effect, from the
point of view of the Dharma, of spreading Tibetan Buddhism to
the west.

Tibetan Buddhism spread into Mongolia and the Himalayan
kingdoms (Nepal, Sikkim, Bhutan) and regions (Kashmir) and
blended with the indigenous traditions, but without producing
any distinctly new lineages.

Buddhism in the West

The latest development in the story of the Dharma is its movement from the eastern hemisphere to other parts of the world, collectively known as "the west." The *International Buddhist Directory* (London: Wisdom, 1985) lists Buddhist groups in Europe, the Americas, Africa, and Australasia, as well as Asia. All Buddhist lineages have now come to the United States, and have found it to be fertile ground. The story is told by Rick Fields in *How the Swans Came to the Lake* (Shambhala, 2nd ed., 1986).

Buddhism entered the United States in two major ways: as part of the culture of immigrant peoples, and by invitation. The most prominent example of an immigrant group is the Buddhist Churches of America, a branch of Jodo Shinshu (see chapter 10), which was brought in by Japanese who settled in Hawaii and California. It now accounts for a large number of the Buddhists in Hawaii, a state where Buddhism is the second largest religion after Christianity, and it has recently become the first religion other than Christianity or Judaism to be allowed to nominate chaplains to the United States Army. The first form of Buddhism to be invited to come to the United States was Zen, and for a long time, it seemed, Zen *was* Buddhism for most white Americans. Today, Tibetan Buddhism has at least as high a profile as Zen, and it is a form that was both brought in by immigrants and invited by residents.

Buddhism is still so new to the United States that Americans who become Buddhist are often required to adopt the customs of one or another foreign culture, according to the lineage they have chosen. An indigenous form of American Buddhism has not emerged, yet there is no reason to think that it will not do so at some time in the future. What form it will take is open to speculation, but some lines of development already appear to be emerging.

The democratic atmosphere of the United States has encouraged lay participation, even in complicated rituals and extended, rigorous retreats, to an extent quite unknown in the east, and an indifference to ancient party squabbles has led to an attempt to see behind the variety of historical forms to the essential message of one main lineage (e.g., "Zen" rather than the traditional concentration on a strict division into, say, Rinzai and Soto Zen) or even of Buddhism as a whole (hence, perhaps, the stimulus for this book). Some westerners are even being identified as reincarnations of Tibetan tulkus. One American boy, one Canadian boy, and (in Europe) one Spanish boy have been so identified. The latest to be recognized is Jetsunma Ahkön Norbu Lhamo, until recently known as Mrs. Catharine Burroughs ("United States Woman Is Named Reborn Buddhist Saint," *New York Times,* October 26, 1988) and whom *People Magazine* could not resist irreverently calling "Buddhism's First U.S. Mama Lama."

The great preoccupation of unhappy Americans is psychotherapy, and since Buddhism deals so directly with the mind, it is able to offer its psychotherapeutic services. When Buddhism is presented to Americans as a therapy rather than as a religion it seems to gain a more ready hearing. But sometimes, practitioners stop there. They meditate so that they can handle stress. Those who see that handling stress brings no more than samsaric relief, however, are ready to go on to final liberation, which, of course, fulfills the intent of the skillful means of psychotherapeutic counseling.

Traditional Buddhism and modern America are friends in the matter of change. In America, contrary to most Old World countries, change is not resisted, it is welcomed and even rewarded. The Utopia of the New World is in the future. It is usually thought of in materialistic, that is, samsaric, terms, but it is a vision that downplays essentialism or the inherent existence of structures (both American and Buddhist) that have been inherited from the past. Thus, it is on the side of Transparency. America, said Thomas Jefferson, is an experiment. So, indeed, is Buddhism, until samsara is emptied.

Select Glossary

Buddhism does not have a language that is distinctively its own, like Sanskrit for Hinduism or Arabic for Islam, that is, it does not have a "sacred" or canonical language. Tradition has it that the Buddha told his disciples, "Teach the Dharma using the language of whatever *desh* (i.e., country or region) you enter." The absence of a single, authoritative language in Buddhism is consonant with the Dharma being "transformation manifesting as information," i.e., skillful means (see chapter 9).

There are, however, many *terms* which, in the course of time, have become distinctively Buddhist, and these have come to be expressed in the *words* of the languages of the various cultures with which Buddhism has mixed (see Appendix: The Story of the Dharma). Since Buddhism is comparatively new to the English-speaking world, the problem arises of not only *how* to translate these terms but, indeed *which* term to translate . . . the Pali, the Chinese, the Tibetan, or what? . . . since often the "same" term is rendered differently.

For example, a being which is not yet enlightened is called **satta** (having existence) in Pali, **sempa** (possessing consciousness) in Tibetan, and **chung-shêng** (many birthed) in Chinese. In this book I have chosen to go with the Tibetan understanding of that particular term and translate it "sentient being." In other cases, I have chosen the understanding of a term favored by some other Buddhist tradition. Why? My selection is necessarily personal, and is open to discussion and possible modification in later editions of this book.

If Buddhism continues to expand in the English-speaking world, it can be expected, in the course of time, to develop its own distinctive vocabulary, as it has done in other cultures. Until then, we need some sort of compromise.

The compromise that I have reached is as follows.

Terms Which Have Become English Words

Certain Buddhist terms, mainly Sanskrit and Japanese (such as nirvana and Zen) have been accepted into English and appear in the standard English dictionaries. There is, in fact, a surprisingly large number of such words, and each new edition of a certain dictionary seems to contain more of them. Whenever I have used an apparently foreign word which is, however, in one of the commonly available English language dictionaries, I have used it *as* an English word, that is, without italicization or diacritical marks, except for the circumflex <ê>, tilde <ñ>, and umlaut <ü>, which are familiar to us from European languages. The reader should, however, beware of taking the dictionary definition as accurate for Buddhism, and should understand it in the context of my explanation in this book.[1]

Non-English Words Which Are Common Terms

Some of the terms which do not yet seem to be regarded as English occur frequently and are common to all forms of Buddhism, without any real difference in interpretative understanding. An example would be *bodhi,* the awakening, or the awoken, mind. In such cases I use the Sanskrit form (as being, so far as possible, a lineage-neutral language) and print the word in *italics* on its first appearance, following it with a suggested translation or two, and an explanation. The absence of diacriticals means

---

[1] For example, nirvana is often defined as negation, extinction, and so forth, but that this is quite misleading should be clear from my discussion of nirvana in chapter 10.

that some distinctions, of concern to specialists, (between, say, <ś> and <ṣ>, both being written as <sh>) are lost. The reader who wishes either to be reminded of the meaning or of the scientific romanization can turn to this glossary, where the term will be found in **bold** as it appears in the text, followed by a letter to denote its language and the romanization of the term in standard transliteration, and then a short explanation.

Infrequently Occurring Terms

Some terms are very important to particular areas of Buddhism but quite unimportant to Buddhism as a whole. An example would be *mano-vijñana,* the term for root consciousness in the Yogachara system. Terms like this I use and explain only as and when they occur. They are omitted from the glossary, since the reader will not meet these technical terms out of the context of their main explanation. A specialist who has momentarily forgotten the standard, scientific romanization (and all of us have such moments!) will, of course, be able to consult the lexicon of the appropriate language.

Phonetic Transcription

The last problem to be addressed is that of "phonetic transcription." I put this phrase in quotation marks since it is, in fact, an impossibility. English is not a phonetically transcribed language, although we sometimes try to fool ourselves that it is. George Bernard Shaw's "phonetic" spelling of fish as *ghoti*[2] is perhaps extreme, but it makes the point: one native English speaker's phonetic spelling is another's perplexity. So, what I have tried to do, in transcribing Sanskrit, Pali, and Tibetan, is to regard the vowels and consonants as having the values they are "supposed" to have . . . which means, perhaps because we borrowed our orthography from the Romans, something like their values in Latin or Italian . . . and hope for the best. However, the reader should note that, for Sanskrit and Pali, the values <th>, <dh> and <ph> are pronounced, respectively, 't', 'd' and 'p'. I suppose I should, logically, have omitted the aspirations (the h's) here,

---

[2]   'Gh' as in 'rough'; 'o' as in 'women'; 'ti' as in 'nation'.

but at this point my professional training cried "Enough!" and I found I could not do it. For Chinese, I have used the Wade-Giles system, because it is the one that is still most commonly found in academic textbooks on Chinese Buddhism. Unfortunately, Wade-Giles is quite unintelligible to the non-specialist, but its suggested replacement, called Pinyan, is no clearer and so, for the reader who does not know Chinese, there is no advantage in using it. Japanese, mercifully, has a romanization system called Hepburn, which is phonetic, and clear to both specialist and non-specialist. I gratefully use it. The terms in the following list are identified by a letter indicating their language thus: **C** Chinese; **J** Japanese; **P** Pali; **S** Sanskrit; **T** Tibetan.

A

abhava <**P, S**>: Non-existence; non-being. The viewpoint that nothing exists (Nihilism) should be carefully distinguished from *Emptiness*.

Abhidharma <**S**>: Further *Dharma* or Advanced Buddhism. With *Madhyamika* and *Yogachara,* one of the three main explanatory systems of Buddhism. Abhidharma analyzes reality into momentary, unique events called *dharmas.* The Sanskrit form of the term, as here, is used for the system as taught in *Hinayana,* where it is seen as a prerequisite for *Mahayana.* In *Theravada,* the system is called *Abhidhamma,* and is the final teaching. See chapter 5.

abhijña <**S abhijña**>: Supernormal skill. A form of high achievement associated with, but not necessary to, *enlightenment.* There are normally said to be six forms of abhijña, including what might be called magical or psychic powers. (See chapter 8.)

ahimsa <**P, S ahimsā**>: Non-harming. A fundamental precept of Buddhism, recommending the gentle treatment, in all actions of body, speech and mind, of any *sattva.*

alambana <**S ālambana**>: Support or basis. In general, any support for the data of the senses, especially as an object of meditative concentration.

alaya-vijñana <**S ālaya-vijñāna**>: Base consciousness. In the *Yogachara* system, the foundation consciousness. Because it stores the seeds of impressions it is known in Chinese as "Store Consciousness" *(tsang-shih).* Its purification is *enlightenment.* See chapter 7.

anuvyañjana <**S**>: Minor mark. Together with the *lakshana,* one of the distinguishing bodily marks of a Buddha.

Arahan <**S**>: In Chinese Buddhism, certain legendary adepts, renowned for their strange, magical behaviour, are known as *Lohan*. The word is derived by transliteration from the Sanskrit root form *Arahan* (worthy one), with the first syllable omitted. *Arahan* is more commonly cited in English as *Arhat* (Sanskrit) or *Arahat* (Pali). For *Theravada*, the Arahat is one who has realized supreme *enlightenment*, differing only from a Buddha in that he has a Buddha for a teacher, whereas a Buddha (whom Theravadins also call an Arhat) has no teacher during the life in which he becomes a Buddha. For *Mahayana*, an Arhat is one who has attained the end of the *Hinayana* path. The Lohan is more of a folk hero than an orthodox teacher of the *Dharma*.

artha <**S**>: A physical object, power, or wealth. When contrasted with *Dharma* it means that which pertains to one's present life, while *Dharma* refers to that which pertains to future lives and to final liberation.

Ashoka <**S Aśoka**>: The name of a king, or emperor, who reigned in what is now the Indian state of Bihar c. 269 BCE. He is regarded as the model Buddhist ruler. See chapter 2.

ashrava <**S āśrava**>: Influx or outflux. The interchange between subject and object, dependant upon which either or both appear to be inherently existing. Normal to defiled mind, it ceases at *enlightenment*. See chapter 8.

asura <**P, S**>: Wrathful deity. One of the states of rebirth. An asura is more powerful and longer-lived than a human, and so can be called a deity, but is constantly wrathful, agitated and ambitious. Wars between the asuras and the *devas* are frequent.

atman <**S ātman**>: The unchanging, inherently existing, or autonomous self, whose existence is denied by Buddhism. Such a self appears to be part of our experience but Buddhism claims that the *feeling* that such a self exists is not borne out by investigation and analysis. It should be carefully noted that Buddhism does not deny the existence of an *empirical* self.

atma-vadopadana <**S ātmavādopādāna**>: Grasping *(upadana)* at the word *(vada)* "I" *(atman)* in the mistaken belief that the word "I" necessarily implies the existence of an *atman* or inherently existing self.

avidya <**S avidya**>: Ignorance. Avidya is not a particular ignorance of this or that thing but an all-pervading disease characteristic of impure mind. At *enlightenment* it is replaced by *vidya*, knowledge or wisdom.

B

bhikkhu <**P**>: Monk or priest of the *Theravada* tradition. Literally "mendicant." Name for a man who has taken full monastic initiation *(upasampada)* and is bound to the observance of the *Vinaya*. See chapter 4.

bhikkhuni <**P bhikkhunī**>: Nun of the *Theravada* tradition. The female equivalent of *bhikkhu*. Strictly, there are no bhikkhunis at present, the Theravadin ordination lineage for them having been broken. There are, however, women who live under precepts very similar to those of nuns. See chapter 4.

bhikshu <**S bhikṣu**>: Monk or priest of the *Mahayana* tradition. See *bhikkhu*.

bhikshuni <**S bhikṣunī**>: Nun of the *Mahayana* tradition. See *bhikkhuni*. The ordination lineage for bhikshunis has been preserved only in the Chinese tradition.

bhumi <**S bhūmi**>: Ground. Commonly used for a level or stage on the *bodhisattva* path.

bodhisatta <**P**>: A being who is on the way to *enlightenment*. Especially used in *Theravada* to refer to Shakyamuni before his achievement of bodhi. See *bodhisattva*.

bodhisattva <**S**>: The Sanskrit form of *bodhisatta*. Especially used in *Mahayana* for any Buddhist who has made a formal resolve to liberate all *sattvas*.

brahmavihara <**P, S brahmavihāra**>: Pure abiding. A group of four virtuous states (friendliness, compassion, sympathetic joy, equanimity). See figure 6.

brahmin <**S**>: In Hinduism, a member of the priestly caste. In Buddhism, one who, whether born as a brahmin or not, possesses the nobility which would be expected of one so born. The correct Sanskrit form is *brahman* but "brahmin" has become common in English.

Buddha <**P, S**>: One who has Awoken. A title given to one who attains full and complete *enlightenment* without, in the life in which enlightenment is attained, having a teacher.

Buddhacharita <**S Buddhacarita**>: *Acts of Buddha*. An account of the life of Shakyamuni Buddha in *kavya* (Court Sanskrit verse), attributed to Ashvaghosha (c. 1st century C.E.).

C

cha-do <**J cha-dō**>: The Way (Tao) of Tea, Tea-ism. The Japanese tea ceremony. See *cha-no-yu*.

chakra <**S cakra**>: Wheel. In the Indian subcontinent, the wheel is a symbol of government and supremacy. An eight-spoked wheel (for the Eightfold Path . . . see pages 210–211) is a common symbol for the *Dharma*.

chakravartin <**S cakravartin**>: World emperor. Literally, "wheel turner," one who exercises supreme government, the wheel being a symbol of sovereignty.

cha-no-yu <**J**>: Teaism. Literally "hot water for tea." See *chado*.

chitta-matra <**S citta-mātra**>: Just mind. In *Yogachara*, the teaching that an object and that same object in a consciousness arise inter-dependently.

chörten <**T mchod rten**>: The Tibetan word for *stupa*.

D

dagoba <**Sinhalese dāgoba**>: A common word for *stupa* in southeast Asia. Derived from the Sanskrit *dhatu-garbha*, "relic-womb" (where *dhatu* is used for *sharira*).

Dalai Lama: The title (being a combination of the Mongolian for "Great Ocean" and the Tibetan for "Teacher") of the principal teacher of Tibetan Buddhism. He is regarded as a *tulku* of Avalokiteshvara, the Bodhisattva of Perfect Compassion. The first Dalai Lama died in 1474 CE. The present Dalai Lama is the fourteenth reincarnation.

dana <**P, S dāna**>: Giving, generosity. One of the principal Buddhist virtues.

deva <**P, S**>: Peaceful deity. One of the states of rebirth. Similar to an *asura*, but calmer of mind.

devaloka <**P, S**>: A divine realm or heaven. A realm inhabited by *devas*. For a list of the devalokas, see the Appendix to chapter 6.

dhamma <**P**>: The Pali form of *dharma*.

dharma <**S**>: One of the richest words in the Sanskrit language. Its two most important meanings in Buddhism are:
    (i) The true nature of reality and the Buddha's teaching about it, i.e., "Buddhism"; as such, it is part of the *Triratna* in which a Buddhist takes refuge and may be used as the antonym of *artha*.
    (ii) In the *Abhidharma* system, the smallest unit of perceived reality (see chapter 5).
In English, it is convenient to write the first meaning with a capital letter (Dharma) and the second meaning with a miniscule letter (dharma). The Pali form of the word is *dhamma*.

Dharmadhatu <**S dharmadhātu**>: Realm of Dharma. Reality as it truly is regarded as a world or universe. The word is favored by Mahayanists.

Dharmakaya <**S dharmakāya**>: Dharma Body. Reality as it truly is regarded as an embodiment of pure, or Buddha, mind. See *Trikaya.*

diachronic model: A suggested model for understanding how, in various Buddhist traditions, Buddhas are said to "come to be" over time rather than to "be" outside of time. The opposite of *synchronic model.*

dibba-chakkhu <**P dibba-cakkhu**>: Divine eye. A supernormal insight in which a person, especially a teacher of Dharma, understands what is the best practice for a disciple to undertake.

duhkha <**S duhkha**>: Suffering, pain, misery, unsatisfactoriness. The first part of the Fourfold Truth. *Samsara* is the experience of duhkha.

dukkha <**P**>: The Pali form of *duhkha.*

dvesha <**S dvesa**>: Aversion. With *raga* and *moha,* one of the three poisons which together drive the wheel of *samsara.*

dynamic synchronic model: A suggested model for understanding how, according to *Mahayana,* Buddhas manifest in the different forms of the *Trikaya* without "coming to be" through time.

E

Emptiness: The commonest English translation of *shunyata,* for which this book also proposes the translation *Transparency.*

enlightenment: The awakening to the nature of reality as it truly is. The commonest English translation of bodhi.

F

Fudo Myo-o <**J Fudō Myō-ō**>: Immovable Wisdom King. The Bodhisattva of Perfect Stability, known in Sanskrit as Achala Bodhisattva.

G

gana <**P, S gana**>: Flock. An early, and now uncommon, name for the *samgha,* especially used for the immediate disciples of the Buddha.

general diachronic model: A suggested model for understanding how, according to various Buddhist traditions, an indefinitely large number of beings are seen as in the process of becoming Buddhas over time.

H

Hinayana <**P, S Hīnayāna**>: Inferior or small vehicle. According to *Mahayana,* the path taken by some Buddhists which leads to an advanced, but still not fully liberated, condition, characterized by great wisdom but small compassion. A dead system, it is superficially similar to *Theravada,* a living system with which it should not be confused.

hongaku <J>: Original or fundamental enlightenment. A term for innate Buddha nature in Japanese Buddhism. See *shikaku.*

I

ikebana <J>: The Japanese art of flower arrangement. Literally "living flowers."

Indra <S>: Literally meaning "Leader," the name of a *deva* regarded by Buddhists as king or leader of the devas. Sometimes also known as Shakra or Brahma. His palace is on top of the cosmic mountain Sumeru. See appendix to chapter 6.

Ishvara <S Īśvara>: Literally meaning "Self-Abiding One," the name of a deity presumed by some non-Buddhists to be the creator and sustainer of the universe. His existence is denied by Buddhism.

J

Jataka <P, S jātaka>: Stories of the previous lives of the entity who was finally born as Shakyamuni and became the "historical" Buddha or the Buddha for our continuum. Literally "pertaining to that which was born."

jiva <P, S jīva>: A word for the inherently existing self, personal life-force or consciousness. Taught as existing by Jainism, it is denied by Buddhism. See chapter 5.

jñana <S jñāna>: Wisdom, true knowledge. Sometimes said to be superior to *prajña,* sometimes inferior to it.

K

kalpa <S>: An age or aeon. A very long period of time. Kalpas are of three kinds: short, medium, long and incalculable, but even the short kalpa is very long in terms of the human time-frame, so the distinctions are not very meaningful to us.

kama <P, S kāma>: Sensuality, sensuousness. Desire associated with the senses. Distinguish kama from *karma.*

Kanthaka <S Kanthaka>: The name of Shakyamuni's horse when he was living as a prince. Literally "Necklace."

karma <S>: Action, deed. In Buddhism, it refers to a universal law according to which any *willed* deed functions as the seed of one or more future events. These future events are called the *fruiting* of karma and, like fruit, are quantitatively larger than the seed. Karma is sometimes misunderstood by non-Buddhists as predetermination but, in fact, it escapes the dichotomy of free will and determinism. Put simply, if I find I can do something, that demonstrates that I have the freedom to do it. My free choice to do that action will then result, at some future time (either during this life or a subsequent one) in an event which, at that time, I experience as predetermined. So, a deed which "just happens," apparently randomly, causelessly, or as a result of fate, is understood by Buddhism as an ordered phenomenon, the fruiting of karma. Since, according to this view, pleasant events ensue upon good (or selfless) acts and unpleasant events upon bad (or selfish) acts, the teaching of karma forms the basis of an ethical system without recourse to a belief in a God, fate, or mere altruism.

kensho <**J kenshō**>: A term for an experience of enlightened insight. Literally "seeing the essential," i.e., seeing Buddha Nature or Transparency. Its use is generally reserved to some Zen lineages and to seeing the Buddha Nature in oneself rather than in reality as a whole. See *satori*.

kshatriya <**S kṣatriya**>: Warrior, soldier or ruler. One of the four castes (with the *brahmin* (priest), the vaishya (the producer, i.e. the farmer or merchant) and the shudra (the cleaner, servant or menial)) of classical Hindu society. The kshatriya is located between the brahmin and the vaishya and has responsibility for the maintenance of order in the physical world. Shākyamuni Buddha was born into the kshatriya caste.

L

lakshana <**S lakṣaṇa**>: Mark, characteristic. (i) When used in reference to the physical appearance of a Buddha it means a major bodily feature, such as the *ushnisha-shirsha* (head bump) which distinguishes a *mahapurusha* from an ordinary human. See *anuvyañjana* and pages 48–52. (ii) When used in *Abhidharma* it means a feature distinctive of and unique to one and one only *dharma:* such a feature is called *svalakshana* ("own-mark") and its existence is maintained in *Hinayana* but denied in *Mahayana*.

lama <**T bla ma**>: A translation of the Sanskrit word *guru* it is used in the Tibetan tradition to address one's teacher. Only certain teachers are called lamas, and they may or may not be monks or nuns. The term "lamaism," which has been used by some scholars in the past to refer to Tibetan Buddhism, is meaningless and should be avoided.

li <**C**>: Essence. Literally, the veins in jade, therefore, the underlying, but hidden, features of something. In Hua-yen Buddhism it is used for the Buddha Nature inherent in all things which is non-dual with *shih*.

lineage: A Buddhist takes refuge in the *Triratna* and therefore becomes, through a particular teacher, part of a heritage which stretches back to Shakyamuni Buddha. Buddhists feel their differences primarily in relation to their teacher and his or her distinctive reception and transmission of the *Dharma*. Differences of doctrine do not control, but are dependent upon, that heritage. The term "lineage" is to be preferred over "denomination" or "sect" (words which imply creedal differences) or "school" (a word which implies a primacy of philosophical differences).

lojong < **T blo sbyong** > : Thought transformation. A technique of mind training in Tibetan Buddhism in which obstacles to progress are transformed into aids.

loka < **P, S** > : World or realm. In Buddhism it means a world as experienced by one or more beings. A world existing by itself, entirely without relationship to conscious beings, is regarded by Buddhists as meaningless and its existence is denied.

Lotus Sutra: One of the earliest and most important of the *sutras* of the *Mahayana*. It is spoken by Shakyamuni Buddha in his *Sambhogakaya* form and is concerned with the differences between the Mahayana and the *Hinayana* paths.

M

Madhyamika < **S Mādhyamika** > : With *Yogachara*, one of the two major theoretical systems of *Mahayana*. It demonstrates Emptiness by means of an examination of language.

Magadhi < **P Māgadhī** > : Since Shakyamuni Buddha came from a region called Magadha it is presumed that he spoke a language called Magadhi. It is then further presumed that this language was close to *Pali*. Both of these presumptions are the subject of learned debate.

Mahapurusha < **S Mahāpuruṣa** > : Hero. Literally "great man" it refers to a very rare and unusual man of great power who can become either a *chakravartin* or a Buddha. The body of a mahapurusha exhibits certain peculiar marks known as *lakshana* and *anuvyañjana*.

Mahayana < **S Mahāyāna** > : The name given to itself by the form of Buddhism dominant in north, central and east Asia. The Chinese translation is *Ta-ch'êng* meaning "Large Vehicle," from which we get the standard English translation "Greater Vehicle." See *yana*.

mandala < **S maṇḍala** > : Circle. In Buddhism, mandala has three meanings:
> (i) the world seen as an ordered universe or *cosmos*—in such a form it is the focus of some meditative visualizations and of certain liturgies of offering;

(ii) the space in which Shakyamuni sat and became the Buddha *(bodhi-mandala)* and, by extension, any area in which Buddhist practice is undertaken;
(iii) the palace of a Buddha, Bodhisattva, or deity who is the focus of worship or other meditative practice.
The precise, technical use of mandala in Buddhism should be distinguished from its use in everyday English where it means something like "symmetrical diagram."

mantra <**S**>: A sound or sequence of sounds, in Sanskrit or quasi-Sanskrit, embodying a particular energy, usually an aspect of bodhi mind.

Mara <**P, S Māra**>: Generally, anything which hinders one's progress to enlightenment can be called a mara. In particular, it is the name of a deity who resides at the top of the sensuous realm (see appendix to chapter 6) and who, with his supporters (called either "the army of Mara" or simply "the maras") attacked Shakyamuni while he sat under the Bodhi Tree and attempted to prevent him from obtaining enlightenment. The name literally means "He of Death."

marga <**S mārga**>: Way, path. Any method leading to enlightenment can be called a marga. The most important is the Eightfold Path which is part of the First Sermon (see chapter 9).

maya <**P, S māyā**>: Illusion. Some systems, especially within Hinduism, teach that reality is maya, a dream or an illusion. Buddhism denies this and teaches that reality is dream*like* or a *delusion,* since it is constructed from, and dependent upon, causes and conditions. See chapter 7.

Mayadevi <**P, S Māyādevī**>: The name of the mother of Shakyamuni Buddha. Literally "Illusion Goddess."

moha <**P, S**>: Confusion. With *raga* and *dvesha,* one (often considered the root one) of the three poisons which together drive the wheel of *samsara.*

moksha <**S mokṣa**>: Liberation. A general term for escape from *samsara,* more frequently used in Hinduism than in Buddhism.

N

nibbana <**P nibbāna**>: The Pali form, used in *Theravada,* of *nirvana.*

Nirmanakaya <**S nirmāṇakāya**>: Transformation body. According to *Mahayana,* a Buddha appearing in human form. See *Trikaya.* The *Dalai Lama* is regarded as a Nirmanakaya.

nirodha < **P, S** >: Stopping, extinction. The third part of the Fourfold Truth, that *duhkha* may be stopped or extinguished. There is also a mental state called *nirodha-samapatti* (extinction-achievement) reported by some non-Buddhists as the state of final liberation from *samsara*. Buddhism teaches that this state is merely one of great mental refinement in which the arising of events is so slow and subtle that nothing appears to be happening.

nirvana < **S nirvāna** >: The Buddhist term for final liberation. It is a negative, meaning "blown out" or "extinguished," but this is a linguistic *upaya* for a condition that is beyond both affirmation and negation. Nirvana should be carefully distinguished from states which are in fact negative such as *abhava* and *nirodha*. In *Mahayana*, nirvana is taught as being non-dual with *samsara*.

nopeti < **P** >: "It is incoherent." Shakyamuni Buddha responded to certain philosophical questions with this word, literally "not *(na)* up *(upa)* thus *(iti)*," i.e., "[the question] cannot come up like that." The intent of the Buddha was to declare that some questions are not conducive to liberation and that, on a deeper level, they may not be questions at all, as if one might ask "What is the shape of a square circle?"

P

pabbajja < **P pabbajjā** >: In *Theravada*, the Pali term equivalent to *pravrajya*.

Pali < **P Pāli** >: A Prakrit language (see *Sanskrit*) in which the texts of *Theravada* are written. Theravada tradition claims that Pali was, or was related to, the language which Shakyamuni Buddha spoke.

pancha-shila < **S panca-śila** >: Fivefold Conduct. The five basic precepts of right action: not to harm sentient beings, not to steal, not to engage in sexual misconduct, not to lie, not to drink alcohol. The precepts are not commandments and are not absolute. They are suggestions which one observes by choice and to the best of one's ability.

paramita < **P, S pāramitā** >: Perfection. Generally, an aspect of *shila* in which a certain conduct is recommended positively rather than negatively, as in the *pancha-shila*. Buddhas manifest the paramitas as true or actual perfections. Other beings aspire to them as perfect ideals. There are lists of six and ten paramitas, differing slightly in *Theravada* and *Mahayana*.

paravritti < **S parāvṛtti** >: Literally "turning around" it is understood as "turning the right way up." A term in *Yogachara* for the transformation of *vijñana* into *jñana*.

pari-nirvana < **S pari-nirvāna** >: Final nirvana. When subsets of nirvana are distinguished, pari-nirvana is identified as the final or most complete. Generally, in *Theravada, pari-nibbana* (as it is written in Pali) is the present state of all Buddhas and arhats (see *arahan*), and in *Mahayana*, it is a state that will only be reached by all *sattvas* when *samsara* as a whole is emptied.

paritta <**P**>: Protection, safeguard. A term for a Theravadin ceremony, usually chanting and often involving a sacred thread (also called paritta), performed to obtain an intra-samsaric blessing such as recovery from sickness. Similar in many respects to *mantra* in *Mahayana*.

Patimokkha <**P** Pāṭimokkha>: A list, preserved in Pali and used in *Theravada*, of 227 rules for *bhikkhus*, recited liturgically every half lunar month. The meaning of the word is disputed.

prajña <**S** prajñā>: Wisdom, true knowledge. Sometimes said to be superior to *jñana*, sometimes inferior to it.

pranidhana <**S** praṇidhāna>: Earnest application of the mind, especially of a *bodhisattva* to liberate all *sattvas*, when it is called the Bodhisattva Vow or Resolve.

prapañcha <**S** prapañca>: The function of mind which divides and classifies holistic reality into parts and mistakes those parts for reality as it truly is. Similar to *vikalpa*.

Pratimoksha <**S** prātimoksa>: A list similar to the *Patimokkha*, used in *Mahayana*. It is longer than the Patimokkha, having more rules concerning proper deportment, and it is not as frequently recited.

pratityasamutpada <**S** pratītyasamutpāda>: Interdependent origination. The teaching that everything that occurs is conditioned by, and conditions, everything else that occurs. Sometimes translated "conditioned co-arising."

pravrajya <**S** pravrajyā>: Going forth. The term for leaving the household life and entering the *samgha* as a monk or nun. The name of one's biological family (surname) is lost and replaced by a Buddhist name indicating that one has entered into the family of the Buddha. In China this re-naming is dramatized by translating pravrajya as *ch'u-chia* or "leaving the family."

preta <**P, S**>: Ghost. One of the states of rebirth. Pretas are consumed by a passionate and insatiable thirst. For this reason they are called in Chinese *o-kuei*, "hungry ghost," and this usage has passed into English.

puja <**P, S** pūjā>: Worship. A general term for a Buddhist liturgy characterized mainly by offerings to Buddhas, Bodhisattvas, or other entities, or to their images, either physically present or visualized.

punya <**S puṇya**>: Merit. A good (selfless) action of body, speech or mind is meritorious and also "meritful," that is, it earns merit. Earned merit may be distributed to assist another *sattva*.

R

raga <**P, S rāga**>: Attachment. With *dvesha* and *moha*, one of the three poisons which together drive the wheel of *samsara*.

Rupakaya <**S rūpakāya**>: Form Body. In the *Trikaya*, the *Sambhogakaya* and *Nirmanakaya* considered as a unit.

S

saddha <**P saddhā**>: Trust. The leading characteristic of one of the three wholesome personality types according to the Theravadin teacher Buddhaghosa. Also, a characteristic of Buddhist practice in general. The Buddha advised that one not believe something on his authority alone, or because it claimed to be a revelation, or because it was logical, or because one had had a vision apparently confirming its truth. Any or all of these considerations might dispose one to investigate the truth of something, but only after testing its truth in one's own experience should one believe it. A Buddhist practitioner, finding that the Buddha is trustworthy in certain things, decides to trust the Buddha in things beyond the practitioner's immediate experience. It is misleading to translate saddha as "faith," since this is a slippery word with many non-Buddhist connotations.

Sakyamuni <**P Sākyamuni**>: The Pali form of *Shakyamuni*.

samadhi <**P, S samādhi**>: Concentration. A term for Buddhist meditation in general and (when used with a qualifier) for a specific meditative state. In Buddhism it does not refer to the state of final liberation.

samanera <**P sāmaṇera**>: A man who has taken *pabbajja*. Literally "one who exerts himself." Often translated into English as "novice" because of a superficial similarity with the novitiate condition in Christian monasticism.

samaneri <**P sāmaṇerī**>: A woman who has taken *pabbajja*. See *samanera*.

Sambhogakaya <**S Sambhogakāya**>: Divine or celestial form. According to *Mahayana*, a Buddha appearing in a form suitable for teaching *devas*. The form is glorious, radiant, gigantic, and fully endowed with the *lakshana* and *anuvyañjana*. Shakyamuni Buddha teaches the *Lotus Sutra* in his Sambhogakaya.

samgha <**S** saṃgha>: Community. Part of the *Triratna* in which a Buddhist takes refuge. In general, "a member of the samgha" is "a Buddhist," but the word may be restricted according to function (e.g., *bhikshu-samgha*, the community of monks, often referred to merely as "the samgha") or attainment (e.g., *arya-samgha*, the community of the holy, i.e., of those who will not again be reborn in an unfortunate or miserable state).

samgha-karma <**S** saṃgha-karma>: Act of the [bhikshu] samgha. A collective decision of the bhikshus of a particular *vihara*.

samkhya <**S** sāṃkhya>: Relating to number, calculation. Especially in *Samkhya Yoga*, a Hindu system purporting to list the elements of which reality is constituted. Shakyamuni, before his enlightenment, is said to have tried a system similar to Samkhya and found it wanting.

samsara <**P, S** saṃsāra>: Cyclic existence. Literally "always moving." A teaching, common to many systems developed on the Indian Subcontinent, that, unless steps are taken to prevent it, life and death continue in an indefinite cycle.

sangha <**P**>: The Pali form of *samgha*.

sangye <**T** sangs rgyas>: The Tibetan translation of *Buddha*. Literally "One who has awoken (or come to his senses) and is fully developed."

Sanskrit: The classical language of the Indian Subcontinent, introduced by the Aryans c. 2500 BCE, who called their own language *samskrita-bhasha*, "ornamented or cultured speech" (hence "Sanskrit") and distinguished it from the indigenous languages which they collectively called *prakriti-bhasha*, "aboriginal speech" (hence "Prakrit"). The Buddha probably spoke a form of Prakrit, perhaps related to *Pali*. By about the first century CE texts (e.g., the *Lotus Sutra*) were appearing in a Prakritized form of Sanskrit called Buddhist Hybrid Sanskrit and (e.g., the *Buddhacharita*) in *kavya* or Court Sanskrit.

satori <**J**>: Awakening. A term used in some Zen lineages for a moment of non-dual awareness. Similar to *kensho* except that it usually refers to an experience of non-duality, or the Buddha Nature, in reality as a whole rather than in oneself.

sattva <**S**>: A being, i.e., a conscious or sentient being. An entity is called a sattva if it manifestly seeks to avoid pain and to obtain pleasure.

Scheduled Caste: A term for persons who were called Untouchables (today usually called Harijans) coined by the British administration in India, who put certain castes and tribes (Scheduled Tribes) who did not fit what appeared to them to be regular society on a special list or schedule. Dr B. R. Ambedkar, who began a reform of Buddhism in India during the early part of this century, came from a Scheduled Caste. In Hindi, members may call themselves *shedulika* (from the British English pronunciation of "schedule") even though the category of Scheduled Caste is no longer legally recognized.

Shakyamuni <S Śākyamuni>: The clan name of the "historical" Buddha or the Buddha for our continuum. Literally "the sage *(muni)* of the Shakya [clan]."

shamatha <S śamatha>: Calming. In Buddhist meditation, the mental stabilization which is the foundation of *vipashyana*.

sharira <S śarīra>: Relic, especially of Shakyamuni. Literally "body."

shih <C>: Manifestation. In Hua-yen Buddhism, everyday reality which is non-dual with *li*.

shikaku <J>: A term in Japanese Buddhism for acquired enlightenment. See *hongaku*.

shila <S śīla>: Conduct, especially as detailed in the *pancha-shila* and the *paramitas*.

shraddha <S śraddhā>: The Sanskrit form of *saddha*.

shramanera <S śrāmaṇera>: The Sanskrit form of *samanera*.

shramanerika <S śrāmaṇerikā>: The Sanskrit form of *samaneri*.

shunyata <S śūnyatā>: According to Buddhism, especially *Mahayana*, the nature of reality as it truly is, regarded from the philosophical standpoints of ontology and epistemology. According to this teaching, whatever exists or does not exist does so *empty of inherent existence*. That is, its existence or non-existence can be known, but the manner of such existence or non-existence cannot be found. Commonly translated into English as *Emptiness*, this book also proposes the translation *Transparency*.

Siddhartha <S Siddhārtha>: The personal or given name of the "historical" Buddha or the Buddha for our continuum. Literally "Aim Achieved" or "Successful."

siddhi <S>: Success, achievement. A skill, such as psychic power, which may be obtained by an advanced meditator as a by-product of Buddhist or other practice.

skandha <S>: Cluster, aggregate. Literally "heap." Especially one of the five skandhas which make up the person.

special diachronic model: A suggested model for understanding how, according to various Buddhist traditions, Shakyamuni Buddha is seen as in the process of becoming a Buddha over time.

static synchronic model: A suggested model for understanding how, according to *Mahayana,* everything is Buddha just as it is.

stupa <**S stūpa**>: Originally a mound of earth covering a *sharira,* it developed more symbolic functions and became, in East Asia, the pagoda.

suññata <**P suññatā**>: The Pali form of *shunyata.*

sutta <**P**>: In *Theravada,* a discourse of the Buddha on a general teaching, preserved in Pali.

sutra <**S sūtra**>: In *Mahayana,* a discourse of a Buddha, Bodhisattva, or other advanced being, regarded as authoritative. The word is the Sanskrit form of *sutta,* but most Mahayana sutras exist as translations (whose authenticity is sometimes disputed) from the Sanskrit into Tibetan, Chinese and other languages.

svabhava <**S svabhāva**>: Essence, inherent existence. Literally "own-being." That objects and beings have svabhava seems obvious to naive consciousness and it is maintained by some philosophies and religions. It is denied by Buddhism.

svalakshana <**S svalakṣana**>: Distinctive or characteristic mark. Literally "own-mark." When, according to the *Abhidharma* of the *Hinayana,* the *dharmas* are said to have *svabhava,* it is claimed that they can be distinguished by their respective svalakshanas. *Mahayana,* on the contrary, maintains that the dharmas are empty of inherent existence.

synchronic model: A suggested model for understanding how, according to the *Mahayana,* Buddhas "are" outside of time, not "coming to be" over time. The opposite of *diachronic model.*

T

Ta Tsang <**C**>: Great Treasury. The name for the collection of authoritative Buddhist texts preserved in Chinese.

tantra <**S**>: An authoritative text, usually a liturgy, specific to *Vajrayana.*

Tao <**C**>: Way. The name for the "way" the universe ultimately is, according to philosophical and religious systems native to China, and variously explained by them. Chinese Buddhism adopted the word as a translation both of *marga* and of bodhi.

tapas < **S** > : Extreme asceticism. Literally "heat." Advocated by some non-Buddhist systems, it is rejected by Buddhism in favor of the middle way between indulgence and denial.

Tathata < **S tathatā** > : Reality as it truly is when it is neither described (pointed at as "this" or "that") nor not described. Literally "Thusness." Synonymous with *shunyata*.

Theravada < **P Theravāda** > : The name given to itself by the Buddhism dominant in southeast Asia (Sri Lanka, Burma, Thailand, Laos, Kampuchea). Literally "Way of the *Theras*." A thera is a *bhikkhu* of at least ten years' standing. According to tradition, Theravada is so called because it was established by a council of five hundred theras soon after the *pari-nibbana* (see *pari-nirvana*) of Sakyamuni Buddha. Theravada, which is a living system, should not be confused with *Hinayana*, a dead system with which it has some superficial similarities.

Tipitaka < **P Tipiṭaka** > : Triple Basket. The collection of texts, preserved in Pali and regarded as authoritative by *Theravada*, which is divided into the *Vinaya*, *Sutta*, and *Abhidhamma* (see *Abhidharma*) baskets or pitakas.

Transparency: A suggested translation of *shunyata*.

Trikaya < **S trikāya** > : Triple Body. According to *Mahayana*, all Buddhas (and some Bodhisattvas and other advanced beings) possess three "bodies" or coherences: the *Dharmakaya*, which is unmanifest, pure mind; the *Sambhogakaya* or divine form; and the *Nirmanakaya* or human form. These three forms are non-dual with each other.

Tulku < **T sprul sku** > : The Tibetan translation of *Nirmanakaya*.

Tushita < **S Tusita** > : Sated. The name of a *devaloka*. Entities who are to be born in the human realm and become Buddhas are born in Tushita immediately beforehand.

U

upadana < **P, S upādāna** > : Grasping. According to Buddhism, *duhkha* is caused by grasping. There are four types of grasping: at sense objects, at viewpoints, at ceremonies and at the word "I."

upasaka < **P, S upāsaka** > : A man who has undergone a formal ceremony to observe the basic precepts of *shila*.

upasika < **P, S upāsikā** > : A woman who has undergone a formal ceremony to observe the basic precepts of *shila*.

upasampada <**P, S upasampadā**>: Completion. The ceremony by which, after having been a *samanera* or *samaneri* for some time, one becomes a full monk or nun bound to the *Patimokkha*.

upaya <**S upāya**>: Skillful means. An abbreviation of *upaya-kaushalya*, "leading out or away with respect to what is good." A fundamental Buddhist virtue, especially emphasized by, but not restricted to, *Mahayana*. It is sometimes regarded as synonymous with compassion and sometimes regarded as the means by which compassion and wisdom are activated.

V

Vajrayana <**S Vajrayāna**>: A form of *Mahayana* found chiefly in Tibet and Japan, characterized by special practices in which reality is approached from pure perspective, i.e., as if one were already enlightened.

Veda <**S**>: The fundamental sacred texts of Hinduism. Literally "Knowledge."

vihara <**P, S vihāra**>: Lodging. A general term for Buddhist temple or monastery buildings and the grounds in which they stand. Literally "pleasure ground" from the fact that the first plot of land to be given to the Buddha for the purpose of building dwellings for *bhikshus* was a park or pleasaunce belonging to a prince.

vijñana <**S vijñāna**>: Consciousness. The function of mind which is aware of its own processes and, therefore, the source of the presumption that a permanent, autonomous and inherently existing self *(atman)* exists. The fifth of the five *skandhas*. Up to eight kinds of vijñana are taught in *Yogachara:* see figure 11 and *alaya-vijñana*.

vikalpa <**S**>: The function of mind which classifies and judges. Similar to *prapañcha*. The word is related to the English word "clip."

Vinaya <**P, S**>: The monastic code. Attributed to the Buddha himself, it is at least the earliest Buddhist literature. Literally "that which leads away [from samsara]." A section of the *Tipitaka* is entirely devoted to Vinaya.

vipassana <**P vipassanā**>: Insight. In Buddhist meditation, the penetrating vision which is founded on *shamatha*.

vipashyana <**S vipaśyanā**>: The Sanskrit form of *vipassana*.

Y

yaksha <**S yakṣa**>: A male fertility spirit which inhabits certain trees. Literally "speeder." A yaksha dwelling in the Bodhi Tree is said to have assisted Shakyamuni as he moved towards enlightenment.

yakshi <S **yakṣī**>: A female fertility spirit. See *yaksha*.

yana <P, S **yāna**>: A general term for a means of moving from one place to another, e.g., a cart, boat or path. Cognate with the English word "go." Commonly used of a method of obtaining *enlightenment*, i.e., of moving from *samsara* to *nirvana*, e.g., *Mahayana*. Often called "vehicle" in English, from the Chinese translation *ch'êng*.

yang <C>: In the indigenous Chinese systems, the cosmic principle, complementary to *yin*, which is responsible for initiating action. An aspect of *Tao*.

yin <C>: In the indigenous Chinese systems, the cosmic principle. complementary to *yang*, which receives the action initiated by *yang*. An aspect of *Tao*.

Yogachara <S **Yogācāra**>: With *Madhyamika*, one of the two major theoretical systems of *Mahayana*. It demonstrates Emptiness by means of an examination of consciousness.

Z

zazen <J>: The term used for sitting meditation in the Zen lineages.

Index